Digital Social Reading and
Second Language Learning and Teaching

AILA Applied Linguistics Series (AALS)
ISSN 1875-1113

The AILA Applied Linguistics Series (AALS) provides a forum for established scholars in any area of Applied Linguistics. The series aims at representing the field in its diversity. It covers different topics in applied linguistics from a multidisciplinary approach and it aims at including different theoretical and methodological perspectives. As an official publication of AILA the series will include contributors from different geographical and linguistic backgrounds. The volumes in the series should be of high quality; they should break new ground and stimulate further research in Applied Linguistics.

For an overview of all books published in this series, please see
benjamins.com/catalog/aals

Editor

Limin Jin
Beijing Foreign Studies University

Editorial Board

Fabiola Ehlers-Zavala
Colorado State University

Susanna Nocchi
Dublin Institute of Technology

Anne Pitkanen-Huhta
University of Jyväskylä

Elke Stracke
University of Canberra, Australia

Antje Wilton
Freie Universität Berlin

Volume 21

Digital Social Reading and Second Language Learning and Teaching
Edited by Joshua J. Thoms and Kristen Michelson

Digital Social Reading and Second Language Learning and Teaching

Edited by

Joshua J. Thoms
Utah State University

Kristen Michelson
Texas Tech University

John Benjamins Publishing Company
Amsterdam / Philadelphia

The paper used in this publication meets the minimum requirements of the American National Standard for Information Sciences – Permanence of Paper for Printed Library Materials, ANSI z39.48-1984.

DOI 10.1075/aals.21

Cataloging-in-Publication Data available from Library of Congress:
LCCN 2024031934 (PRINT) / 2024031935 (E-BOOK)

ISBN 978 90 272 1813 1 (HB)
ISBN 978 90 272 4637 0 (E-BOOK)

© 2024 – John Benjamins B.V.
No part of this book may be reproduced in any form, by print, photoprint, microfilm, or any other means, without written permission from the publisher.

John Benjamins Publishing Company · https://benjamins.com

Table of contents

List of contributors   VII

CHAPTER 1. Introduction   1
Kristen Michelson & Joshua J. Thoms

SECTION I. **Focusing on learners**
CHAPTER 2. Examining graduate students' positioning identities in collaborative digital annotation tools   22
Elif Burhan-Horasanlı

CHAPTER 3. Critical historical literacy in world languages through digital social reading   48
Claudia Baska Lynn & Sibel Sayılı-Hurley

CHAPTER 4. Incorporating mindfulness into multiliteracies pedagogy: Contemplative digital social reading and writing   74
Carl Blyth

SECTION II. **Texts, tasks, and teachers**
CHAPTER 5. Addressing text difficulty in novice L2 digital social reading   104
James Law, David Barny & Rachel Dorsey

CHAPTER 6. Digital social reading annotations as evidence of L2 proficiency   128
Frederick J. Poole & Joshua J. Thoms

CHAPTER 7. Developing digital social reading in source-based writing: A second language teaching and learning account   153
Inanç Karagöz & John I. Liontas

CHAPTER 8. Conclusion: Insights for research and praxis around DSR   179
Kristen Michelson

Index   193

List of contributors

David Barny is a PhD candidate in French Linguistics at the University of Texas at Austin. After an M.A. in English Studies form the University of Orléans (2010) and an M.A. in the Teaching of Languages from the University of Southern Mississippi (2012), David worked as a language lecturer of French at the University of Southern Mississippi, at the New York French Institute Alliance Française, and at New York University. David's research interests are in Applied Linguistics, primarily in Second Language Learning and Second Language Acquisition, with a focus on L2 Pragmatics, Computer Assisted Language Learning (CALL) and Digital Game-based Language Learning (DGBLL). His work explores innovative approaches to instructional pragmatics, with research focusing on how L2 learners negotiate meaning, agency and identity via Computer Mediated Communication; from social reading tools and social media, to collocated and networked digital gaming.

Dr. Claudia Baska Lynn is Language Program Director and Lecturer of Foreign Languages at the University of Pennsylvania. Her teaching practice motivates her research interests in curriculum design, critical content-based instruction, digital humanities, technology in language education, as well as intercultural and sociocultural theories of learning. She has presented on topics related to her research at regional, national and international conferences and given invited workshops. She is co-author with Sibel Sayılı-Hurley of *Bewegungen: Contemporary Social, Cultural, and Political Movements in the German-Speaking World. Bewegungen*, a content-based German textbook and curriculum, is currently piloted at the University of Pennsylvania and was awarded the 2016 *SAS Language Teaching Innovation Grant First Place Award*.

Dr. Carl S. Blyth (PhD, Cornell University) is Associate Professor of French and Director of the Center of Open Educational Resources and Language Learning (COERLL) at the University of Texas at Austin. His research interests include computer-mediated discourse, intercultural pragmatics, and open education. He has authored and co-authored journal articles in venues such as the *Modern Language Journal, L2 Journal, CALICO Journal, Journal of Educational Computing Research, ALSIC Revue* and *Language & Dialogue*. In 2023, he and his co-editor Joshua Thoms received the Mildenberger Prize honorable mention for their 2021 book *Open Education and Second Language Learning and Teaching: The Rise of a New Knowledge Ecology* (Multilingual Matters). In addition to traditional forms of scholarship, he has been involved in the development of many open educational resources (OER). Finally, he has served on the editorial boards of *Intercultural Pragmatics, Language Learning & Technology,* and *Second Language Research & Practice.*

Dr. Elif Burhan-Horasanlı, as a Fulbright scholar between 2015–2020, completed her PhD degree in Second Language Acquisition and Teaching at the University of Arizona. She currently works as an assistant professor in the English Language Education Program at TED University in Ankara, Türkiye, and teaches various courses to undergraduate and master's students. Her research interests include reflective practice in language teacher education, (academic) language socialization, and sociocognitive perspectives in second language acquisition. She has published in *Teaching and Teacher Education, Linguistics and Education, International Review of Applied Linguistics in Language Teaching*, and *Studies in Higher Education*.

Dr. Rachel Dorsey completed her PhD in French Linguistics at the University of Texas at Austin where she studied second language acquisition and language processing. She now applies her research experience in adult learning theory and cognitive science by designing online courses for Special Education teachers as an Instructional Designer.

Dr. Inanç Karagöz has instructed a diverse range of English as a Foreign Language (EFL), English as a Second Language (ESL), and English for Academic Purposes (EAP) classes in both Turkish and American higher education settings. Holding a PhD in Technology in Education and Second Language Acquisition, she explores ways to employ technology in a manner that improves the language learning process and fosters efficacy. The focus of her research pertains to reading engagement, peer support, and the potential of innovative digital tools for language learning. Currently, she serves as a faculty member at Bartin University, Turkiye, in the department of English Language Teaching.

Dr. James Law is an Assistant Professor of French at Brigham Young University. His research centers on semantic and pragmatic change in the Romance languages. Although lexical variation and change is notoriously idiosyncratic, his work aims to identify trends in lexical semantic shifts. This contributes to a better understanding of the mind while facilitating broader historical linguistic and philological research. He works within the cognitive linguistic tradition, notably Construction Grammar and Frame Semantics, and uses quantitative corpus methods. He also carries out research on applied pragmatics as well as linguistic variation in computer-mediated communication and teaches courses on semantics, pragmatics, historical linguistics, and corpus linguistics.

Dr. John I. Liontas is an Associate Professor of ESOL and FL education at the University of South Florida. He served as the director of the Technology in Education and Second Language Acquisition (TESLA) doctoral program at the University of South Florida from 2014 to 2021 and held the position of Coordinator of TESOL and Foreign Language Education from 2023 to 2024. Dr. Liontas is an active member of (inter)national learned societies and is widely recognized as a thought leader in the fields of idiomatics, digital technologies, applied linguistics, and second language acquisition. He has received numerous teaching and research awards and honors, totaling over four dozen at the local, state, regional, national, and international levels. Additionally, Dr. Liontas is the Editor-in-Chief of the award-winning encyclopedia, *The TESOL Encyclopedia of English Language Teaching* (Wiley, 2018), which is the first print and online encyclopedia for TESOL International Association since its founding in 1966.

Dr. Kristen Michelson is Associate Professor of French and Applied Linguistics in the Department of Classical and Modern Languages and Literatures at Texas Tech University, where she also directs the first- and second-year language program in French. Her scholarly work is anchored in multiliteracies pedagogies and has ranged from exploring global simulation frameworks as a way to foster multiliteracies, to tracing how foreign language teachers co-construct knowledge through digital social annotated reading, to investigating how second language learners of French interpret everyday internet texts. In this latter work, she has employed various methodologies in solo and collaborative research projects, including digital social annotated reading and prompted think-alouds. Her work aims to raise awareness of how particular representational choices are made with agency and intention against a backdrop of broader social contexts, and to provide opportunities for second language learners to understand and participate flexibly in cultural discourses of target language cultures.

Dr. Frederick Poole, Assistant Professor of Master of Arts in Foreign Language Teaching at Michigan State University, received his PhD in Instructional Technology and Learning Sciences in the College of Education at Utah State University in 2020. He earned a Master of Second Language Teaching Degree in 2015. His research investigates the implementation of technology for improving and assessing second language literacy skills and the effect of well-designed games on second language learning, teaching, and classroom dynamics. His work has been published in *Foreign Language Annals, System,* and *Language Learning & Technology*. Frederick has taught both English and Chinese as a Foreign language as well as graduate-level courses related to second language teaching methods, educational technology, and using games for learning.

Dr. Sibel Sayılı-Hurley is Lecturer of Foreign Languages at the University of Pennsylvania. Her research focuses on language and technology, curriculum design, digital humanities, and critical pedagogy. She has presented on topics related to her research at regional, national and international conferences and given invited workshops. She is also co-author with Claudia Baska Lynn of *Bewegungen: Contemporary Social, Cultural, and Political Movements in the German-Speaking World. Bewegungen*, a content-based German textbook and curriculum, is currently piloted at the University of Pennsylvania and was awarded the 2016 *SAS Language Teaching Innovation Grant First Place Award.*

Dr. Joshua J. Thoms is Professor of Applied Linguistics and Spanish at Utah State University where he researches issues related to second language (L2) digital social reading/literacy practices, open education, and L2 learning and teaching issues in hybrid and fully online environments. In 2013, he published a co-edited volume (Cengage) with Dr. Fernando Rubio on hybrid language learning and teaching in L2 contexts. He also co-edited a volume with Dr. Carl Blyth entitled *Open Education and Second Language Learning and Teaching: The Rise of a New Knowledge Ecology* with Multilingual Matters in 2021. In addition, he has published several articles appearing in journals such as *Language Learning & Technology, System, Modern Language Journal, Canadian Modern Language Review, Foreign Language Annals*, and *Second Language Research and Practice.*

CHAPTER 1

Introduction

Kristen Michelson & Joshua J. Thoms
Texas Tech University | Utah State University

Over the last decade, the fields of applied linguistics and second language education have seen a renewed interest in socially oriented perspectives on second language (L2) learning and teaching (Dubreil & Thorne, 2017; Paesani, Allen, & Dupuy, 2016; Warner & Michelson, 2018). Similarly, researchers working in the field of computer assisted language learning have increasingly examined digitally-mediated communication and collaborative online learning with respect to language and literacy development (e.g., Kern, 2021; González-Lloret, 2020) given the ubiquitous nature of technological tools in the social and academic lives of students at all levels of education. Traditional notions of literacy continue to be re-conceptualized due to the myriad ways in which texts are produced, accessed, and interpreted. The aforementioned changes have had significant impacts on L2 reading as technologies such as digital annotation tools have afforded students and teachers to re-envision L2 reading as a more social/collaborative activity. This introductory chapter therefore begins with definitions of some key terms and a brief overview of empirical work related to digital social reading (DSR) in L2 learning and teaching contexts carried out over the last decade. Next, we include information about the theoretical perspectives that frame the work included in the book. We then provide a brief summary of each chapter.

Introduction

Rapid changes in communication channels, tools, and conventions of interaction over the last three decades have paved the way for increasingly digital learning environments. In second language (L2) education, a growing number of courses have shifted from traditional face-to-face classrooms to hybrid or online formats (Blake & Guillén, 2020; Goertler, 2019), where learners are co-convened through a virtual platform for part or all of the course. These pre-pandemic shifts toward digital learning were intensified during the pandemic and many such formats are here to stay. At the same time, a growing interest in socially oriented pedagogies in

https://doi.org/10.1075/aals.21.01mic
© 2024 John Benjamins Publishing Company

L2 learning and teaching is prompting many L2 researchers and practitioners to investigate new research areas and explore post-communicative language teaching pedagogies that engage learners more deeply with cultural texts, using a range of semiotic and linguistic resources. One area that has been affected by both the aforementioned technological advances and increasing interest in social perspectives on L2 learning and teaching is L2 reading.

The activity of reading a text in community through a virtual platform has been called by many names and has been researched from a range of disciplinary perspectives in both first language (L1) and second language (L2) educational settings. Some of these terms emphasize learner activities, such as anchored discussions (Eryilmaz, Chiu, Thoms, Mary, & Kim, 2014; van der Pol, Admiraal, & Simons, 2006; Wolfe, 2008); social annotation (Novak, Razzouk, & Johnson, 2012); digital social reading (Blyth, 2014); digital social annotated reading (Michelson & Dupuy, 2018). Others foreground the social setting, referring to book clubs or literature circles (Kupfer, 2018; Sambolin & Carroll, 2015) or virtual literature circles (Pei, 2018). Still others emphasize the tools through which these activities are facilitated, for example, through the term digital annotation tools (Solmaz, 2020a); Thoms, Sung, & Poole, 2017). Regardless of the terminology, these pedagogical interventions share a common interest in promoting learning by integrating into pedagogical practice technologies that afford simultaneous annotating and dialoguing in community around the same text. In this book, we adopt the term digital social reading (DSR), foregrounding the learner.

The benefits of using digital platforms for collaborative reading activities extend beyond the obvious, such as the ability to co-convene readers and learners from various geographical locations, or the ability for teachers to observe and intervene in the learning processes of multiple students simultaneously. The aforementioned benefits are primarily in service of institutions (i.e., the capacity-building that is afforded by hybrid or online learning) and instructors (i.e., the efficiency of observing and monitoring student learning). However, the digitization of collaborative reading also confers benefits to students in that annotations from multiple readers are layered on top of the same text, such that readers' own interpretations can be scaffolded in vivo. More specifically, benefits from DSR center around the affordances of interacting with the text (annotations) and interacting with other readers (dialogues). Theoretically, annotations can: help learners make note of key information for later revisiting; help learners process text meanings toward more successful comprehension (Reid, 2014); and expose intersubjective interpretations, both for the benefit of other readers and for instructors. Dialogues can allow readers to: question passages that are ambiguous or contain unfamiliar cultural or linguistic references, thus co-constructing knowledge (Li, Pow, & Cheung, 2015); deepen readers' interpretations through extended discussion of a passage; and promote deeper reflection on a passage through the benefit of a slowed-down, written communication process (Pei, 2018).

By definition, DSR moves reading and learning beyond the realm of individual cognitive efforts and outcomes. Rather than reading framed as an exercise in readers getting meaning from texts, DSR affords co-construction of textual meanings through collaborative interpretation, where one reader's interpretation might be enhanced or extended — i.e., scaffolded — through comments made by a peer or instructor. DSR also makes learning visible to learners themselves, to peers, and to instructors. Due to the written nature of interactions, DSR comments lend themselves to further analysis of various aspects of learning, particularly in terms of learner-learner relations and learner-text relations and help reveal aspects of the complex learning ecology that traditional classroom discourse may obscure. We now briefly summarize research carried out to date related to DSR and L2 learning and teaching across a variety of educational environments.

Literature review

The overwhelming majority of research that has investigated DSR in L2 contexts has focused on its use in English as a Second or Foreign Language (ESL/EFL) learning and teaching environments. Of this subset of work, much attention has involved analyzing the effects of DSR and/or the use of digital annotation tools on students' overall L2 reading comprehension abilities (e.g., Azmuddin et al., 2020; Chen, Wang, & Chen, 2014; Tseng & Yeh, 2018; Tseng, Yeh, & Yang, 2015; Yang & Lin, 2015) and their developing linguistic competence in English (e.g., Liu, & Lan, 2016). An illustrative example of research on DSR and its effects on L2 reading comprehension in an EFL environment includes Yeh, Hung, and Chiang's (2017) study, which investigated the use of online annotations and their impact on 54 EFL low intermediate students enrolled in an English course at a Taiwanese university. Students were trained via a 'reciprocal teaching' approach which involved illustrating to students how to predict, clarify, question, and summarize digital texts. Students then were placed in small groups of three and collectively read, annotated, and discussed (i.e., via text-based chat) six articles using Google Docs over an eight-week period. The researchers found that based on pre- and post-test measurements of L2 reading proficiency, students' overall reading comprehension improved over the course of the study and the DSR environment increased learners' engagement with their peers and instructor. The researchers also found that the groups of learners who demonstrated the most progress over the course of the study frequently reviewed their generated online predictions, clarifications, questions, and summaries in the Google Doc and were also more active with respect to providing peer feedback. This study underscores one of the primary benefits of DSR in that learners are generally more engaged with the text and each other when compared to traditional approaches to reading and analyzing L2 texts via in-person classroom environments. Hypothetically, students have the potential to read more in DSR environments given that they are reading both the digital text(s) and fellow students' written annotations.

Two other notable areas of inquiry of researchers working in ESL and EFL contexts focus on students' perceptions of DSR-based activities (e.g., Benedict, 2022; Zhao, Gao, & Yang, 2018) and how DSR affects students' motivation (e.g., Liu & Lan, 2016). For example, Akhand (2023) investigated the use of a 'collaborative reading annotation system' with low-achieving ESL and EFL learners in Bangladesh over the course of four months. After receiving training on how to use Google Docs, 30 students collaboratively read a variety of short stories and were administered questionnaires at the end of the semester to understand how students perceived the digital collaborative reading experience and how they perceived their own development in English. Focus group discussions were also conducted and analyzed. The researcher reported that students found DSR activities to be 'interesting and appealing'. A handful of students also responded that collaborative social reading allowed them to be more confident in their L2 reading abilities. However, some students in the study did report that they did not feel comfortable reading and annotating, especially when they knew others would read what they wrote.

The final main area of research of DSR use in ESL/EFL contexts investigates the myriad social ramifications of this kind of reading experience on L2 learners. Framed via a second language socialization perspective (Duff, 2008), Solmaz (2020a) sought to understand how EFL learners' collaborative reading practices affect their L2 socialization in a digital environment. A small group of 12 EFL students who were majoring in English language teaching at a university in Turkey participated in the study. Participants were divided into groups of three students and discussed assigned readings that were read and annotated outside of class over the course of eight weeks. Students also were eventually able to take on the role of 'leader' of some of the discussions and uploaded a text of their choosing that other students would read via the digital annotation tool SocialBook. Students' reflections showed that by using a digital annotation tool and engaging in DSR, there were ample opportunities for learners to collaborate with each other and gain multiple perspectives on the various topics presented in the digital texts/readings. The researcher also illustrates, via analysis of learners' annotations, that some of the 'novice' students became 'experts' when leading discussions on their chosen text(s). One of the primary conclusions of the study indicated that via DSR, a new kind of community of practice was formed where learners could collaborate, co-construct meaning, socialize, and adopt different identities (e.g., novice vs. expert) more easily when compared to traditional L2 EFL classroom environments.

Similar work in this vein has also found that DSR-based activities can facilitate both EFL/ESL students' and teachers' social presence in digital spaces (Cui & Wang, 2023), and lead to students being more engaged with the digital texts and each other (Solmaz, 2020b). In addition, some (Solmaz, 2021) have also found that DSR activities can yield a number of social affordances in ESL/EFL classrooms, such as gaining access to different perspectives about the text(s) being read and annotated, engaging in socialization practices as previously highlighted, and collaborating with fellow students in a more socially relaxed and open environment. In sum, EFL/ESL scholars are some of the first researchers to make use of and investigate DSR and its effects on L2 learning and teaching and have generally reported positive benefits of DSR in those specific L2 contexts.

Regarding work that looks at DSR in L2 classrooms other than English, far fewer empirical studies have been carried out to date. As of this writing, the only L2 contexts other than English where DSR has been investigated involve Chinese, French, and Spanish L2 classrooms; although, Chapter 3 in this book includes the first DSR study carried out in an L2 German classroom. As a result, there remains a paucity of empirical work that needs to be carried out regarding the effects of DSR activities in a variety of L2 contexts other than English. To begin filling the research void, Thoms, Sung, and Poole's (2017) article represented the first DSR study carried out in an L2 Chinese classroom environment (the second one appears in this volume; see Chapter 6). The small-scale exploratory study involved 11 students in a beginning college-level L2 Chinese language classroom reading two texts via the eComma digital annotation tool. The results indicate that students predominantly used the DSR experience to query fellow students about the meaning of vocabulary/Chinese characters. Evidence is also presented in the study that shows that eComma allowed students to co-construct meaning and scaffold their learning while engaged in close readings of the Chinese literary texts outside of the physical classroom. A number of pedagogical suggestions resulted from this study, including the importance of adding timing constraints to promote more virtual interaction among students, better integrating students' virtual comments into face-to-face (FTF) classroom discussion, and offering more structure for novice learners in the DSR environment.

Work with DSR in L2 Spanish classrooms has involved understanding the overall benefits for learners and teachers alike. For example, Zapata and Morales (2018) had 44 undergraduate students in an Intermediate Spanish L2 classroom use eComma to read and annotate two poems that were related to themes tied to the class's instructional units. The researchers analyzed students' annotations as well as their responses to a short online survey to better understand students' experience(s) with eComma and DSR in general. The authors found evidence for learners collaborating when offering their interpretation(s) of the poems and when annotating the texts to better understand lexical items in the poems. In addition, students also drew on a range of semiotic resources in their annotations, such as links to videos and music referenced in the poems. One of the main criticisms of the DSR experience voiced by students related to some technical issues with eComma, which primarily related to the slowed and sometimes glitchy nature of interactions when learners were synchronously annotating the texts with the tool. Some characterized eComma as not being user-friendly.

Two other studies (Thoms & Poole, 2017; Thoms & Poole 2018) also analyzed the effects of DSR on 15 college-level advanced L2 Spanish learners. Data for the studies involved (a) the annotations of students using the digital annotation tool Hylighter to read 3–5 poems per week in Spanish over the course of a four-week period, (b) feedback from students regarding their perceptions about engaging in DSR-based activities, and (c) interview data from the cooperating instructor. The Thoms and Poole (2017) study delineated three types of affordances (van Lier, 2004) that emerged in the data: literary (i.e., annotations dealing with some aspect of interpretation or analysis of the poems); linguistic (i.e., annotations that focus on grammar and/or vocabulary items in the poems); and social (i.e., annotations that sought to agree or disagree with others' reactions to the poems or comments that were not directly related to the texts). In addition to operationalizing the three aforementioned affordances in the context of a DSR environment, the researchers found that the number of literary and social affordances outnumbered the linguistic affordances over the course of the study. Regarding students' responses to the DSR activities, the primary challenges included other students' comments impeding some students' understanding of the text and having to make one's comments distinct from others' comments to avoid being socially viewed as an inactive reader or student. From a pedagogical perspective, the primary benefits of incorporating collaborative reading in an L2 Spanish poetry course involved the ability to establish a more open learning community and allowing students to carry out a closer reading of literary texts.

The Thoms and Poole (2018) study built on the findings in Thoms and Poole (2017) by looking at the relationship between L2 text difficulty and the linguistic, literary, and social affordances that emerged in the data. The primary conclusions of this second study pointed to the idea that factors beyond the learners themselves can affect the types of affordances that emerge in the DSR environment. For example, one of the findings from the study suggests that when the lexical diversity of the poems increased, the number of literary affordances that emerged in learners' annotations decreased. The study also found that when two types of affordances emerged in a single annotation, they tended to be both social and literary in nature. Finally, some students resorted to using their L1 in order to express some literary interpretations.

With regard to work in French L2 classrooms, two notable studies are worth highlighting. Michelson, Abdennebi, and Michelson's (2023) study was framed via multiliteracies and ecological theoretical perspectives and sought to compare and contrast text-centered discourse in FTF and digital social annotated reading (DSAR) contexts. Fourth-semester university L2 French students in the United States were divided into the two aforementioned groups and read the same articles with discussions guided by the same reading questions. Students' discussions in both groups were coded based on various types of discursive moves that emerged in both environments and were analyzed via social, textual, and linguistic affordances (Thoms & Poole, 2017). The researchers found that more social than textual affordances were present among learners in the FTF context while textual affordances were the most used among students in the DSAR group. Linguistic affordances (i.e., discursive moves that had a focus on grammar or lexical queries) were relatively infrequent in both groups. The authors conclude that one of the primary benefits of DSAR tools is that they allow for more 'anchored discussions' versus FTF classroom discussions. However, they also signal the important role of the teacher in facilitating in-depth discussions via DSAR. In other words, simply using DSAR in an L2 classroom will not automatically result in more substantive discussion(s) of texts but needs to be implemented carefully by the instructor.

Law, Barny, and Poulin's (2020) study also looked at the use of DSR with college-level French L2 learners in the United States from a multiliteracies perspective. 216 beginning-level French students from across 11 French language sections and taught by 10 instructors participated in the study. Students used the digital annotation tool eComma to read and annotate six different sets of song lyrics that related to the themes of the units found in their textbook. For each song, learners in each section were instructed to simply make at least five annotations in either the L2 or their L1 (English). After categorizing each student's annotations as either literary, linguistic, or social affordances, the researchers' analyses found that some of the sections' discussions in eComma reached a level of 'rich and interactive discussion'. They also discovered that the number of social affordances did not generally increase over the course of the study, contrary to what they expected. Even when social affordances are at a minimum, the researchers contend that DSR may still be more beneficial than solitary reading given that the DSR environment can still allow learners to collaborate — oftentimes, asynchronously — with the digital text. Specifically, the authors mention how students in their study asynchronously provided translations of multiple lines of text to each other to gradually and collectively build meaning over time. Finally, the researchers also found that the DSR environment allowed for students to not only discuss linguistic features of the texts/lyrics, but it also allowed them to more fully explore the pragmatic and cultural aspects of the songs.

Finally, it's worth mentioning that some work on DSR has been carried out with learners in L1 settings, where students and teachers make use of DSR to analyze texts written in learners' L1 with an aim to improve students' L1 literacy skills (e.g., Chen, Chen, & Horng, 2021; O'dell, 2020). In addition, a handful of studies have also looked at DSR-based issues in L2 contexts that go beyond traditional analyses related to linguistic development or the social, literary, and overall literacy-based effects of DSR on learners' L2 development. Examples of these kinds of studies include Benitez et al.'s (2020) project that studied the digital annotation features of the Nota Bene software on EFL pre-service teachers' academic performance and Burhan-Horasanlı's (2022) study that explored issues related to the use of DSR and the unfolding academic discourse socialization of nine students enrolled in a second language acquisition doctoral program in the United States. In short, work on DSR is slowly starting to encompass new L2 contexts and more learner- and teacher-related issues are being explored from a variety of theoretical lenses; an important aspect that we now consider in the context of this volume.

Theoretical framings

At the outset, this book and its respective call for chapters was framed in the intersections between sociocultural theoretical (SCT) perspectives and multiliteracies (ML) pedagogies and their application to research and praxis around DSR. Our original conceptualization of this volume saw a clear synergy between ML perspectives and SCT approaches. Not only do both perspectives prioritize learning and development through social experiences in dynamic contexts, but in their broadest conceptions, both focus on cognitive, linguistic, and social development, seeing sign-making as fundamental to developmental processes. From an ML perspective, the kind of semiosis that is foregrounded is one where users take a sign complex and re-shape it based on their own identities and purposes, using their available representational resources. From an SCT perspective, sign-making mediates development. Multiple and overlapping sign-making activities are inherent — and indeed amplified — in DSR. Highlighting points to relevant passages of text that are meaningful for particular readers, annotations afford opportunities to make explicit individual interpretations and simultaneously provide a prompt for other readers in the community. Reading and writing activities become synergistic, as texts are interpreted through the written down thoughts of readers, made in the margins of the virtual page.

Whether one departs from the New London Group's (1996) original proposal, or Cope and Kalantzis' (2009) Learning by Design framework or via any number of derivatives of ML pedagogies (e.g., Paesani, Allen & Dupuy 2016; Paesani & Menke, 2023), a foundational pedagogical design principle within multiliteracies pedagogies is the engagement between learners and texts. ML sees textual engagement as opportunities to reflect critically on rhetorical purposes of authors, the concomitant design choices made for these rhetorical purposes, and the way that identities and ideologies are manifest in texts, whether explicitly or subtly. The agile interpretation and production of texts — in other words, in ways that are recognized as socially acceptable — is seen as foundational to being 'literate.' In DSR, learners and texts inhabit the same virtual space, and learning can emerge through scaffolded interactions between other peers or between readers and the text. From an SCT perspective, literacy and learning are mediated through cultural tools that include texts, highlighting, annotating, and dialoguing with peers. Annotations and written dialogues serve as mediational affordances: annotations help learners take note of key information for later revisiting, allow instructors to orient reading of particular passages, and reveal readers' interpretations. Written dialogues can allow learners to question ambiguous passages due to unfamiliar cultural or linguistic references, share and debate differing interpretations, thereby deepening readers' interpretations. From an SCT perspective, mediation is a key driver of development and includes the notion that actions, cognitions, and overall human development are mediated by social relations, artifacts, and tools; the latter of which include language and other symbolic systems.

Thus, we believed — and still believe — that SCT and ML perspectives are particularly suited to the pedagogies and scientific inquiries around digital social reading. As in many scholarly projects, we never could have imagined the ways that the call for this volume would be interpreted, nor the vast and expansive kind of work that this collection would bring together around DSR. Many of the chapters in this book draw upon ML pedagogies. In Chapter 2, the course that is the locus for the study reported has been designed around ML pedagogies (Allen & Paesani, 2010; Cope & Kalantzis, 2009), with an emphasis on critical literacy and identity. Chapter 5 proposes ML (Cope & Kalantzis, 2009; New London Group, 1996) as a pedagogical framework for enhancing textual awareness and draws on multimodality in highlighting students' sensitivity to the visual designs in music videos, used as advance organizers for interpreting written language texts (i.e., song lyrics). In Chapter 7, authors highlight principles of cultural awareness, digital literacy, and critical thinking (New London Group, 1996) as well as awareness of linguistic designs that can emerge through carefully scaffolded literacy activities involving reading and writing. Finally, Chapter 4 reports that the course was designed through principles of Learning by Design (LbD) (Cope & Kalantzis, 2009) with an emphasis on multilingual reading and writing practices. The experience of leading students in reflective, mindful, interpretive work leads Blyth to ultimately propose an expansion of the LbD framework beyond the things you do to know to include a focus on the things you do to feel.

The theoretical framings for the diverse projects in this book are far more expansive and innovative than we could have imagined. Nevertheless, they are linked through the shared focus on not only using DSR as a way to mediate language and literacy development, but on laying bare some of the learning processes emerging in FL educational settings. The contributions in this book reflect a diverse set of dialogically-oriented and socio-constructivist theories and converge around three distinct yet complementary themes: the discursive construction of self in relation to others; the integration of affect and cognition, both in response to and as driver of action; and dynamic approaches to teaching and assessing learning.

Two early chapters reflect the theme of discursive constructions of self by drawing on positioning theory (Chapter 2) and stancetaking (Chapter 3). Positioning theory is considered to be a socio-constructivist view of language learning and is anchored in narrative and discourse analysis (Kayi-Aydar & Steadman, 2021). Initially proposed by Davies and Harré (1990), the concept arose out of a desire to move away from the notion of role in "developing a social psychology of selfhood" (p. 43). Role was seen as static while position offered a way to move beyond a notion of the self in terms of personal identity, and instead reflect a notion of 'multiple selfhood', understood as ever-changing in relation to one's interlocutors and the specific expectations of a particular social setting. Positioning theory is especially helpful for educational contexts, as the positions taken up by individuals can have the effect of affording or constraining certain positions for others in the same social setting (Kayi-Aydar & Steadman, 2021). As both an analytic lens and an exploratory theory (Green et al., 2020, as cited in Kayi-Aydar & Steadman, 2021, p. 16), positioning theory helps understand social dynamics, including who has the power or legitimacy to say certain things or act in certain ways. As such, it is related to questions of access. Similarly, stancetaking shares with positioning theory that it is a discursively constructed activity that is sensitive to the social context in which the interaction takes place. Keisanen (2007) asserts that stancetaking is performative and may be characterized through alignment or disalignment with a previous speaker in the context of an interaction. Like positioning theory, stancetaking is a useful analytical lens applied to educational settings, as it reveals complex interpersonal relationships between and among learners, and sheds light on learners' responses to the subject matter they are encountering through texts.

Affective dimensions of interpreting and producing texts are foregrounded in Chapter 4 through the lens of the Vygotskyan concept of *perezhivanie*. Chapters 5, 6, and 7 reflect dynamic aspects of teaching and learning through the ecological theory of affordances (Chapter 5), a formative assessment approach (Chapter 6), and sets of literacy scaffolds that can be flexibly applied in different DSR settings based on pedagogical purpose (Chapter 7). While most scholars who have encountered Vygotskian socioconstructivist theories are familiar with the concepts of mediation and scaffolding, and particularly the Zone of Proximal Development, a lesser-known but nevertheless robust concept within Vygotskian theory is *perezhivanie*. A term without a single-word translation in English, *perezhivanie* signifies a convergence of cognitive and affective responses of individuals to events and reflects a core belief of Vygotsky of the inseparability of affect and cognition (Mok, 2015). *Perezhivanie* has often been referred to through the metaphor of a prism (Johnson & Golombek, 2016; Mok, 2015) through which an individual processes their experiences; as prism, it can both refract experience and shape development (Agnoletto et al., 2021). Consistent with Vygotsky's approach, *perezhivanie* resides within a dynamic relationship between an individual and their environment and signifies a unity between thought and experience.

Affordances, which are relational, provide opportunities for action; in educational contexts, affordances create learning opportunities that are taken up differently by learners. In van Lier's (2004) ecological approach, affordances are semiotic. Thus, the use of particular affordances becomes an activity of sign-making. In the context of a DSR environment, a number of affordances are made available to the learner (e.g., linguistic, literary, social affordances across students' annotations). Relatedly, the affordance-rich DSR environment coupled with a learner's engagement within that digital context result in learners making use of an array of semiotic resources (e.g., pictures, videos, links to related texts) when collaboratively making meaning with others. These resources are not available to learners when collectively discussing texts in traditional face-to-face L2 classrooms.

When looking at how DSR might be used to assess learners' L2 abilities, the authors of Chapter 6 adopt an assessment for learning approach. Different from summative assessment (assessment of learning), formative assessment (assessment for learning) rests upon a dialogic relationship between a teacher and learner. Evaluation of a learner is not made for the purpose of sorting or ranking students, nor determining whether a student has met pre-established criteria for passing an exam or a course. Instead an assessment is made with the purpose of providing feedback to a learner to inform their future development. Thus, assessment for learning is a form of mediated action that has the intention of driving development. In this paradigm, the learner is central; goals for development are jointly constructed between teacher and student and are made visible and tangible in the process.

Organization of book

The chapters in the first section of the book focus on learners, foregrounding the interactions that emerge through DSR and the way that identities and inter-subjectivities are developed and put on display through DSR. In Chapter 2, Elif Burhan-Horasanlı unveils the discursive interactions that emerge among multilingual graduate students and the positioning identities they take up throughout their collaborative reading of scholarly articles carried out in one of their doctoral seminars. In Chapter 3, Claudia Lynn and Sibel Sayılı-Hurley show how German L2 learners discuss and position themselves vis à vis historical events while reading literary and scholarly texts about experiences of belonging by Germans who identify as Black and People of Color. Finally, in Chapter 4, Carl Blyth illuminates the way DSR can slow down reading processes among advanced French L2 learners in a course on the multilingual self, and thus foster reflection and mindfulness.

Elif Burhan-Horasanlı's chapter presents a qualitative classroom-based investigation of the positioning identities that multilingual doctoral students enact while reading scholarship from applied linguistics with their peers through the DSR tool, Social Book. Drawing on classroom data from one group of three doctoral students, Burhan-Horasanlı traces their discursive interactions with each other and with the articles they are reading, focusing on both the content and the language choices (pronouns, adjectives, sentence structure) of their annotations. She unveils the patterns in each of three learners' discursive moves throughout the semester, demonstrating how these moves enact and reflect particular situated identities of each learner: the critical reader, the forever teacher, and the EAL (English as an Additional Language) reader and knowledge seeker. Discursive analyses are triangulated through interviews with each participant, which further reveal that participants' written comments in the DSR activity were sensitive to the anticipated responses and perceptions of their colleagues. Further, Burhan-Horasanlı demonstrates the way that reading practices and patterns of engagement are also shaped by learners' interests with respect to the content of the articles.

Claudia Lynn and Sibel Sayılı-Hurley's chapter also outlines a classroom-based study, this time with undergraduate students, in an effort to foster critical historical thinking. In their study, DSR was implemented in an advanced undergraduate German L2 course that focused on questions of home and belonging, particularly for Black Germans and people of color. Students collaboratively read German literary and scholarly texts through the DSR platform, Perusall, for the duration of the semester. The authors analyzed students' discursive moves from a theoretical framework of stancetaking, which foregrounds individual's interactions vis-a-vis an object of study (e.g., the texts) as well as others in the social setting. Their study effectively demonstrates how alignment, affect, and investment emerge through DSR and how these mediate patterns of collaboration. Their study is particularly striking for the way they demonstrate, linguistically, how individual thinking can become collective thinking through the emergence of community norms within the DSR space.

Carl Blyth's chapter consists of a descriptive report of implementing DSR in an advanced French course entitled "Narrating the Multilingual Self." Drawing on the concept of perezhivanie from Vygotskyian sociocultural theory, which refers to individuals' emotional reflections on and interpretations of events (Agnoletto et al., 2021), Blyth implements a contemplative approach to reading, designing instructional activities that ask learners to slow down in their process of annotating their own and others' texts. Differently from traditional social annotation activities which often take place uniquely in virtual settings, Blyth implements DSR as a synchronous in-class activity, then projects the annotated text on the board as a point of departure for in-class discussion, where students are invited to share a follow up comment about their annotation. Throughout this chapter, Blyth demonstrates how the slowed down reading process allowed students to unpack layers of meanings in the texts they read, beginning with referential meanings, then stylistic meanings, and ultimately interacting with the texts on a subjective level, becoming aware of their own affective responses to these texts. Further, Blyth demonstrates how DSR can be used in annotating one's own texts as a form of self-reflection on writing.

The second set of chapters focuses on texts, tasks, and teachers. In Chapter 5, Jim Law, David Barny and Rachel Dorsey demonstrate from empirical data how glossing can aid in fostering more literary discussion among novice L2 French learners while interpreting song lyrics through DSR. In Chapter 6, Fred Poole and Joshua Thoms illustrate how DSR can lay bare the learning process for teachers in supporting an assessment-for-learning approach. Finally, in Chapter 7, Inanç Karagöz and John Liontas present reading tasks that can be used in conjunction with DSR activities, demonstrating the adaptability of DSR to reading-to-writing tasks.

The chapter by Jim Law, David Barny, and Rachel Dorsey reports on a study exploring the relationship between text difficulty and the emergence of literary affordances among novice French L2 learners ($n = 200$) as they annotate a series of song lyrics using the DAT eComma throughout their semester-long French course. Songs were selected and sequenced by the course coordinator, and tasks were open-ended: learners were instructed to make five comments or tags per song, without specific instruction on the type of comments. Texts were glossed within the DAT environment, anticipating unfamiliar vocabulary. Drawing on ecological frameworks and the theory of affordances and building on previous research using this framework for understanding learners' engagement with texts, the researchers coded affordances according to literary, linguistic, and social affordances. By looking at the emergence of literacy affordances with respect to text difficulty as measured through three different standard measures (K1/100, (frequent vs. infrequent words), type-token ratio (TTR), and professor difficulty rating (PDR), and number of glosses as a fourth measure, authors set out to examine whether glosses effectively counteract text difficulty. Through a linear regression model with the four difficulty measures and the proportion of literary affordances for each text, authors found that glossing did effectively "level the playing field" for texts. In other words, the proportion of literary affordances did not appear to be related to the inherent difficulty of the texts (as measured by traditional measure of text difficulty). Next, they investigated what other textual factors might be contributing to emergence of literary affordances and identified factors such as the cultural content of the song, and prior viewing of the accompanying music video. Furthermore, they found that figurative language was not an affordance for literary annotations, contrary to expectations. Authors conclude with recommendations, drawn from multiliteracies pedagogies, for training students in textual interpretation.

Fred Poole and Joshua Thoms propose using DSR for assessment purposes, specifically in an assessment-for-learning approach. They problematize traditional and mainstream assessment practices, including the fact that assessment is time consuming and that there is often a disconnect between classroom teachers and assessment creators. Furthermore, they remind us that summative assessments for language learning are fraught, because they provide a static measurement of a complex and dynamically evolving skill. Drawing on data from prior studies around DSR, the authors present purposeful examples of student annotations from Chinese L2 courses in which DSR was used, representing annotations that demonstrate novice, intermediate, and advanced proficiency levels. Students' comments are interpreted using ACTFL performance indicators. They proceed to advocate for using the evidence-centered design (ECD) framework in designing assessment tasks and provide a list of sample highlighting and annotation tasks at each proficiency level (novice, intermediate, advanced). Further, they discuss the potential expanded affordances of using DSR for assessment in that assessing students' contributions in a social setting takes into account the learning that can occur within social contexts. Thus, DSR can expand the possibilities and potentials for assessment beyond mere assessment of individual cognitive abilities.

In their descriptive chapter, Inanç Karagöz and John Liontas propose using DSR for source-based reading and writing activities. Departing from social constructivist theories of teaching and learning, and drawing on principles from multiliteracies pedagogies, authors advocate for DSR as a way to enhance both collaboration and textual awareness. They propose eight task sequences designed to promote reading comprehension, but more importantly textual awareness, as a precursor to successful writing, and structure these on a continuum from less cognitively challenging to more cognitively challenging. Task sequences include: Noticing Grammatical Structures, Applying Vocabulary Glossing (designed to promote lexical inferencing), Instigating Reading Content Conversations, Engaging Critical Thinking on Arguments, Making Inferences, Dissecting Model Texts, Reconstructing Ideas, Crafting Source-Based Writing (which includes evaluating credibility of texts). Throughout these task phases are prompts and questions that aim to focus learners' attention on global and local features of texts, and to link language forms with rhetorical purposes through close reading and analysis of texts. Additionally, several task sequences are designed to foster students' critical thinking around texts including assessing credibility of a text, identifying objective and subjective statements, and linking linguistic forms to rhetorical purposes. Sample tasks and question prompts are designed to be adaptable to many different text types and are used to scaffold students' textual analysis. They also propose literacy-based activities that involve textual production — including textual borrowing — demonstrating how learners can be guided to re-appropriate language forms for their own purposes in designing their own texts. The authors argue that doing these activities through DSR enhances conscious awareness of textuality due to the visibility of annotations and comments, and to the collaborative nature of the reading tasks. Finally, their chapter includes a discussion of best practices for educators wishing to implement DSR, including considerations for orienting learners to the tool, scaffolding the activities beginning with simple low-stakes annotations, modeling comments, and limiting group sizes.

In the concluding chapter, Kristen Michelson presents an overview of where we currently sit with respect to research in digital social reading by providing a critical synthesis of the findings and implications of the chapters in this collection and making a case for future research areas around DSR. She then pivots from research to praxis by offering an overview of technical and pedagogical considerations practitioners might wish to make when selecting a DAT for integrating DSR activities into L2 teaching and learning. Technical issues such as cost and accessibility, privacy and visibility, text types supported, and user experience are discussed, followed by pedagogical considerations for optimally matching texts, tools, and techniques.

The chapters in this volume extend the field of research around DSR through an expansive set of theoretical orientations applied to DSR in L2 contexts and by introducing a new L2 (German) into the field. Nevertheless, the field of research around DSR in languages other than English remains narrowly focused on a few languages (Chinese, French, Spanish), and narrowly anchored in educational settings in the United States. We hope that this volume serves as a further call to researchers and practitioners alike to make use of DSR in their work.

References

Agnoletto, M., Dellagnelo, A., & Johnson, K. (2021). Perezhivanie in action: A novice teacher's refraction of mediated dramatic events. *Language and Sociocultural Theory*, 8(2).

Akhand, M. (2023). Impact of collaborative reading annotation system on EFL/ESL learners on a digital platform: A case study of tertiary level students in Bangladesh. *Journal of Education and Practice*, 14(18), 40–50.

Allen, H., & Paesani, K. (2010). Exploring the feasibility of a pedagogy of multiliteracies in introductory foreign language courses. *L2 journal*, 2(1), 119–142.

Azmuddin, R., Nor, N., & Hamat, A. (2020). Facilitating online reading comprehension in enhanced learning environment using digital annotation tools. *Journal of Education: Technology in Education*, 8(2), 7–27.

Benedict, T. (2022). Digital social reading and annotation in the Japanese university classroom: A case study using Perusall. *Kwansei Gakuin University Research in Higher Education*, 12, 67–77.

Benítez, C., Quinones, A., González, P., Ochoa, C., & Vargas, A. (2020). The impact of online annotation tools on students' academic performance in a distance education program. *Turkish Online Journal of Distance Education*, 21(2), 167–177.

Blake, R., & Guillén, G. (2020). Brave new digital classroom: Technology and foreign language learning (3rd ed.). Georgetown University Press.

Blyth, C. (2014). Exploring the affordances of digital social reading for L2 literacy: The case of eComma. In J. Pettes Guikema & L. Williams (Eds.), *Digital literacies in foreign and second language education* (pp. 201–226). Calico.

Burhan-Horasanlı, E. (2022). Digital social reading: Exploring multilingual graduate students' academic discourse socialization in online platforms. *Linguistics and Education*, 71, 101099.

Chen, C., Chen, L., & Horng, W. (2021). A collaborative reading annotation system with formative assessment and feedback mechanisms to promote digital reading performance. *Interactive Learning Environments*, 29(5), 848–865.

Chen, C., Wang, J., & Chen, Y. (2014). Facilitating English-language reading performance by a digital reading annotation system with self-regulated learning mechanisms. *Educational Technology & Society*, 17(1), 102–114.

Cope, B., & Kalantzis, M. (2009) 'Multiliteracies': New literacies, new learning. *Pedagogies: An International Journal*, 4(3), 164–195.

Cui, T., & Wang, J. (2023). Empowering active learning: A social annotation tool for improving student engagement. *British Journal of Educational Technology*, 55, 712–730.

Davies, B., & Harré, R. (1990). Positioning: The discursive production of selves. *Journal for the Theory of Social Behaviour*, 20(1), 43–63.

Dubreil, S., & Thorne, S. (Eds.). (2017). *Engaging the world: Social pedagogies and language learning.* Cengage.

Duff, P. (2008). Language socialization, participation, and identity: Ethnographic approaches. In N. Hornberger (Ed.), *Encyclopedia of language and education* (Vol. 3, pp. 107–119. Springer.

Eryilmaz, E., Chiu, M., Thoms, B., Mary, J., & Kim, R. (2014). Design and evaluation of instructor-based and peer-oriented attention guidance functionalities in an open source anchored discussion system. *Computers & Education*, 71(c), 303–321.

Goertler, S. (2019). Normalizing online learning: Adapting to a changing world of language teaching. In N. Arnold & L. Ducate (Eds.), *Present and future promises of CALL* (3rd ed.) (pp. 52–92). San Marcos, TX: CALICO Monograph Series.

González-Lloret, M. (2020). Collaborative tasks for online language teaching. *Foreign Language Annals*, (53)2, 260–269.

Green, J., Brock, C., Baker, D., & Harris, P. (2020). Positioning theory and discourse analysis: An explanatory theory and analytic lens. In N. Nasir, C. Lee, R. Pea, & M. Royston (Eds.), *The handbook of the cultural foundations of learning.* London: Routledge.

Johnson, K., & Golombek, P. (2016). *Mindful L2 teacher education: A sociocultural perspective on cultivating teachers' professional development.* Routledge.

Kayi-Aydar, H., & Steadman, A. (2021). Positioning Theory for English-Medium Instruction (EMI) praxis: Insights and implications for teaching and research. *Ibérica*, 42, 15–32.

Keisanen, T. (2007). Stancetaking as an interactional activity: Challenging the prior speaker. In R. Englebretson (Ed.), *Stancetaking in discourse: Subjectivity, evaluation, interaction* (pp. 253–281).

Kern, R. (2021). Twenty-five years of digital literacies in CALL. *Language Learning & Technology*, (25)3, 132–150.

Kupfer, C. (2018). *Literature circles: Their effectiveness in developing literacy skills in a foreign language* (Unpublished doctoral dissertation). Grand Canyon University.

Law, J., Barny, D., & Poulin, R. (2020). Patterns of peer interaction in multimodal L2 digital social reading. *Language Learning & Technology*, 24(2), 70–85.

Li, S., Pow, J., & Cheung, W. (2015). A delineation of the cognitive processes manifested in a social annotation environment. *Journal of Computer Assisted Learning*, 31(1), 1–13.

Liu, S., & Lan, Y. (2016). Social constructivist approach to web-based EFL learning: Collaboration, motivation, and perception on the use of Google Docs. *Educational Technology & Society*, 19(1), 171–186.

Michelson, K., & Dupuy, B. (2018). Teacher learning under co-construction: Affordances of digital social annotated reading. *Alsic Apprentissage des Langues et Systèmes d'Information et de Communication*, 21, 1–16.

Michelson, K., Abdennebi, M., & Michelson, C. (2023). Text-centered "talk" in foreign language classrooms: Comparing the affordances of face-to-face and digital social annotated reading. *Foreign Language Annals*, 56(3), 600–626.

Mok, N. (2015). Toward an understanding of perezhivanie for sociocultural SLA research. *Language and Sociocultural Theory*, 2(2), 139–159.

New London Group. (1996). A pedagogy of multiliteracies: Designing social futures. *Harvard Educational Review*, 66(1), 60–92.

Novak, E., Razzouk, R., & Johnson, T. (2012). The educational use of social annotation tools in higher education: A literature review. *The Internet and Higher Education*, 15(1), 39–49.

O'dell, K. (2020). Modern marginalia: Using digital annotation in the composition classroom. *Computers and Composition*, 56, 1–19.

Paesani, K., & Menke, M. (2023). *Literacies in language education: A guide for teachers and teacher educators*. Georgetown University Press.

Paesani, K., Allen, H., & Dupuy, B. (2016). *A multiliteracies framework for collegiate foreign language teaching (theory and practice in second language classroom instruction)*. Pearson.

Pei, L. (2018). *Impact of virtual literature circles on Chinese University EFL students; independent English reading* (Unpublished doctoral dissertation). Oakland University.

Reid, A. (2014). A case study in social annotation of digital text. *Journal of Applied Learning Technology*, 4(2), 15–25.

Sambolin, A., & Carroll, K. (2015). Using literature circles in the ESL college classroom: A lesson from Puerto Rico. *Colombian Applied Linguistics Journal*, 17(2), 193–206.

Solmaz, O. (2020a). The nature and potential of digital collaborative reading practices for developing EFL proficiency. *International Online Journal of Education and Teaching*, 7(4), 1283–1298.

Solmaz, O. (2020b). Examining the collaborative reading experiences of English language learners for online second language socialization. *The Reading Matrix: An International Online Journal*, 20(1), 20–35.

Solmaz, O. (2021). The affordances of digital social reading for EFL learners: An ecological perspective. *International Journal of Mobile and Blended Learning*, 13(2), 36–50.

Thoms, J., Sung, K., & Poole, F. (2017). Investigating the linguistic and pedagogical affordances of an L2 open reading environment via eComma: An exploratory study in a Chinese language course. *System*, 69, 38–53.

Thoms, J., & Poole, F. (2017). Investigating linguistic, literary, and social affordances of L2 collaborative reading. *Language Learning & Technology*, 21(2), 139–156.

Thoms, J., & Poole, F. (2018). Exploring digital literacy practices via L2 social reading. *L2 Journal*, 10(2), 36–61.

Tseng, S., & Yeh, H. (2018). Integrating reciprocal teaching in an online environment with an annotation feature to enhance low-achieving students' English reading comprehension. *Interactive Learning Environments*, 26(6), 789–802.

Tseng, S., Yeh, H., & Yang, S. (2015). Promoting different reading comprehension levels through online annotations. *Computer Assisted Language Learning*, 28(1), 41–57.

van der Pol, J., Admiraal, W., & Simons, P. (2006). The affordance of anchored discussion for the collaborative processing of academic texts. *International Journal of Computer-Supported Collaborative Learning*, 1(3), 339–357.

van Lier, L. (Ed.). (2004). *The ecology and semiotics of language learning: A sociocultural perspective.* Springer.

Warner, C., & Michelson, K. (Eds.). (2018). Living literacies: L2 learning, textuality, and social life. *Special Issue of L2 Journal,* 10(2). https://escholarship.org/uc/l2/10/2

Wolfe, J. (2008). Annotations and the collaborative digital library: Effects of an aligned annotation interface on student argumentation and reading strategies. *International Journal of Computer-Supported Collaborative Learning,* 3, 141–164.

Yang, Y., & Lin, Y. (2015). Online collaborative note-taking strategies to foster EFL beginners' literacy development. *System,* 52, 127–138.

Yeh, H., Hung, H., & Chiang, Y. (2017). The use of online annotations in reading instruction and its impact on students' reading progress and processes. *ReCALL,* 29(1), 22–38.

Zapata, G., & Morales, M. (2018). The beneficial effects of technology-based social reading in L2 classes. *Lenguas en Contexto 9 (Suplemento 2018–2019),* 40–50.

Zhao, N., Gao, F., & Yang, D. (2018). Examining student learning and perceptions in social annotation-based translation activities. *Interactive Learning Environments,* 26(7), 958–969.

SECTION I

Focusing on learners

CHAPTER 2

Examining graduate students' positioning identities in collaborative digital annotation tools

Elif Burhan-Horasanlı
TED University, Ankara

Digital annotation tools (DATs) are one of the recent digital platforms in which multiple users can read and annotate a shared document. Scholars have explored the use and impacts of DATs on peer interaction and documented that collaborative annotation enables a more learner-centered academic space where students can facilitate peer learning and socialization. The present study, on the other hand, shifts the focus and explores the roles of peer interaction to document three multilingual doctoral students' micro-level positioning identities in a semester-long DAT activity. The study's data involved students' collaborative annotations on 11 scholarly articles, semi-structured interviews, and demographic information questionnaires. The data were analyzed with discourse analysis techniques. Findings indicate that students' previous teaching experiences, linguistic and educational backgrounds, and research interests shaped their annotation behaviors and discursive choices and thus led to taking different positioning identities. The study offers pedagogical implications that might cultivate and foster quality peer interaction and involvement in collaborative DAT activities.

Digital annotation tools

Digital annotation tools (DATs hereafter) can be defined as "new discussion spaces that can support sustained on-topic discussion, ... by allowing direct links from participants' shared annotations to a text ... synchronously or asynchronously" (Michelson & Dupuy, 2018, p.3). They not only allow readers to document their reading acts with multiple multimodal annotation affordances such as highlighting, underlining, and commenting features but also help them share these acts and follow others' reading processes in smaller or larger reading communities via social media networks (Blyth, 2014). In addition to these critical aspects, DATs, in a way, turn the individualistic reading practice into a shared

https://doi.org/10.1075/aals.21.02bur
© 2024 John Benjamins Publishing Company

social activity in a cognitively and socially distributed online community of (reading) practice.

DAT activities emerged in the last century but have gained popularity with the increasing interest and emphasis on digital literacies (Michelson & Dupuy, 2018). They differ from conventional discussion boards (e.g., Moodle discussion boards), enabling learners to pinpoint and draw attention to specific text parts at the word or sentence level (Sun & Gao, 2017). Rather than organizing annotations in chronological order as in conventional asynchronous discussion boards, DATs allow users to create direct links to texts through which readers can engage in more focused, on-topic, sustained conversations (Burhan-Horasanlı, 2022; Lambiase, 2010).

Scholars have explored the use of DATs in higher education contexts to explore students' language learning (e.g., Thoms & Poole, 2017), reading comprehension (e.g., Nor, Azman & Hamat, 2013), and (academic) discourse socialization within the last decade (e.g., Burhan-Horasanlı, 2022; Solmaz, 2020). To exemplify, Lo, Yeh, and Sung (2013) explored the use of online annotation tools on reading comprehension of English-as-a-foreign-language students at Chung Hua University in Taiwan. The researchers utilized an experiment design and asked one group of students to read an essay with the Paragraph Annotator — a web-based collaborative annotation tool. The other group was asked to read the essay in a web-based environment with access to an online dictionary. A comparison of the cued recall test and free recall test showed that the students who used Paragraph Annotator indicated higher reading comprehension. Shifting the focus, Thoms, Sung, and Poole (2017) conducted a study to explore the linguistic and instructional advantages and difficulties associated with using eComma in a Chinese language course at the second-semester undergraduate level. During two weeks, students engaged in collaborative reading of two short stories written in Chinese characters. The predominant usage of eComma involved students asking their peers about vocabulary and the meanings of Chinese characters. Overall, these studies showed that DATs served as interactive spaces where students engaged in a collective endeavor to interpret and understand texts at the word or paragraph level.

In recent studies, scholars have approached DATs for exploring Digital Social Reading (DSR hereafter) activities from ecological and sociocultural theoretical perspectives to see whether or how peer interaction facilitates language socialization practices in higher education contexts. Using van Lier's (2000) ecological perspective as their conceptual lens, Thoms and Poole (2017) conducted an empirical research study to analyze learner-learner and learner-text interactions within a DAT setting called *Hylighter*. Exploring the collaborative reading practices in a college-level Hispanic literature course, the scholars identified linguistic, literary, and social affordances. The results showed that students' engagement in social and literary affordances outnumbered linguistic affordances; few annotations were centered around linguistic elements, such as asking their peers questions about vocabulary or grammar. Solmaz (2020), on the other hand, employed language socialization theory and examined the DSR activities of English as a foreign language learners *on SocialBook* in an advanced-level reading course over a semester. The findings indicated that students were socialized into multiple genres and networks with the reading practice and had the chance to step into expert and novice roles to assist each other in the DSR processes.

Shifting the focus to academic language socialization, Burhan-Horasanlı (2022) explored nine doctoral students' semester-long collaborative annotation practices of 11 scholarly articles on *SocialBook*. The findings of the study indicated that by pinpointing different aspects of scholarly articles (e.g., language use, research design), students invited each other to participate in digital social reading and engaged in thought-provoking conversations, yielding socialization into research and academic writing practices. Finally, Michelson and Dupuy (2018) explored the use of DATs on professional growth among four graduate teaching assistants of French in a methods course. The students were asked to complete the course readings on multiliteracies through *SocialBook*. Findings indicated that via collaborative annotation, students demonstrated deeper reflections on content, felt more confident to confirm their understandings, and built a learning community with active participation. In short, these studies indicated that DATs served as active social and academic spaces where students could share their expertise, take different roles, and go beyond textual interpretation with collective knowledge construction.

The present study builds on existing research on DATs to approach online interaction with post-structuralist perspectives on identity, specifically positioning identity, and explores three multilingual doctoral students' DSR activities. It explores how students engage in reflexive and interactive positionings and construct positioning identities via multimodal collaborative annotation over a semester. The following section will present the study's conceptual framework, bridging the connection between identity and positioning theory.

Conceptual framework

Identity and positioning theory

Poststructuralist perspectives have played a prominent role in revising the definition of identity, which was traditionally believed to be a rather structured and fixed unitary phenomenon, in second language acquisition and applied linguistics (De Costa, 2010). With seminal work on five immigrant women in Canada (see Norton, 2000), Norton (2014) revisited identity "as multiple, changing, and a site of struggle, frequently negotiated in the context of inequitable relations of power" (p.60). Following this reconceptualization, scholars have approached identity as a social construct that helps one understand their relationship to the world and is shaped and reshaped across time and space (e.g., Norton & Toohey, 2011; Pavlenko, 2003). Rather than a single and structured aspect, identity is now defined as an unstable, ongoing, constructed, co-constructed, and negotiated phenomenon.

Positioning theory has been utilized as a theoretical and methodological tool to analyze narrative discourses and social interaction in applied linguistics (Kayi-Aydar, 2019). It is intertwined with identity, as positioning theory captures the smallest building blocks of identities — positions or positionings. Davies and Harré (1990) define positioning as a "discursive process" that accumulates "in conversations ... in jointly produced storylines" with discourse moves and multimodal acts such as gestures, facial expressions, and intonation. (p.48). It is highly observable in interactions with a focus on how individuals attune to and attain conversations in the multimodal communicative world.

Davies and Harré (1999) put forward two modes of positioning. The first mode, *reflexive positioning* (or self-positioning), refers to individuals' acts to position themselves. Deppermann (2015) noted that reflexive positioning is not a private or invisible phenomenon remaining in individuals' minds; it is still tied to and enacted with social actions within diverse settings. The second mode, *interactive positioning*, refers to when an individual positions the other(s) with verbal or multimodal communication. To exemplify, asking a question to someone in a conversation can position the question-receiver as a source of knowledge. In a different case, one can avoid an addressee in a discussion and position them as outsiders. Collecting these recurring modes either separately or jointly constructs the positioning identities. In other words, constant positioning practices of individuals accumulate in time and space within different situations or conversational practices and lead to the emergence of various identities.

Researchers have documented how language learners and teachers engaged in positioning and constructed positioning identities by exploring classroom interactions (e.g., Anderson, 2009; Pinnow & Chval, 2015; Wagner & Herbel-Eisenmann, 2009; Wood, 2013) or narratives (e.g., Deppermann, 2013; Kayi-Aydar, 2018). For instance, Kayi-Aydar's (2014) study conducted within an ESL classroom over a semester exemplifies the positioning identities of two international students who took active roles in interacting with the course instructor and creating learning opportunities for themselves but at the same time, denied access to their peers' learning opportunities by overtaking the conversations in collaborative group work. The recursive positionings within the two students' immediate turn-taking structures, interruptions, or ignorance of peers constructed their 'talkative student' identities. Highlighting the excessively dynamic nature of positioning, Wood's (2013) study demonstrates the multiple micro identities (e.g., mathematical explainer, menial worker) a fourth-grade student constructed within a single class period. Findings also documented these micro identities' positive and negative influences on the student's learning process. For instance, the focal participant actively attuned to the course content by using disciplinary discourse as a mathematical explainer and communicating his ideas but engaged in passive roles as a note-taker of mathematical terms when he stepped into the shoes of a menial worker. The findings of these studies show not only the situated and fluid natures of positions and positioning identities but also their impacts on other interactants involved in the learning/teaching processes.

Since DATs allow online interaction on shared documents synchronously or asynchronously, they might serve as spaces where individuals engage in annotation activities in specific ways and construct positioning identities with the storylines built in between annotations or by underlining/highlighting specific parts in texts. However, there is a dearth of research focusing on micro-level interactions to see how participants construct discursive positioning identities. Therefore, using positioning theory as its conceptual lens, the present study delves into this underexplored area by examining how three multilingual doctoral students construct positioning identities in DATs using the multimodal (e.g., highlighting, underlining) and interactive affordances[1] (e.g., commenting) and addresses the following research question:

1. How, if at all, do three multilingual doctoral students engage in discursive positioning and (co)construct micro-level fluid identities through multimodal affordances in their collaborative DAT practice?

The study

Setting and participants

The study was conducted in an applied linguistics doctoral program with first- and second-year doctoral students in a research-intensive university in the U.S.

---

1. Following Michelson & Dupuy (2018), the term *affordance* addresses the contributions of highlighting/underlining and commenting features on building focused conversations around texts.

At the time of the study, 14 students were taking the compulsory course Introduction to Applied Linguistics. The course aimed to inform the students about four main areas: (second/multilingual) language acquisition, linguistics, cognitivist perspectives on SLA, and pedagogical aspects of language teaching/acquisition. Out of these 14 students, three students from one of the three collaborative reading groups were chosen as the focal participants.

Within the scope of the graduate course, the instructor asked the students to read 11 scholarly articles on the four aforementioned areas over a semester. *SocialBook,* a free collaborative annotation website, was utilized as the digital social reading platform (see Figure 1 for a screenshot). SocialBook enabled students to read and annotate articles in groups by writing and responding to each other's comments and questions. It also allowed the students to highlight/underline articles, and these highlights/underlining were visible to all group members.[2] In addition, SocialBook offered virtual reading rooms through which the students could be grouped in smaller numbers and only see their group members' shared texts and annotations. Using this affordance, the course instructor divided students into three virtual reading groups to create a more effective and interactive ecology and asked the students to read and annotate one scholarly article every week. The course instructor organized the students' DSR activity in two stages. In the first stage (Mondays and Tuesdays), students would only read and annotate the text. In the second stage (Wednesdays and Thursdays), students would respond to their classmates' comments and questions. The course instructor did not restrict the students' participation with minimum or maximum number of annotations and remained mostly invisible by posting only 13 comments in the entire semester. DATs were graded to reinforce students' involvement in collaborative reading and constituted 20 percent of the overall course grade.

The focal participants of the present study were chosen from one of these groups for the study after the approval of the Institutional Review Board. These students were selected intentionally, as they only knew each other after the course. More importantly, all three of them had completed their M.A. degrees in different programs and conducted their master's theses in various areas of applied linguistics. Therefore, each student, in a way, had diverse expertise. It should be noted that all three of these students were multilingual speakers. Two of the students were English as an additional language (EAL) speakers, and one of the students was an English L1 speaker. In addition, their experience in teaching varied. I chose these three students, in particular, to see whether or how greater cultural, linguistic, and experiential differences might afford more overt demonstrations of positioning identities reflected in their annotation behaviors.

---

2. SocialBook shows underlined sentences with highlights when the cursor is on the underlined text. That is why, I use these two features interchangeably in the entire chapter.

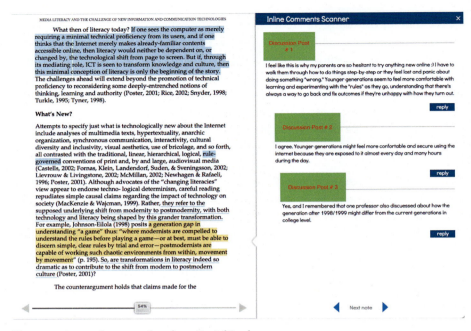

Figure 1. A sample screenshot from SocialBook

Table 1. Demographics of the participants[a]

Name	Age	Language background	M.A. degree	Teaching background
Lina	28–30	English L1 speaker	Language teaching	4 years
Max	33–35	EAL speaker	Curriculum and instruction	7 years
Mira	30–32	EAL speaker	Linguistics	2 years

a. Participants of the study are presented in alphabetical order. For confidentiality purposes, the year of the students in the program was not included in the table. Similarly, the data collection year remains undisclosed. The names of the focal participants have been replaced with pseudonyms.

Data collection and analysis

The data of this study comes from a larger project that explored graduate students' academic reading and socialization practices. The data collection period started in the third week of the semester after I received the IRB approval and participant consent. Data for the present study came from three sources: annotations of 11 articles, questionnaires, and semi-structured interviews. The students read one article and annotated it with their group members each week. After each week's DSR practice, I transferred the students' annotation comments, underlining, and highlights to separate Microsoft Word documents, as the DAT's interface did not allow me to download students' annotations as a Word or PDF document for coding purposes. The second portion included demographic information questionnaires asking about students' educational and professional backgrounds. The third part of the data came from semi-structured interviews. The interviews had two parts; in the first part, the students were asked to reflect on their demographic information and overall DSR experiences. Some of the sample questions regarding demographics were as follows: How do you define yourself (e.g., a language teacher, an interdisciplinary researcher, a linguist or applied linguist? How, if at all, did your teaching experience influence your collaborative reading practice? As someone holding a degree in Linguistics, how did you navigate yourself while reading articles from three other subfields of applied linguistics? The second part focused on students' responses regarding their annotation behaviors. Both interview sections played prominent roles in understanding the rationale behind the students' positioning identities. These interviews were conducted at the end of the course so as not to influence students' annotation behaviors. The duration of the interviews varied between 30 and 52 minutes.

Data were analyzed through discourse analysis and completed in four consecutive stages. In the first stage, I treated the students' annotation features (e.g., highlighting, commenting) as multimodal positioning elements. I believe they were not random practices but rather deliberate choices indicating their reading behaviors. I then created correlations between these reading behaviors and students' positioning identities (e.g., note-taker, detail-oriented reader) by coding and checking the frequencies of each student's annotation types (e.g., highlighting, commenting). I revisited these initial correlations in the second analysis stage.

In the second stage, I coded students' turn-taking strategies by coding their comments or questions (e.g., Kayı-Aydar, 2014) to identify how they position themselves in the participation structures. For instance, it was important to see when students initiated a new turn with a comment (e.g., Mira: It is really interesting how the author compares language. (visual, digestive or immune systems), asked a question (e.g., asking for clarifications) as in the following example: "Max: I did a corpus-based study using film language. Do y'all consider this authentic language?", and/or when they stepped in to answer their partners' questions (e.g., informative explanations) as exemplified in Lina's response to Mira's question:

> **Mira:** Why does the author continuously repeat that she considers herself a CL?
> [Annotation, October 27]

> **Lina:** Trying to emphasize his position? Similarly, I find it interesting how much 1st person voice is used here! [Annotation, October 30]

Such discursive moves informed my analysis in terms of students' areas of expertise and how they created room for each other to take various positions as, for instance, novices and experts. In addition, I also counted the number of annotations per participant to see if there were any connections between the participants' research interest and the content of the annotated articles.

In the third stage, I focused on the content of the students' annotations with detailed analyses of word choice (e.g., use of pronouns, adjectives, sentence structure) and annotation content to understand what kind of information the students shared with each other and whether or how this information was associated with their positioning identities. It should be noted that the findings of these three analytical processes on the annotations were triangulated with interview data to see parallels and differences between what the students enacted in their DAT practice and their perceived rationales behind their participation. In addition, I intentionally avoided using a priori codes and categories in these three analysis stages to utilize a bottom-up approach to detect and depict the focal participants' salient positioning identities carefully.

In the fourth stage of analysis, which occurred while writing the cases, the previous detailed discourse analysis stages were reinterpreted according to whether or how they might serve as reflexive and discursive positioning. In the writing stage, I also utilized within and cross-case analysis (Merriam & Tisdell, 2015) (1) to compare the positioning identities of the three focal participants and (2) to identify the differences between participants' micro-level positioning identities.

Researcher positionality

I believe that my academic situation at the time I conducted the study might have influenced my research motivation and design. As Patton (2014) suggested, to increase the research process's transparency, it is essential to disclose some dispositions that I might have brought into play and how I overcame them. I was a doctoral student in applied linguistics when I conducted the study. I had already taken classes for various semesters and experienced the reading-oriented nature of postgraduate programs. Almost all of my classes involved multiple weekly readings discussed within the classroom context. Even though the classroom discussions helped me approach the reading materials with different lenses with the help of my classroom community, the overall reading process had always felt like a lonely, individual practice during which I struggled with understanding and interpreting articles with critical lenses.

Hearing in the first week of the semester that the focal participants would engage in semester-long collaborative DAT sessions, in which I could see the students' while-reading activities, I decided to start my research project. In the participant recruitment process that occurred in the third week of the semester, I approached the students as one fellow doctoral student interested in the interactional nature of their DAT use and academic reading. I believe my position as a student researcher encouraged them to participate and consent to the study. I could easily see this in the semi-structured interviews, where the students seemed to feel comfortable opening up about their experiences more conversationally without the need to be directed questions only by the researcher. I had no background information about the students or their potential approach to DATs. It was also my first time encountering a DAT tool and DSR practice. I believe all these helped me analyze the data without bias and in a curious way. In addition, to avoid any potential influences I could create on the participants, I only attended the DATs as an observer. I avoided taking part in any of the collaborative reading processes.

Findings

Findings indicated that students demonstrated variations in their use of DAT affordances. To exemplify, among all three participants, Mira used underlining as a frequent annotation behavior in her DSR activities. Max and Lina, on the other hand, underlined less content. Regarding the use of commenting feature, Mira demonstrated more active participation in initiating a comment, asking questions, and responding to comments. On the other hand, Lina and Max enacted much similar numbers of instances while asking questions and responding to comments. Table 2 demonstrates the number of underlining and commenting instances for each participant.

Table 2. Numbers of underlining and commenting instances per participant

Participants	Underlining	Commenting		
		Initiating a comment	Asking Questions	Responding to comments
Lina	78	63	22	43
Max	47	48	21	37
Mira	154	111	43	65

Analysis of the comments indicated that the topics of the article played a prominent role in students' participation. To exemplify, Lina and Max left more annotations on the articles covering language use (e.g., identity, agency) and language teaching pedagogies. However, they decreased their participation when they started annotating articles on language analysis and language processing in L2 teaching. On the other hand, the quantity of Mira's annotations remained more stable throughout the semester, leaving more than 30 comments on nine of 11 articles. Table three presents the number of annotations per article per participant.

Table 3. Number of annotations for each participant per article

Participants	Number of annotations per article[*]										
	A 1	A 2	A 3	A 4	A 5	A 6	A 7	A 8	A 9	A 10	A 11
Lina	23	30	25	24	23	15	13	11	10	14	12
Mira	38	37	41	43	31	21	34	36	32	28	32
Max	21	19	22	17	18	13	8	9	10	9	7

[*] Articles 1, 2, and 3 (A1, A2, A3) covered topics on language use. Articles 4, 5, and 6 (A4, A5, A6) covered topics on language teaching pedagogies. Articles 7, 8, 9, 10 and 11 (A7, A8, A9, A10, A11) covered topics on language analysis and language processing in L2 learning and teaching.

In light of these, the analysis of students' annotations, interview responses and demographic information questionnaires as individual cases showed that their cumulative DAT behaviors reflected different online positioning identities presented as three separate cases. The first case shows that Lina's recursive critical comments about the content, language use, and research methods positioned her as *the critical reader*. Max, the second case, acted as *the forever teacher* by annotating articles referencing his previous teaching experiences and research interests in language teaching. Mira, as the third case, was documented as *the EAL reader and knowledge seeker* of the reading group with frequent annotations that are underlining details in the articles and involving questions about terminology and relevant content.

Lina: The critical reader

Lina had received her degree in language teaching. She wanted to pursue her doctoral studies to focus on social and pedagogical aspects shaping language learning/teaching processes. It was her first time taking a postgraduate course with an online component for collaborative reading in which she was introduced to DATs. When asked how and for what purposes she annotated articles, she mentioned the following statements.

Extract 1.
```
01  I think I tried to look for ideas that were either surprising or interesting
02  to me and also parts of the articles that were maybe confusing. And
03  usually, I tried to write whatever thoughts it made me think of but also
```

Chapter 2. Examining graduate students' positioning identities **33**

```
04  asked a question so that it would engage other students so sometimes
05  I'd be like, "ohh this is similar to what so and so says, did it make you
06  guys think of that or anything else?" And hopefully open it up for more
07  discussion. [Interview, February 16]
```

The interview quote shows that Lina approached the readings from two perspectives; (1) as a personal space reflecting the thinking process through which she engaged in *reflexive positioning*, and (2) as a dialogic process with the texts and peers through which she engaged in *interactive positioning*.

It was evident in Lina's comments that both of her positioning types were reflected in her recurring annotation behaviors. The following extract (Extract (2)) demonstrates the reflexive positionings she engaged in while reading an article on identity and agency.

Extract 2.
```
01  Lina:  This is really interesting! I've never thought of laughter as a
02         form of resistance. It makes sense, though! [Annotation, September 25]
03         (Annotation # 1)
04  Lina:  So as long as you don't speak your ideas to others, they don't
05         exist? They don't shape your actions? I find this hard to accept.
06         [Annotation, September 25] (Annotation # 2)
```

The annotations shared in Extract (2) were retrieved from the same article and represent a purposive example of Lina's reflexive positionings. Her use of "I never thought of ..." (line 01), and "I find this hard to accept" (lines 05) with references to the information presented in the articles exemplify how she questioned the content and evaluated it with her personal perspectives — as supported by the use of the first-person pronoun. With such comments, Lina depicted her challenged thoughts through which, in a way, she engaged in new learning experiences. In the interview, Lina also mentioned that her critical annotations were mostly motivated by her purpose "to understand the theoretical aspects" as she "[did]n't understand a lot of theory behind teaching" [Interview, February 16] in her master's studies. With her annotations, she thus might have attempted to delve more into the reading material and merge it with her thinking process.

Lina's interactive positioning occurred mostly to meet the course requirements for which the course instructor told the students to take active roles in creating engaging conversations. In this respect, Lina saw the DATs as an extra burden which would bring another dimension to her reading practice. She stated in the interview that normally she "would take rather quick notes to [herself]"; however, in DATs she needed "to think how other people [were] going to view [her] notes and find ways for other people to interact with [her] notes." [Interview, February 16]. However, she still asked questions as a discursive strategy to create an engaging learning environment. She posed questions to her classmates —

which can be interpreted as Lina's invitations for interaction. Extract (3) exemplifies one of these discursive strategies.

Extract 3.

Annotated Excerpt: *Sylvia said of herself and her husband, "We came with open eyes," meaning that they knew they had to abandon an important aspect of their identities.* (Vitanova, 2005, p. 161).

```
01  Lina:   What do you guys think about this interpretation of her
02          statement? I feel like it could just mean that they came ready
03          to observe and learn. I don't think that this would necessarily
04          mean abandoning "important aspects of their identities"
05          unless she personally clarified this later in the interview.
06          [Annotation, September 28]
07  Mira:   I think they must have a context. But yes, I agree with you.
08          [Annotation, September 28]
```

Lina starts her comment with an open invitation to interpret the author's statement (line 01). Then, she reports her critique on the author's descriptions of the research participants' language learning behaviors and the identity formation processes. With this invitation, Lina engages in interactive positioning by positioning her classmates as knowledgeable others who could help her understand the author's claim. It should be noted that even though Lina did not always receive strong responses from her peers, she kept asking questions and demonstrated persistent behavior to create engagement in their DAT reading activity, as seen in Extract (4).

Extract 4.

Annotated Excerpt: *An infant from a Stone Age tribe in the Amazon, if brought to Boston, will be indistinguishable in linguistics and other cognitive functions from children born in Boston who trace their ancestry to the first English colonists; ...* (Berwick & Chomsky, 2011, pp. 19–20).

```
01  Lina:   This is very strange to think about. Is it really true? Has our
02          modern environment really had no biological influence on
03          our linguistic and cognitive functions over such a long period
04          of time? [Annotation, October 23]
05  Mira:   I think they might argue that, in terms of maybe lexical items,
06          or phonological change, etc. yes, but in terms of the innate
07          syntactic structure, maybe not. [Annotation, October 24]
08  Lina:   That's a good distinction. I wish they would've clarified that
09          more... [Annotation, October 25]
```

The annotation sequence occurred when Lina questioned a sentence that claimed no effects of the modern world on the biolinguistics evolution. Her questions given in lines 01 through 04 (e.g., is it really true?) might be conceptualized as encouraging Mira's involvement in the discussion through which she shared her own interpretation of the potential changes in the linguistic aspects. Lina's turntaking with the approval of Mira's comment with "a good distinction" (line 09) and not letting the conversation pass without notice might indicate Lina's intentions for cultivating an active, peer-led learning platform.

One thing that limited Lina's reflexive and interactive positioning was the reading materials. Even though she was quite immersed in the articles at the beginning of the semester, her participation decreased over time when the students were given studies on cognitive dimensions of language learning. She explained this decrease as follows:

Extract 5.
```
01  Because most of my background has been language use in context
02  and teaching, the other half of the course was kind of foreign to me,
03  and I just didn't have like the scholarly connections to other research
04  and stuff that other people were bringing, and because it wasn't really
05  interesting to me either. I had a hard time engaging and being
06  thoughtful in my comments. So yeah I really struggled because my
07  background is mostly language use and language teaching pedagogy.
08  [Interview, February 16]
```

Such disconnection between her background and some of the subfields of applied linguistics had a negative impact on Lina's participation. Her adjective use in her statements ("it wasn't really *interesting* to me", "hard time", etc.) (lines 04 & 05) shows the reasons that made her move towards silence and individualization in her annotation practice, by positioning herself as a scholar of language teaching pedagogy and drawing boundaries between her research-areas and other subfields.

Max: The forever teacher

Max was an international student who had received his undergraduate and master's degrees from prestigious universities. It was his first time studying in the U.S. Max had been working as an English teacher in international contexts "as a practitioner," and he "thought it was time for [him] to develop as a researcher as well" [Interview, February 22]. For this reason, he decided to continue his doctoral degree. It was Max's first time using a DAT platform.

Analysis indicated that Max's professional experiences as a language teacher strongly influenced his annotation behaviors. Unlike Lina and Mira, while responding to his friends' comments and questions, Max referenced his teaching experiences as his "go-to" source for instance, to provide concrete examples to support the reading materials. Such discursive reflexive positionings of Max as an invested teacher and practitioner ignited engaging online discussions among the group members. Since everyone in the group had teaching experiences to a certain degree, they could relate to the ideas and think from learners' perspectives. The following extract exemplifies one of these instances.

36 Elif Burhan-Horasanlı

Extract 6.

Annotated Excerpt: *The hugely significant skills of reading and writing have been augmented by the also-significant skill of "reading" audiovisual material from the mid-twentieth century onward.* (Livingstone, 2004, p.3).

```
01  Max:   It is also important to train learners in a way that they are
02         able to "read" non-linguistic messages that texts have. 4)
03         [Annotation, September 4]
04  Lina:  To add onto Max's point, we should also get students to critically
05         analyze why non-linguistic messages are crafted as they are. Sometimes
06         how texts convey a message is just as important as what the text says.
07         [Annotation, September 5]
08  Mira:  Yes, I think intertextuality is really vital for students and using
09         multimodal resources we could help the students to engage in, and develop
10         their awareness of messages embedded. [Annotation, September 5]
```

The annotated excerpt was given to show that even though the quote did not include any information about teaching in particular, Max still tied it to teaching practice. As shown in the extract, Max built onto the annotated excerpt by sharing his opinions about the importance of "train[ing] learners" towards reading non-linguistic messages. His choice of the word "train" — the synonym of 'teach' — might signal how he approaches the content of the article — media literacy — from a teacher's perspective. In line 4, Lina stepped in to contribute to Max's comment, emphasizing the critical analysis of nonlinguistic elements for students. Last, Mira joined the conversation by addressing the importance of intertextuality and multimodal literacy skills for reading the textual meaning between the lines. To summarize, even in the fourth week of semester, Max's comment did not receive simple affirmative responses but rather deep and critical insights from the group members.

Max's responses to his peers were also interwoven with his teacher identity, providing his friends' abstract questions with concrete examples drawn from his previous in-class teaching experiences when and if possible. More specifically, he mostly acted like a teacher in his explanations and used "exemplification" as one of the common discursive strategies of teachers (e.g., Bozbıyık & Morton, 2023; Zodik & Zaslavsky, 2008) to help his peers overcome confusion regarding some of the concepts. Regarding interactive positioning, Max located his fellow DAT friends as classmates with diverse expertise due to the rich diversity in their research and educational backgrounds. He stated:

Extract 7.

```
01  I was very happy with this collaborative reading, I really liked it because
02  I learned a lot from others because the funny thing is that you read the
03  same paragraph even the same sentence and you could see that 10
04  different people can interpret in ten different ways or they associate it with
05  something else. So some people might just start talking about Bourdie, and
06  you might have never heard it or you start talking about Kumaravadivelu
07  who some other people have never heard, so I think it goes mutually
```

Chapter 2. Examining graduate students' positioning identities   **37**

```
08  beneficial. So how did I use the [DAT]? I used it to ask my friends about
09  research and theory, because their expertise could help me understand new
10  things and expand on my knowledge. [Interview, February 22]
```

Analysis of Max's interview response showed that he could turn the diversity of the group members into new learning experiences. His use of *a lot* in line 02 in his sentence, "I learned a lot from others," might indicate the rich learning ecology cultivated by the differences in the students' backgrounds. In the response, he did not simply engage in interactive positioning by positioning his peers as *experts* in "research and theory," as in line 09. However, he still signaled the potential contributions that each person could offer and thus play equally important "mutually beneficial" (lines 07 & 08) roles in the collaborative reading processes of each other.

Max's awareness of equal distribution in peer contribution might have helped him create a safe zone where he could easily ask his peers questions about research and theory when needed. The following extract exemplifies one of the instances in which he directed a question to differentiate two issues: *corpus* and *native speaker judgments.*

Extract 8.

Annotated Excerpt: *In the absence of corpus data for the metonymic patterns investigated in this experiment, we rely on native speaker judgments to establish regularity through acceptability ratings.* (Slabakova, Cabrelli Amaro, & Kyun Kang, 2016, p. 181).

```
01  Max:   It sounds as if they contrast corpus data and "native speaker
02         judgments". "What makes corpus, then? Isn't it the collection
03         of written and spoken texts by native speakers of that
04         language? [Annotation, November 12]
05  Lina   I think the idea is that "native speaker judgments" of a certain
06         linguistic aspect are based on an individual's subjective
07         intuitions, which can be wrong, while a corpus can have
08         thousands of examples of the linguistic phenomenon, which
09         offers a more objective and representative analysis.
10         [Annotation, November 13]
11  Max:   Thanks, Lina! [Annotation, November 14]
```

As seen in the extract, Max directly posed a question to first understand 'corpus', one of the key terms referenced in the reading material (lines 02–04). However, he did not leave it simply as a 'what is this' question, he also reflected on his knowledge by sharing his understanding of corpus. With this turn-taking move, Max did not simply leave the stage to his classmates to fill in his question but rather fed into the collaborative ecology by providing information on which his classmates could build. In lines 05 through 09, Lina explained the difference between *native speaker judgments* and *corpus data* with her own ideas and examples. In the last line (line 11) Max thanked Lina for the explanation. Max's last turn the next day after Lina's comment might show that he followed the response sequences and did not leave questions for the sake of doing the DAT task but to learn from his peers. The following extract shows another instance in which Max directs a question to his peers about the lack of visual proof in a scholarly article.

Extract 9.

Annotated Excerpt: *Statistically speaking, for whatever that is worth, the overwhelming use of language is internal — for thought.* (Berwick & Chomsky, 2011, pp. 25–26).

```
01  Max:    Is it only me who expected to see some figures :) ?
02          [Annotation, October 23]
03  Mira:   Yeap! Some illustrations would help! [Annotation, October 24]
04  Lina:   Yes! You can't say that this is statistically the case without
05          referencing WHAT those statistics are, WHERE they came
06          from, or HOW they got them... [Annotation, October 29]
```

Max's use of 'is it only me' in line 01 might have sounded as if he was looking for allies for his claim and motivated his peers to respond to his question. Both comments approved his point, and Lina, as seen in lines 4, 5, and 6, built on Max's claims by explaining how scholars should present ideas based on statistics. It should be noted that as in Extract (8), in Extract (9), Max again grounded his questions on his reflection. Rather than posing a 'what do you think' question, he first shared what he expected to see in the article. This can also exemplify his approach to DATs as a space of collaborative learning and distributed peer contributions.

Similar to Lina, Max's reflections decreased towards the end of the semester when the class started to focus on other fields of applied linguistics (e.g., corpus linguistics, cognitivist perspectives in SLA). His strong research plans and interests on language teaching worked as a barrier towards his participation and he mostly aimed to perform the course requirements. Overall, Max's reflexive positioning revolved around his teaching and teacher-oriented positioning identity. However, in addition to positioning himself as a "teacher" in his annotations, he also stepped into the shoes of learners via interactive positioning to create an active learning atmosphere in which he valued his peers' contributions and treated them as sources for learning.

Mira: The EAL reader and knowledge seeker

Mira had completed an M.A. in linguistics. Even though she had been introduced to some areas of applied linguistics in her master's years, it was her first time taking a semester-long, comprehensive class solely based on various subfields of applied linguistics (e.g., cognitive sciences, corpus linguistics). She stated her intentions as follows:

Chapter 2. Examining graduate students' positioning identities   39

Extract 10.
```
01  I wanted to study [applied linguistics] because I wanted to learn more
02  about the field, it is a big field. I was reading some things because I
03  was curious to learn more about it, but I don't think it is enough. So I
04  took the class. [Interview, February 25]
```

Enrolling in the class, she was happy to see that DAT was going to be used for two reasons; first, she had already used it before and enjoyed the nature of collaborative discussions; second, as an EAL speaker and learner, she was hesitant to read and comprehend articles by herself, so DATs would allow her to seek help from her peers when needed. She stated:

Extract 11.
```
01  English articles are not easy, and I know I don't understand some things.
02  So I could get help from my friends because some of them maybe have
03  better English, and some are native speakers" [Interview, February 25].
```

Pinpointing her friends who might have "better English" (line 3), Mira positioned herself as a less competent English user and engaged in interactive positioning by situating her other EAL and English L1-speaking friends as more 'capable' others. These statements might show that Mira actually did not approach the DSR activity as a distributed learning space in which everyone might play an active role in the learning ecology but as a top-down structured platform where 'linguistically experienced' or 'capable' ones play a more significant role in helping other students. In a way, Mira reduced DAT's scope to reading comprehension. Extract (12) reflects Mira seeking help from the 'knowledgeable others' when she detected unclear parts in the article.

Extract 12.
Annotated Excerpt: *Second, there are the physio-chemical constraints of the world, necessities that delimit biological possibilities, like the near-impossibility of wheels for locomotion due to the physical difficulty of providing a nerve control and a blood supply to a rotating object.* (Berwick & Chomsky, 2011, p. 22).
```
01  Mira:  This is a little bit absurd to me, what is your understanding
02         towards this paragraph? [Annotation, October 21]
03  Lina:  I agree — I don't see how it directly relates to the topic of
04         language variation. [Annotation, October 23]
```

Noticing a less relevant paragraph, Mira wanted to hear her peers' opinions (lines 01 & 02). What is important here is that she did not simply ask for help with interpretation but also shared her opinion about the article (e.g., absurd to me), engaging in an evaluative role and positioning herself as an active reader who did not simply ask for passive confirmations. Lina confirmed Mira's evaluation by elaborating on the irrelevance of the topic (lines 03 & 04). Such conversations frequently occurred between Mira and her reading partners, Lina and Max, especially in the initial parts of the semester. However, towards the end of the semester,

Mira's questions about clarity diminished. When I verbally reported this change in her annotation behaviors and asked the rationale behind it in the interview, she stated the following:

Extract 13.
```
01  I think my questions changed about article language because I saw
02  that my friends had the same question like 'what is this, what do they
03  mean?' I was thinking that I was the only one when I didn't understand
04  because I am an EAL speaker. Sometimes articles have sophisticated
05  words. I thought that I didn't understand them because of the
06  academic language. But I know it is not because of my English
07  anymore (laughs). [Interview, February 25]
```

As seen in the quote, DAT helped Mira to reposition herself; rather than foregrounding her language background as the basis of her reading struggles, witnessing her friends asking similar questions on meaning (lines 02 & 03), she started to understand the potential misinterpretations that could result from the article itself. This might indicate that her positioning identity as a less competent EAL user changed over time with her involvement in the DAT and observations of her peers' annotations. She became assertive in her claims and evaluations about authors' language use and avoided asking her friends' opinions. Extract (14) exemplifies one of these instances in which she critiqued the author's use of referential pronouns.

Extract 14.
Annotated Excerpt: *Turning to what we and scholars from other disciplines see from, and think about, each other, I think there are several things that make corpus linguistics less attractive to the observer from theoretical linguistics (apart from very time-consuming retrieval and coding operations).* (Gries, 2010, p. 330).
```
01  Mira:  This made me almost want to do a discourse analysis on the author's use
02         of "referential pronouns"... [Annotation, November 2]
```

The second finding about Mira indicated a stronger positioning identity — the knowledge seeker. In the interview, Mira mentioned that she enjoyed reading a lot and kept her reading range broad to get familiar with different concepts. She followed the same attitude in the DATs and approached the readings as a new source for learning and bridging more connections between different concepts. She thus "highlight[ed] important things probably for [her] to quote in the future [when] maybe [she] had another suggestion or connection for different areas [Interview, February 25]". Her approach to the DATs as a site for learning accumulated in her reflexive positioning when she offered information about additional sources by providing specific references and created multiple (intertextual) connections across various fields throughout the semester. The following extract (Extract (15)) exemplifies one of these instances:

Chapter 2. Examining graduate students' positioning identities   **41**

Extract 15.

Annotated Excerpt: *Although philosophers, anthropologists, and psychologists have increasingly used Bakhtin's notions of dialogue and subjectivity, his ideas remain largely unexplored by second language researchers.* (Vitanova, 2005, pp. 149–50).

```
01  Mira:  I do think even now there are a huge amount of work that are
02         done by sociologists and anthropologists haven't been explored
03         by second language researchers, especially for researchers that
04         are focusing in (language) use. [Annotation, September 25]
05  Lina:  I agree! Was there anything in particular that you were
06         thinking of? [Annotation, September 27]
07  Mira:  I think there are a lot research in social science that will benefit
08         our studies as well. For example, the studies of social networks
09         are quite mature in sociology. We mention "social networks"
10         a lot, but do not have much studies regarding this particular
11         issue. Also, another example is that Indexicality, enregisterment
12         which are talked a lot in anthropology, they often talk about
13         native language instead of second language. Something like that
14         I think. [Annotation, September 28]
```

The conversation started when Mira detected the need for more research interaction between different fields (e.g., anthropology and sociology). Her use of "I do think" in line 01 might indicate that she did not simply engage in brainstorming but took a determinist position about the cross-references in research fields. She later built on her comment upon Lina's request via examples involving specific terminology rooted in different areas (e.g., social networks, enregisterment). In addition, her frequent use of quantifiers (e.g., a lot, much) (e.g., lines 07, 11, 12) and preference for simple present tense helped her engage in reflexive positioning of a competent self who was not simply brainstorming but proposing strong claims with confidence.

It should be noted that despite the frequent intertextual references and interdisciplinary connections that Mira built in her DAT annotations, she was not aware of her emerging discursive self as a *knowledge seeker*. She was more concerned about her EAL reader positioning identity, due to which she might have overshadowed the contributions she offered in the DSR activities (e.g., bridging rich connections). She reported "I post some things like just random things. I don't think I write for something important (laughs)." [Interview, February 25]. Mira's approach to her comments as unimportant, random posts might be seen as the unawareness of her contributions.

Discussion

The present study emerged from scholars' call for studies on learner-based explorations of DATs as research sites (e.g., Thoms & Poole, 2018). Approaching the social affordances of DAT from a positioning theory perspective, the study explored how three multilingual doctoral students constructed positioning identities of *critical reader, forever teacher,* and *EAL reader and knowledge seeker* via collaborative reading and annotation over the course of a semester.

First, the study's findings demonstrated that all three participants engaged in different annotation practices and discursive strategies, thus building three different positioning identities. To exemplify, Max, with relatively thick teaching experience, used his professional background as a source and reference in his annotations and built a "forever teacher" positioning identity. On the other hand, Mira, who approached the course as a space to expand her knowledge in applied linguistics, treated course materials as sources for a learning experience and thus demonstrated a more active presence in DAT as a "knowledge seeker". In addition, her concerns regarding her language background played a role in her positioning identity as an EAL reader who asked her peers to help interpret language use in the articles. These findings might exemplify the situated nature of social reading activities that is highly attuned to the variation in collaborative readers' professional, educational, and linguistic backgrounds (Burhan-Horasanlı, 2022). Therefore, DAT ecologies should not be conceptualized as standard annotation practices but rather active and dynamic spaces that can be shaped through the variety of dialoguing offered by the readers.

Second, the findings of the study highlight the dialogic nature of DATs and concur with existing research in terms of students' annotations pointing out specific parts of the texts to seek help from their peers and create learning opportunities (e.g., Burhan-Horasanlı, 2022; Thoms & Poole, 2017, 2018). Building onto this, the study also demonstrates how students' questions about scholarly texts provided their peers the time and space to show their expertise in content while co-constructing meaning (Lantolf & Poehner, 2014). As Thoms (2014) put forward, with collaborative annotation, learners aim to be "intelligible and more accessible not only to [one learner or interactant] but to others as well" (p.739), and thereby cultivate a dialogic interactive space. In this respect, DATs might train learners to realize and accept the existence of a larger crowd, forming a rich learning/teaching ecology, and this way, they might reduce their concerns of becoming intelligible to one addressee — the course instructor.

Third, the findings indicated that the participants' annotation frequencies also served as a tool for their positioning identities. Mira actively participated throughout the semester regardless of the content, which constructed her positioning identity as a knowledge seeker. On the other hand, Lina and Max reduced the number of their annotations when the content of the reading material did not align with their research interests or purposes. This finding might offer an alternative view to language-proficiency-oriented learner participation approaches.

Existing scholarship on classroom discourse has documented that course instructors associate international students' lack of attention and participation with learners' linguistic capacities (e.g., low proficiency in speaking and listening), culture, and gender (e.g., Morita, 2009) rather than willingness to communicate (e.g., Sang & Hiver, 2021; Zhong, 2013). However, the study's findings showed that the students intentionally avoided participation when they did not find parallelism between their research scopes and the content of the articles. Thus, the study indicated that decreasing participation is not solely correlated with linguistic, cultural, or social elements but can be more of a selective act forming one's positioning identity.

Pedagogical implications

Value diversity. As seen in the findings, all three participants had diverse educational and professional backgrounds and research directions reflected in their annotation behaviors. These differences helped students create a diverse and lively ecology where they could take various reflexive positionings. The focal participants were grouped randomly, not with a particular intention to enrich diversity in terms of educational or professional background. However, the positive outcomes of the students' DAT discussions might encourage other instructors or educators to form reading groups with diverse participants. In online platforms, instructors might hesitate to bring students from various geographic and even disciplinary areas together as they might be afraid that students cannot find common ground to engage in interactions. Instead, the present study shows that when teachers approach DSR as a shared practice with distributed cognition or cognitive load (Blyth, 2014), students can then contribute with collective support, recycling their previous knowledge and practices for interpreting and consuming the new reading material.

Assign readings that align with learners' interests. The study demonstrated that the focal students' participation rates were highly associated with their research areas. Lina and Max's involvement in the DATs decreased when the students were assigned readings that were not of interest to their potential research directions. Only one of the students, Mira, valued being exposed to articles outside of her field as she had already liked reading materials from different subfields. For doctoral students, it might not be realistic to reduce the reading range to a particular area as the nature of working towards a doctoral degree requires philosophical and intellectual investment, which is partly accomplished via reading different sources. However, for younger age groups of undergraduate or master's programs, reducing the array of the readings mostly, if not only, towards the learners' interest or providing a choice among readings might play a substantial role in increasing students' participation.

Help learners see their peers as 'intellectual partners'. DAT has reinvented the definition of reading as a social practice in which readers can share, ask and answer questions, take individual notes that are open to the reading community, summarize, synthesize, and create connections between different types of information with intertextual references. All these acts and benefits are cultivated and fostered by learners, not teachers or course instructors. Therefore, teachers should encourage their learners to see their classmates as potential guides and resources in the learning process. By exemplifying the positive outcomes of DSR practices to their students, teachers can materialize the contributions of various learners. To achieve this, teachers can create a list of topics that students shared in annotations and present it as learning outcomes of collaborative reading, or they can lead whole class discussions in which they elicit what students learned from each other in DAT activities. One additional way could be transforming students' DSR discussions into bubble maps or mind maps, in which teachers put the reading material into the center of the map and create nodes to show what topics students discussed in their annotations and whether or how they went beyond the course reading with intertextual connections. Showing these maps and intertextual connections to the whole class can easily materialize the diversity that students bring into the learning setting. In short, these approaches help teachers create a learner-centered classroom ecology where learners do not treat teachers as the only 'go-to' source for information but as intellectual partners.

Help learners see their strengths and empower them. Students, especially international students, might join their academic programs with hesitations and fear that they will not be able to contribute to their classmates' learning processes. Some of these thoughts might derive from the ideologies imposed by the native-speaker dichotomy. As seen in Mira's case, students might see their linguistic background and proficiency as drawbacks and feel ready to accept and consume the work of published scholars. Moreover, their concerns regarding their language level might shadow all other potential intellectual insights they might offer their classmates. With DAT use, teachers should inform their students about the linguistic support they might receive from their peers but also underline that every student in the classroom comes to school with something to share, teach, and add onto the learning/teaching process. To show students' contributions, teachers can go over some of the comments in the classroom setting every once in a while and highlight each student's input.

Conclusion

This study explored three multilingual doctoral students' positioning identities as they engaged in collaborative annotations around scholarly literature through a free DAT called SocialBook over a four-month period. Findings from the analyses of the students' annotations, semi-structured interviews, and demographic information questionnaires indicated that all three participants enacted various discursive strategies and constructed three positioning identities. The study highlights the situated and dialogic nature of DAT spaces in that variations in students' interests and approaches to collaborative reading activities build unique positioning identities. Despite this variation, collaborative readers still acknowledge and value what their peers offer for the learning ecology. The study suggests that DATs are potentially valuable platforms for higher education settings to create lively, rich, student-centered learning and even teaching spaces.

References

Anderson, K. (2009). Applying positioning theory to the analysis of classroom interactions: Mediating micro-identities, macro-kinds, and ideologies of knowing. *Linguistics and Education*, 20(4), 291–310.

Berwick, R., & Chomsky, N. (2011). The biolinguistic program: The current state of its development. In A. M. Di Sciullo & C. Boeckx (Eds.), *The biolinguistic enterprise: New perspectives on the evolution and nature of the human language faculty* (pp. 19–41). Oxford University Press.

Blyth, C. (2014). Exploring the affordances of digital social reading for L2 literacy: The case of eComma. In J. Guikema & L. Williams (Eds.). *In Digital literacies in foreign language education: Research, perspectives, and best practices* (pp. 201–226). Calico.

Bozbıyık, M., & Morton, T. (2023). Lecturers' use of examples in online university English-medium instruction: A micro-analytic classroom interaction and knowledge-building perspective. *Language and Education*, 1, 1–20.

Burhan-Horasanlı, E. (2022). Digital social reading: Exploring multilingual graduate students' academic discourse socialization in online platforms. *Linguistics and Education*, 71, 1–12.

Davies, B., & Harré, R. (1990). Positioning: The discursive production of selves. *Journal for the Theory of Social Behaviour*, 20(1), 43–63.

Davies, B., & Harré, R. (1999). Positioning and personhood. In R. Harré & L. Van Langenhove (Eds.), *Positioning theory* (pp. 32–52). Wiley-Blackwell.

De Costa, P. (2010) Let's collaborate: Using developments in global English research to advance socioculturally-oriented SLA identity work. *Issues in Applied Linguistics* 18(1), 99–124.

Deppermann, A. (2013). How to get a grip on identities-in-interaction: (What) does 'positioning' offer more than 'membership categorization'? Evidence from a mock story. *Narrative Inquiry*, 23(1), 62–88.

Deppermann, A. (2015). Positioning. In A. De Fina & A. Georgakpoulou (Eds.), *Handbook of narrative analysis* (pp. 369–387). Wiley.

Gries, S.T. (2010). Corpus linguistics and theoretical linguistics: A love – hate relationship? Not necessarily. *International Journal of Corpus Linguistics*, 15(3), 327–343.

Kayi-Aydar, H. (2014). Social positioning, participation, and second language learning: Talkative students in an academic ESL classroom. *TESOL Quarterly*, 48(4), 686–714.

Kayi-Aydar, H. (2018). "If Carmen can analyze Shakespeare, everybody can": Positions, conflicts, and negotiations in the narratives of Latina pre-service teachers. *Journal of Language, Identity & Education*, 17(2), 118–130.

Kayi-Aydar, H. (2019). *Positioning theory in applied linguistics* (pp. 41–69). Springer.

Lambiase, J. J. (2010). Hanging by a thread: Topic development and death in an online discussion of breaking news. *Language@ Internet*, 7(9). http://www.languageatinternet .org/articles/2010/2814

Lantolf, J., & Poehner, M. (2014). *Sociocultural theory and the pedagogical imperative in L2 education: Vygotskian praxis and the research/practice divide*. Routledge.

Livingstone, S. (2004). Media literacy and the challenge of new information and communication technologies. *Communication Review*, 7(1), 3–14.

Lo, J., Yeh, S., & Sung, C. (2013). Learning paragraph structure with online annotations: An interactive approach to enhancing EFL reading comprehension. *System*, 41(2), 413–427.

Merriam, S., & Tisdell, E. (2015). *Qualitative research: A guide to design and implementation* . Jossey-Bass.

Michelson, K., & Dupuy, B. (2018). Teacher learning under co-construction: Affordances of digital social annotated reading. *Apprentissage des Langues et Systèmes d'Information et de Communication*, 21, 2–16.

Morita, N. (2009). Language, culture, gender, and academic socialization. *Language & Education*, 23(5), 443–460.

Nor, N., Azman, H., & Hamat, A. (2013). Investigating students' use of online annotation tool in an online reading environment. *3L: The Southeast Asian Journal of English Language Studies*, 19(3), 87–101.

Norton, B. (2000). *Identity and language learning: Gender, ethnicity, and educational change*. Pearson Education.

Norton, B. (2014). Identity and poststructuralist theory in SLA. In S. Mercer, & M. Williams (Eds.), *Multiple perspectives on the self in SLA* (pp. 59–71). Multilingual Matters.

Norton, B., & Toohey, K. (2011). Identity, language learning, and social change. *Language Teaching*, 44(4), 412–446.

Patton, M. (2014). *Qualitative evaluation and research methods* (4th ed.). Sage.

Pavlenko, A. (2003). "I never knew I was a bilingual": Reimagining teacher identities in TESOL. *Journal of Language, Identity, & Education*, 2(4), 251–268.

Pinnow, R. J., & Chval, K. Bouchard. (2015). "How much You wanna bet?" Examining the role of positioning in the development of L2 learner interactional competencies in the content classroom. *Linguistics and Education*, 30, 1–11.

Sang, Y., & Hiver, P. (2021). Using a language socialization framework to explore Chinese students' L2 reticence in English language learning. *Linguistics and Education*, 61, 1–12.

Chapter 2. Examining graduate students' positioning identities

Slabakova, R., Cabrelli Amaro, J., & Kyun Kang, S. (2016). Regular and novel metonymy: Can you curl up with a good Agatha Christie in your second language? *Applied Linguistics*, 37(2), 175–197.

Solmaz, O. (2020). Examining the collaborative reading experiences of English language learners for online second language socialization. *The Reading Matrix: An International Online Journal*, 20(1), 20–35.

Sun, Y., & Gao, F. (2017). Comparing the use of a special annotation tool and a threaded discussion forum to support online discussions. *Internet and Higher Education*, 32, 72–79.

Thoms, J. (2014). An ecological view of whole-class discussions in a second language literature classroom: Teacher reformulations as affordances for learning. *The Modern Language Journal*, 98(3), 724–741.

Thoms, J., & Poole, F. (2017). Investigating linguistic, literary, and social affordances of l2 collaborative reading. *Language Learning and Technology*, 2(21), 139–156.

Thoms, J., & Poole, F. (2018). Exploring digital literacy practices via L2 social reading. *L2 Journal*, 10(2), 36–61.

Thoms, J., Sung, K., & Poole, F. (2017). Investigating the linguistic and pedagogical affordances of an L2 open reading environment via eComma: An exploratory study in a Chinese language course. *System*, 69, 38–53.

Van Lier, L. (2000). From input to affordance: Social-interactive learning from an ecological perspective. In J. P. Lantolf (Eds.), *Sociocultural theory and second language learning: Recent advances* (pp. 245-259). Oxford University Press.

Vitanova, G. (2005). Authoring the self in a non-native language: A dialogic ap-proach to agency and subjectivity. In J. K. Hall, G. Vitanova, & L.A. Marchenkova (Eds.), *Dialogue with Bakhtin on second and foreign language learning: New perspectives* (pp. 149–169). Lawrence Erlbaum Associates.

Wagner, D., & Herbel-Eisenmann, B. (2009). Re-mythologizing mathematics through attention to classroom positioning. *Educational Studies in Mathematics*, 72, 1–15.

Wood, M. (2013). Mathematical micro-identities: Moment-to-moment positioning and learning in a fourth-grade classroom. *Journal for Research in Mathematics Education*, 5(44), 775–808.

Zhong, Q. (2013). Understanding Chinese learners' willingness to communicate in a New Zealand ESL classroom: A multiple case study drawing on the theory of planned behavior. *System*, 41(3), 740–751.

Zodik, I., & Zaslavsky, O. (2008). Characteristics of teachers' choice of examples in and for the mathematics classroom. *Educational Studies in Mathematics*, 69(2), 165–182.

CHAPTER 3

Critical historical literacy in world languages through digital social reading

Claudia Baska Lynn & Sibel Sayılı-Hurley
University of Pennsylvania

This exploratory study reports on digital social reading (DSR) interactions in an advanced collegiate German course. Using a stancetaking perspective, we examine how learners linguistically conceptualize, discuss, and draw on historical thinking strategies of continuity and change to evaluate historical, social, and cultural patterns in texts and how their interactions mediate peer-to-peer learning. Preliminary findings suggest that DSR can mediate peer-to-peer interaction in a critical content-based course. We conclude with suggestions for future research and teaching. The results of this study indicate that an interactional analysis of stancetaking can help researchers and instructors understand how such peer-to-peer mediation of disciplinary language and thinking approaches emerges in DSR.

Introduction

The exchange in Figure 1 is taken from a Digital Social Reading (DSR) thread of an advanced undergraduate collegiate German course that examined how Germans who identify as Black or People of Color renegotiate *Heimat* and *Belonging*. Brittany and Diana, students in the course, were responding to the introductory chapter of *Undeutsch*[1], Fatima El-Tayeb's (2016) critique of revisionist historical narratives in Germany. El-Tayeb's scholarly text challenged the students linguistically and conceptually.

Brittany announces her challenges by explaining her conundrum *I understand the words but I do not understand the concept of this sentence so much* and then asks for help: *Can someone help me and explain a little?* With the addition of the hashtag *#Clarificationquestion*, Brittany reinforces her requests and adds to a repository of such requests on the course's DSR site, Perusall. Diana responds

---

1. El-Tayeb, F. (2016). *Undeutsch. Die Konstruktion des Anderen in der postmigrantischen Gesellschaft*. Transcript Verlag.

https://doi.org/10.1075/aals.21.03lyn
© 2024 John Benjamins Publishing Company

Chapter 3. Critical historical literacy in world languages through digital social reading 49

Figure 1. Excerpt from Digital Social Reading exchange

BRITTANY	Ich verstehe die Wörter aber ich verstehe die Konzept dieses Satz nicht so gern. Kann jemand mir helfen und erklären ein bisschen? #Verstaendnisfrage
	I understand the words but I do not understand the concept of this sentence so much. Can someone help me and explain a little? #Clarificationquestion
DIANA	Wenn ich richtig verstehe, bedeutet der Satz, dass es eine Version der Geschichte gibt, die gemeinhin akzeptiert ist. Es gibt auch andere Versionen der Geschichte, aber die deutsche Mehrheit verwirft die andere Versionen, um ihre "Hauptgeschichte" zu schuetzen. (z.B. vielleicht ist Kolonialismus versteckt in die "Hauptgeschichte" aber erkennt in eine andere Versionen der Geschichte, die POCs vorschlagen) Dass bedeutet, dass es "unser Geschichte" und "ihre Geschichte" gibt — wieder eine Grenze zwischen die deutsche Mehrheit und Migranten/POCs.
	If I understand correctly, the sentence means that there is one version of history that is commonly accepted. There are also other versions of history, but the German majority rejects the other versions to protect their "main history". (e.g. maybe colonialism is hidden in the "main story" but recognized in other versions of history that POCs propose) That means that there is "our story" and "their story" — again a boundary between the German majority and migrants/POCs.
BRITTANY	Ah verstehe ich, jetzt. Es ist ein anderes Beispiel von "Wir gegen sie". Danke schön!
	Ah I now understand. It is another example of "Us against them". Many thanks!

with her interpretation *If I understand correctly, the sentence means that there is one version of history that is commonly accepted.* She then rephrases her understanding again and gives an example. As she draws her conclusion *That means that there is "our story" and "their story"*, Diana alludes to the fact that this passage illustrates an example of social boundaries, a topic of a previous class,... *again a boundary between the German majority and migrants/POCs.* Concluding the thread, between exclamations that proclaim her improved understanding and gratitude, Brittany proposes *It is another example of "Us against them"*, signaling her own ability to draw intertextual connections between this new text and previous class discussions.

Brittany might simply be restating Diana's intertextual insight. Yet, her intersubjective alignment (Kärkkäinen, 2006) with Diane, mirrored in the parallelism of "I understand" in all three annotations, suggests she is focused on understanding the troublesome passage, namely putting the words together into a meaningful message. In contrast, the deictic reference in "It is another example..." suggests that Brittany, referring to "it" as the text rather than Diana's annotation, takes an epistemic stance as author of this conclusion. The analysis of stance in this dialogic exchange reveals how Brittany incorporates — rather than simply mimics — Diana's intertextual thinking processes. Diana, in other words, mediates in peer-to-peer interaction a model of sophisticated disciplinary thinking that Brittany was ready to take up (Gergely & Csibra, 2007; Lantolf, 2006; Tomasello, 1999).

How do learners come to engage with each other in DSR? What types of engagement mediate learning? For any engagement to happen learners must recognize an annotation as a certain type of social interaction with certain types of social conduct (Agha, 2007). As Kiesling (2009) demonstrated, interlocutors draw on linguistic and semiotic resources to communicate their stance towards a discursive figure talked about in their interaction (e.g., a person, an idea, a text) and each other. Thus, through stancetaking, interlocuters signal complex relationships to the discursive figure, or stance object (Du Bois, 2007), and to each other, thereby making the interaction recognizable as a specific communication event.

This exploratory study — a practitioner and researcher collaboration — examines learners' peer-to-peer mediation in DSR as they engage historical thinking strategies. The study was conducted as part of a departmental curricular initiative,[2] led by the authors. This initiative responds to calls by the profession (Geisler et al., 2007; Lomicka & Lord, 2018) for a curricular transformation at the postsecondary level that develops "deep translingual and transcultural competence" (Geisler et al., p. 236) at all levels of the curriculum. Any implementation of such a curricular transformation, must scrutinize the content of world languages education and its pedagogical delivery with renewed determination for its suitability to meaningfully engage learners.

Inviting historical complexity and diverse perspectives into the classroom requires pedagogic strategies that decenter the teacher as expert (Kubota, 2016). Instead, the teacher as facilitator must bring diverse knowledges into conversation with each other. A multiliteracies pedagogy (Allen & Paesani, 2010; Cope & Kalantzis, 2009; NLG, 1996) coordinates such multiple entry points into the complexities of language and content, while historical thinking approaches provide learners disciplinary tools to analyze, construct, and critique narratives of the past (Lévesque & Clark, 2018), and thereby navigate the tensions of multiple perspectives. DSR tools decenter the teacher as expert and allow for learners to become active participants in knowledge creation (Gao, 2013; Thoms, Sung, & Poole,

---

2. This curriculum reform targets beginning to low-advanced German courses in our department -those courses that have traditionally been conceptualized as language focused courses or bridge courses to content courses. The goal of the reform is to implement a critical content-based curriculum supported by a social view of language (Fairclough, 1999; Johnson, 2009) and a multiliteracies pedagogy (NLG, 1996; Cope & Kalantzis, 2009; Allen & Paesani, 2010).

Chapter 3. Critical historical literacy in world languages through digital social reading 51

2017) and mediate learning in peer-to-peer interaction. As the exchange in the opening vignette affirms, student interactions in DSR have the potential to foster learning through peer-to-peer mediation (Vygotsky, 1986; Lantolf, 2006; Lantolf et al., 2014) in the world language classroom.

Literature review

DSR in world languages

Digital tools enable learners to participate in DSR and digital social annotation (DSA) allow learners to engage collaboratively with texts, peers, and instructor in a community of learning. To date DSR research has focused primarily on L1 or ESL contexts. While DSR studies in FL contexts are still limited, they generally report on the positive effects of DSR on motivation and learning. An early descriptive report (Blyth, 2014) indicated that DSR had a beneficial impact in two undergraduate French courses. Learners used "interpretive strategies" (p. 215) in the 1st semester course to evaluate vocabulary, co-construct meaning, and reflect on intercultural differences. DSR resulted in "nuanced and creative" (p. 216) commentary in the 4th semester course. Thoms, Sung, and Poole (2017) investigated the linguistic and pedagogical impact of DSR in an undergraduate Chinese (L2) course, and similarly demonstrated that learners mediated the meaning of vocabulary and co-constructed meaning of literary texts. Thoms and Poole (2018) explored digital literacy practices in a college level Hispanic literature course and found that literary and social affordances outnumbered the linguistic affordances in their DSA. This demonstrates that students are focused on and engage more with the content and each other instead of only the linguistic aspects of language. The language/culture bifurcation is not replicated. In other words, DSR can help overcome the language-content bifurcation by unifying the "study of literature and the study of literary-cultural content" (Paesani, Allen, & Dupuy, 2016, p. 22), and serving as a "scaffold or mediate the learning of peers in addition to fostering social connections" (Paesani & Menke, 2023, p. 96). Law, Barny, and Poulin (2020) examined patterns of interaction in DSR across multiple sections of beginning French courses and reported collaborative co-construction of meaning.

Overall, studies suggest that DSR (1) increases motivation and promotes learning as a social practice (Adams & Wilson, 2020; Chen, Chen & Horng, 2021); (2) improves reading comprehension (Chen & Chen, 2016; Chen & Chen, 2014; Chen, Chen, & Horng; 2021; Jan, Chen & Huang, 2016; Yang, Yu, & Sun, 2013; Yeh, Hung, & Chiang, 2017); and (3) engages learners as active participants in collaborative processing of the texts and knowledge construction through anchored discussion (Eryilmaz et al., 2014; Gao, 2013; Plevinski, Weible, & DeSchryver, 2017; van der Pol, Admiraal, & Simons, 2006). These studies suggest that DSR turns reading into an interactive, social process, where meaning is socially constructed through social interactions, which may lead to deeper/higher knowledge.

Stancetaking in digital social reading

Stance is enacted through a range of linguistic, paralinguistic and other semiotic resources such as lexical items, grammatical constructions, and code choice. As an analytic tool, stance or stancetaking (Kiesling, 2022) captures how interlocutors take perspective in discourse (Johnstone, 2007) and "claim relationships to their talk, the entities in their talk, and their audience and interlocutors" (Kiesling et al., 2018, p. 684). Du Bois (2007) elaborates the multidirectionality and intersubjectivity of stancetaking:

> Stance is a public act by a social actor, achieved dialogically through overt communicative means (language, gesture and other symbolic forms), through which social actors simultaneously evaluate objects, position subjects (themselves and others), and align with other subjects, with respect to any salient dimension of the sociocultural field. (p. 163)

Thus, alignment between interlocuters unfolds while each interlocuter evaluates and takes position vis-à-vis the stance object in a given period of discourse. Within this framework, evaluation and positioning are conceptualized through affective stance and epistemic stance respectively. Following Jaffe (2009), affective stance relates to emotional states of the speaker and epistemic stance conveys degrees of certainty. Importantly, the evaluation and positioning moves of affective and epistemic stance are "socially grounded and consequential" (Jaffe, 2009, p. 7), meaning that both stances are presupposed and entailed by the alignment of the interlocutors. The stance act, thus, constructs and negotiates social relationships.

Kiesling et al. (2018) examined stancetaking through the dimensions of alignment, epistemic stance (investment), and affective stance in online discussion forums on Reddit. Their analysis revealed that alignment emerges as the dimension with the most persistence across threaded conversations. Like all dimensions of stancetaking, alignment was operationalized on a 1 to 5 scale, where 1 indicates very low, 3 indicates neutral, and 5 indicates very high. Yet, for alignment to persist throughout a threaded discussion it did not require a high positive score; it was most persistent or "sticky" on the neutral level. Perhaps counterintuitively, for alignment to persist throughout a threaded online discussion it did not require a high positive score evidenced by explicit expressions of agreement. Instead, alignment was most persistent or "sticky" on the neutral level which means that participants expressed neither strong agreement nor strong disagreement, but rather acknowledged each other's points or asked questions. As the authors conclude, neutral alignment, rather than positive or negative, facilitates cooperativeness, giving evidence that the cooperativeness principle (Grice, 1975) holds in online interactions.

Historical literacy in a world language

Without carefully attending to how content is integrated, language instruction runs the risk of trivializing content or, worse, leading students to draw problematic conclusions (Kubota, 2012). While history in world language education is not taught as stand-alone, disciplinary content, it is increasingly an integral content component in critical content-based curricula. Historical thinking strategies (Lévesque, 2008; Seixas, 2017), articulated for the teaching of history, respond to the needs of learners in diverse societies to engage agentively in principled historical inquiry. They foreground the procedural knowledge of how historical knowledge is constructed, while substantive or content knowledge — what history is about — serves merely as background information (Lévesque, 2011, p. 118). In this framework, historical thinking includes a series of procedural habits of thought, such as historical significance, evidence, cause and consequence, historical perspective-taking, ethical dimensions, continuity and change.

Historical thinking strategies are transferrable into critical content-based world language curricula and may help overcome the questionable moral conclusions or silences when learners discuss contested histories (Kubota, 2012; Tocaimaza-Hatch & Bloom, 2019). A typical activity is the reconstruction of chronologies, where learners must match images and/or text to dates as a prereading activity. Such activities, when only engaging substantive knowledge such as dates, names, and place can lead to false conclusions on causality between events and illusions of completeness. Engaging procedural knowledge that considers dimensions of continuity and change develops synoptic judgement (Lévesque, 2008), the ability to trace the relationships between events in the past so that "contemporary people [can] compare and assess the meaning and significance of past events and ultimately for the present" (p. 66).

Because our primary concern as teachers is the transformational potential of our instruction, we, as researchers, are interested in how learners apply such conceptual tools when they are "in charge" of talk. DSR provides a forum that centers learners and their expertise. Our concern in this study is to understand in what ways learners engage with each other and in what ways these engagements have the potential to mediate learning between peers as documented in the opening vignette.

Description of the course

This advanced collegiate German Studies course explores themes of cultural and historical significance in contemporary German-speaking countries. In the fall 2022 semester, twelve learners of diverse backgrounds, from first-year undergraduates to PhD level, were enrolled: learners of color, international learners, heritage speakers with varying degrees of German proficiency. The course was anchored in a multiliteracies pedagogies framework (Allen & Paesani, 2010; Cope & Kalantzis, 2009) that engages students in critical literacy "that is the purposeful questioning of text for prejudice or silences" (Cole & Pullen, 2009). The course had interrelated goals: (1) to develop critical disciplinary skills, such as literary and historical literacy through exploration of complex concepts such as *Heimat* (home, homeland), identity, and belonging in relation to Black and Peoples of Color (BPoC) in the German context, and (2) to develop learners' transcultural and translingual competence as defined by the MLA.

Learners engaged with each other and the primary materials asynchronously through a Learning Management System, LMS, the DSR platform *Perusall*, Google Slides, and Etsy StoryMaps. They annotated multimodal texts on *Perusall* throughout the semester in preparation for class discussions and interactive group activities. The *Perusall* assignments introduced learners to Germany's colonial and migration histories and their continuing legacies in today's Germany, while also promoting reflection on language, culture, and history. In this chapter, we focus on the interactions that illustrate mediation of historical thinking through stancetaking in DSR.

The design of the study

In the following sections, we provide a brief overview of *Persusall*, the DAT used in our study. We also discuss our methods for selecting and analyzing the data we selected from learners' DSR interactions in *Perusall*.

Digital social reading in Perusall

The DAT used in our study is *Perusall*, a digital social annotation platform that is integrated into our LMS and available to all learners. It allows instructors and learners to collaboratively annotate texts in multimodal ways: e.g., through images, hyperlinks, and audio-video files, hashtags, and emojis. When learners pose questions, other group members are alerted to it by a question mark (Figure 2). Posts can be upvoted, indicated by the check mark. Learners can choose to mention individual community members in their posts directly by using the @, they can address @Everyone, or choose to make their post anonymous to others. When learners respond to an initial post, a thread is created. Threads are indicated by a bubble with the number of responses (Figure 2).

Figure 2. Perusall Interface

Methods

Viewing language learning as social, locally situated, and emergent (NLG, 1996), we examine how language in and of a community of learners engaging in collaborative DSR constructs an emergent referential system (Lin, 1994, p. 403). To capture learners' emerging interactional relationships vis-à-vis the assigned DSR course readings, we drew on the concept of stance or stancetaking (Kiesling, 2022). Stance refers to the relationships that speakers indicate to each other and to the objects of their attention. Through stance interactants negotiate their evolving relationships both to each other and the focus object.

We performed a qualitative data analysis of learner annotations in the course. The collective annotations for a total of 30 textual and visual media annotated by learners in *Perusall* are part of an extended research project. Because we are interested in DSR interaction that focused on historical thinking, this study concentrated on annotation threads — not single posts — for three pivotal texts that were assigned at crucial points in the instructional cycle of the semester: *Das Schlüsselereignis des modernen Kolonialismus* (about the Berlin Conference on Africa) as a baseline text at the beginning of the semester, *Undeutsch: Die Konstruktion des Anderen in der postmigrantischen Gesellschaft* (monograph about the construction of the Other in post-migrant German society), as the foundational text in the fourth and fifth week, and *Willkommenskultur in Deutschland* (introducing specific concepts, e.g., Willkommenskultur, asylum, refugees) in week 12, close to the end of the semester, referred to as *Schlüsselereignis*, *Undeutsch*, and *Willkommenskultur* respectively from this point on. The annotations were translated by the authors without mirroring linguistic errors, as they are not pertinent to this study. To code the data for stancetaking patterns, we adopted Kiesling et al.'s (2018) thread structure analysis that codes for stance focus as well as degrees of alignment, affect, and investment. For our qualitative analysis, however, we simplified Kiesling et al.'s (2018) multipoint 1 to 5 scale, and instead coded stance focus for affect, investment, and alignment at high (H), neutral (N), and low (L) to represent the following:

Table 1. Coding Scale adapted from Kiesling et al. (2018)

Score	AFFECT (how strongly or not student feels about the stance focus)	INVESTMENT (how strongly is student invested in their talk, i.e., annotation)	ALIGNMENT (how much interlocutor aligns/ disaligns with their interlocutor
H (High)	Positive affect (e.g., appreciation, approval)	strongly invested in their talk	strongly aligns with interlocuter (e.g., agreement, elaboration)
N (Neutral)	Neither positive nor negative affect	Neither strong nor weak investment in annotation/ talk	no marked alignment or disalignment
L (Low)	Negative affect (e.g., dislike, disapproval)	Low investment; uncertainty	strong disalignment (e.g., disagreement, criticism)

To develop reliable consistency in our analysis, we individually coded "practice" data from student annotations of texts not included in this study. We compared our results and developed a scheme based on our mutual understanding of stancetaking dimensions. After individually coding the selected texts, we met to compare our analysis and to achieve consensus on the threads in the data set. We report the data from students using pseudonyms to protect their identities.

Results and analysis

In this section, we first discuss our analysis of learners' stance taking as they begin to engage with history narratives and relate past events to the present. The analysis of stance sheds light on emerging cooperative actions and community norms

Chapter 3. Critical historical literacy in world languages through digital social reading   **57**

in learners' threaded DSR interactions. We then discuss how stancetaking analysis of DSR interactions captures the ways in which guided-reading questions posed by the instructor mediated the development of historic thinking skills.

Beginning to read history and coming to terms with the present

Community norms characteristic of this class emerged early. In their annotation threads to *Schlüsselereignis*, learners created hashtags and provided links to other media resources. In addition, learners interacted with each other in annotation threads, albeit in lower frequency than in later texts, six threads compared to an overall average of twelve threads per text. While neither affect nor investment scores reflected a consistent pattern, alignment consistently scored neutral except in two posts where learners addressed their interlocutors by name and used predicated discourse markers, such as "I agree with you, Brittany" (Table 2) or "I agree with Grace" (Table 3). As noted earlier, alignment persistence is an indicator for cooperativeness in interaction (Kiesling et al., 2018). When following the rules of cooperative interaction (Grice's cooperative principle), interactants seek relevant, truthful, and clear, information rather than overtly emotional (dis)agreements. Because foreign language learners are not always intelligible to each other or because they prioritize individual written or oral language output rather than collaborative understanding of content, cooperativeness in interaction is a desired but elusive achievement in foreign language instruction. However, such cooperativeness is a precondition for developing and applying historical thinking strategies. We, thus, further analyzed the annotations for linguistic features that may indicate mediation of historical thinking.

A plethora of semiotic and linguistic tokens, such as dates, temporal adverbials, temporal clausal connectors, and temporal prepositions construct *Schlüsselereignis* as a temporal chronological account. Yet, as the stance foci illustrate, leaners did not orient to the chronological narrative. Instead, learners' stances focused primarily on singular ideas such as "scramble for Africa", protection, and contest.

As the stance focus in Diana, Brittany, and Clara's interaction (Table 2) indicates, all three posts primarily gloss the word meaning for "scramble for Africa". Yet, in Diana's and Brittany's glosses a tentative agent-patient parallelism (Jakobson, 1960; Urban, 1991) emerges. Parallelism — or linearily co-occuring elements (Lempert, 2008) — was theorized by Jakobson as an example of how the "poetic function" in everyday interactions reflexively foregrounds the message form. Tannen (1987, 1989) and Johnstone (1994) demonstrated not only the ubiquity and variation of poetic functions in conversation but also their pragmatic construal in interaction. In the interaction below, "the people of Africa", "the Europeans" and "Africa" (or "these countries and nations") are cast in triad of agents in conflict over belonging and land possession of "this place" or "homelands of the Africans". Their agreement and desire to cooperatively elaborate an understanding of the text is, thus, not only signaled by overt agreement idioms but also reflected in the text-metricality of parallelisms. Clara, however, does not join into this parallelism and instead only glosses the word meaning as "the end of African independence" and then moves on to reminisce about her learning of the term.

Table 2. *Schlüsselereignis* — Thread #2

Diana	Dieser Ausdruck ist problematisch weil es andeutet, dass Africa erhaeltlich fuer europaeischen Besitz war, obwohl es eigentlich zu einheimische Afrikaner gehoert.
Brittany	Ich bestimme mit dir, Brittany. Diese Länder und Nationen nicht war "neue" ohne Leute. Die Leute des Afrikas hat in diesem Ort gelebt und die Europäern hat die Heimaten der Afrikaners genehmen.
Clara	#HistorischesThemReferenzen: "Wettlauf um Afrika" bedeutet das Ende der afrikanischen Unabhängigkeit. Ich kann mich. noch erinnern, als ich dieses Wort in meinem Geschichtsunterricht vor ein paar Jahren gelernt habe.

		Stance focus	Alignment	Affect	Investment
Diana	This expression is problematic because it implies that Africa was available for European ownership, even though it actually belonged to native Africans.	"scramble for Africa"	N	N	H
Brittany	I agree with you, Brittany. These countries and nations were not "new" without people. The people of Africa lived in this place and the Europeans took the homelands of the Africans.	"scramble for Africa"	H	N	H
Clara	#HistoricalThemReferences: "Scramble for Africa" means the end of African independence. I can still remember when I learned this word in my history class a few years ago.	"scramble for Africa"	N	N	H

Although Diana, Brittany, and Clara primarily focus on word meaning, the emerging parallelism in their glosses indicates their joint attempt to reconstruct

Chapter 3. Critical historical literacy in world languages through digital social reading   **59**

the past. This effort is what Reisman (2015) has called the "historical problem space". In this reconstruction of the past

> ...the strangeness of the past butts up against the human desire to render it familiar. When the desire for familiarity pulls too strongly, one runs the risk of presentism, or the application of anachronistic, present-day standards, values, or worldviews to the past. At the same time, one can never completely abandon one's historical perspective. (Reisman, 2015, p.116)

We see these students negotiating this historical problem space. They astutely critique the "problematic" terminology, in which they recognize an embedded Eurocentric perspective. Yet, they also apply anachronisms such as land ownership, nativeness, "homelands", and "independence". The difficulty of coming to terms with this conundrum is illustrated in the last annotation thread between Diana, Brittany, and Clara.

The annotation threads for *Schlüsselereignis* conclude with Grace and Jack referencing Churchill's well-known dictum on the supposed workings of history (Table 3). This type of voicing (Bakhtin, 1986) of historical figures is not uncommon in the annotations; elsewhere, for example, reference is made to Santayana's dictum that "Those who cannot remember the past are condemned to repeat it." As indicated by their stance focus, Grace and Jack voice — directly and indirectly — Churchill as author (Goffman, 1981) which proposes that the past determines a singular outcome in the present. The parallelism of Grace and Jack's stance focus is reflected in the parallelism of their utterance. Aside from Jack's positive alignment discourse marker "I agree with Grace", their interactions both begin with an epistemic stance "Here I must think of..." and "I believe" which are then followed with the direct quote as well as its paraphrased version. Both Grace and Jack comment on the relationships between past and present but they do so obliquely.

The annotation passage in *Schlüsselereignis*, indexed by Grace as "here", performs a similar rhetorical move. *Schlüsselereignis* concludes its chronological overview with an excerpt of a 1970 poem by Burundian author Michel Kayoya which voices the perspectives of the formerly colonized peoples of Africa. Thus, *Schlüsselereignis*, like Grace and Jack, animates another author to relate past and present. Parallelism of co-occurring signs creates a cohesive texture within an interaction (Silverstein, 1998) from which interlocutors derive significance. In this interaction, for Grace and especially Jack, who aligns his stance with Grace, authorship on assessing colonial legacies on the present was deferred.

Clearly, as these young learners read academic secondary literature about German colonialism in their second or other language, they cannot be expected to also be experts on African history. Yet, if we do take seriously the call to inte-

Table 3. *Schlüsselereignis* — Thread #6

Grace	Hier muss ich an Winston Churchill's Kommentar denken: "History is written by victors." #HistorischesThema				
Jack	Ich stimme Grace zu. Ich glaube, dass die mächtigeren Länder die Gegenwart kontrollieren und die Gewinner die Geschichte schreiben.				
		Stance focus	Alignment	Affect	Investment
Grace	Here I must think of Winston Churchill's comment: "History is written by victors." #HistoricalTopic	victors of history	N	N	H
Jack	I agree with Grace. I believe that the mightier countries control the present and the winners write history.	victors of history	H	N	H

grate content and language and do so in a meaningful, critical way, then challenging topics and texts will be the norm and not an exception. As our analysis shows, when tracing historical continuities and change from the past to the present, learners do not have unhampered access to these temporal spaces. We also showed, however, how leaners' stancetaking provided evidence that cooperative interaction and community norms emerged early in DSR. This social cohesion is reflected in textual cohesion of the linguistic parallelism that emerged in the annotations. In the next section, we discuss how learner interactions unfolded as the instructor offered mediational tools in DSR.

Guided reading questions as mediation

As discussed in the preceding section, considering continuities and change over time is not a practiced habit of thought (Barton 2001; Jay & Reisman, 2019). Yet, this practice emerged in *Undeutsch* with the mediation of the instructor who posted guided reading questions throughout the text. Prompted by the instructor's question, Clara, Henry, and Emma discuss the meaning of "German migration amnesia" (Table 4). This discussion reflects several interactional characteristics identified earlier for this DSR community. Again, stance dimensions were relatively stable, and the stance focus throughout the thread centered on a singular concept (Amnesia). The collaborative social cohesion indicated by the stance persistence is linguistically reflected in Henry's use of a discourse marker "I agree with Clara" and the parallelism within his own utterances "I would also say...I would also say..", as he adds to Clara's preceding comment.

Chapter 3. Critical historical literacy in world languages through digital social reading   61

Table 4. *Undeutsch*, 1 — Thread #9

Clara	Vielleicht hat diese Amnesie eine Beziehung zu Rostock und die Pogrome die wir im Unterricht geredet haben. Deutschland hat oftmals Menschen ausgegrenzt und die Folgen danach erfahrt. Wieso ist das jetzt ein ganz neues Problem?
Henry	Ich stimme Clara zu. Ich würde auch sagen, dass vielleicht diese Amnesie auch beschreibt, wie Deutschland seit langer Zeit schon eine Einwanderungsgesellschaft ist. Deshalb macht es überhaupt keinen Sinn, dass die Leute jetzt mit Panik auf die sogenannte Flüchtlingswelle reagieren. Ich würde auch sagen, dass diese Amnesie beschreibt, wie die Leute nur ein Problem bemerken, wenn sie einige der Auswirkungen sehen. Aber wenn es weit weg ist, wollen sie nicht darüber nachdenken oder die Existenz des Problems zugeben.
Emma	Diese Amnesie ist gesellschaftlich, geschichtlich, und kulturell. PoCs in Deutschland sprechen über diese Probleme mit Rassismus in Deutschland jeden Tag. Wie kann Mann es vergessen?

		Stance focus	Alignment	Affect	Investment
Clara	Maybe this amnesia has a relation to Rostock and the pogroms we talked about in class. Germany has often marginalized people and experienced the consequences afterwards. Why is this a whole new problem now?	Amnesia	N	N	N
Henry	I agree with Clara. I would also say that maybe this amnesia also describes how Germany has been an immigration society for a long time. So, it doesn't make any sense at all that people are now reacting with panic to the so-called wave of refugees. I would also say that this amnesia describes how people only notice a problem when they see some of the effects. But when it's far away, they don't want to think about it or admit the existence of the problem.	Amnesia	H	N	N
Emma	This amnesia is social, historical, and cultural. PoCs in Germany talk about these problems with racism in Germany every day. How can one forget?	Amnesia	N	N	H

Clara, Henry, and Emma's discussion also exemplified two new patterns emerging in annotations threads for *Undeutsch*: One, the use of temporal linguistic tokens and, two, the posing of rhetorical questions. Learners started to use linguistic tokens that mark temporal states of affairs. In thread 9 (Table 4) temporality is expressed through adverbials "often", "afterwards", "now", "a long time", "every day" as well as temporal connectors "since" and "when". After reading several texts that provide historic roots of cultural and social phenomena and thus provide chronologies of events, learners temporally enregister (Agha, 2007) such phenomena in their own utterances. This is important, as the understanding of the central concept, "German racial amnesia", hinges on the temporalities of continuity (marginalization and immigration) and change (German perception of these phenomena). In their discussion of these, Clara and Henry ponder about their "consequences" and "effects" on German society in the present. They also discuss change. Henry does so with temporal linguistic tokens:

Table 5. *Undeutsch*, 1 — Discussion Excerpts with Temporal Linguistic Tokens

Henry	"macht es überhaupt keinen Sinn, dass die Leute jetzt mit Panik auf die sogenannte Flüchtlingswelle reagieren."
	"wie die Leute nur ein Problem bemerken, wenn sie einige der Auswirkungen sehen.".
Henry	"it doesn't make any sense at all that people are now reacting"
	"they only notice a problem *when* they see some of the effects"

Clara and Emma, however, conclude their posts with rhetorical questions:

Table 6. *Undeutsch*, 1 — Discussion Excerpts with rhetoric questions

Clara	"Wieso ist das jetzt ein ganz neues Problem?"
Emma	"Wie kann Mannes vergessen?"
Clara	"Why is this a whole new problem now?
Emma	"How can one forget?"

As Kiesling et al. (2018) argued, questions are multifunctional and can be high investment (p. 717). Because cognitively demanding (Pienemann, 1998), it is noteworthy that Clara and Emma take a strong epistemic stance, in form of a question, to morally censure present-day "German racial amnesia".

The last threaded annotation for *Undeutsch* stands out for its singular persistence of positive alignment. Responding to the instructor's guided reading question, the interlocutors point out textual passages, pose comprehension questions, and create hashtags as they puzzle out an intricate, and most likely unfamiliar, argument about double standards and justice.

Chapter 3. Critical historical literacy in world languages through digital social reading 63

Table 7. *Undeutsch*, 1 — Thread #12

Sibel	Vergleich wird hergestellt. Was wird verglichen?
Diana	El-Tayeb verglichtet die Reaktion zu muslimische Terror gegen weissen Europaer und die Reaktion zu europaeische Terror gegen Migranten und POCs. Wenn Europaer die Opfer sind, glauben sie, dass alle muslimische Leute sind gefaehrlich, aber wenn sie die Taeter sind, wollen sie kein Schuld nehmen; sondern sagen sie dann, dass die Terror von einzelnen Menschen ist. #Scheinheiligkeit
Henry	Am Ende des Satzes wird ein Gegensatz zwischen "Osten und in der Unterschicht" und "den aufgeklärten Räumen des Feuilletons oder der Universität" gezogen. Ich weiß nicht, ob ich das richtig verstanden habe, aber bezieht sich das auf die falsche Annahme, dass gebildete Menschen und die Oberschicht nie rassistisch sind? #Verstaendnisfrage
Jack	Danke Diana…! Eure Kommentare haben mir wirklich geholfen, zu verstehen. Dieser Vergleich der Reaktion der Europäer als Opfer und als Prälaturen zeigt deutlich die Scheinheiligkeit. Ich hoffe, dass die Autorin die Lösungen in künftigen Kapiteln ansprechen kann. Wie können wir das Verhalten der Menschen ändern? Wie können wir den Teufelskreis durchbrechen? Wie können wir die "selektive Farbenblindheit" beheben?

		Stance focus	Alignment	Affect	Investment
Sibel	Comparison is made. What is compared?				
Diana	El-Tayeb compares the reaction to Muslim terror against white Europeans and the reaction to European terror against migrants and POCs. When Europeans are the victims, they believe that all Muslim people are dangerous, but when they are the perpetrators, they don't want to take blame; but then they say that the terror is from individual people. #Hypocrisy	Prejudice in categorization of offenders	H	N	N
Henry	At the end of the sentence, a contrast is drawn between "the East and in the lower class" and "the enlightened spaces of the feuilleton or the university." I don't know if I understood this correctly, but does this refer to the false assumption that educated people and the upper class are never racist? #understandingquestion	Prejudice in categorization of offenders	H	N	N

Table 7. *(continued)*

| Jack | Thank you Diana ...! Your comments really helped me to understand. This comparison of the reaction of Europeans as victims and as prelatures clearly shows the hypocrisy. I hope the author can address the solutions in future chapters. How can we change people's behavior? How can we break the vicious cycle? How can we fix the "selective color blindness"? | Prejudice in categorization of offenders | H | H | N |

The thread concludes with Jack first effusively thanking his peers for the support he received by reading their annotations. Jack then finishes with three beseeching questions:

Table 8. *Undeutsch*, 1 — Excerpt with parallel structures

Jack	<u>Wie können wir</u> das Verhalten der Menschen ändern?
	<u>Wie können wir</u> den Teufelskreis durchbrechen?
	Wie können wir die "selektive Farbenblindheit" beheben?
Jack:	<u>How can we</u> **change** people's behavior?
	<u>How can we</u> **break** the vicious cycle?
	<u>How can we</u> **fix** the "selective color blindness"?

The striking parallelism in this set of three questions begins each question with the same question word (how), modal verb (can) and personal pronoun (we), and then asks for a series of actions (change, break, fix) that could be taken. This positive alignment expressed in these emphatic series of questions signals not only Jack's earnest engagement with the textual materials but also his sense that he is communicating with actively engaged conversation partners in DSR.

Becoming an expert through collaboration

Two noteworthy changes emerged in *Willkommenskultur*. One, the semantic tokens of epistemic stance indicated a shift from individual, associative knowledge to collective, expert knowledge. Two, the stancetaking focus of most annotations indicated greater internal complexity within individual posts as well as greater divergence within threads. However, our analysis also showed that learners did not adopt historical thinking as a consistent practice.

In contrast to *Schlüsselereignis,* learners' epistemic stancetaking in *Willkommenskultur* frequently invoked their collective knowledge construction. Rather than using discourse markers such as "I think" or "I believe" as they had in the earlier text, learners now used discourse markers such as "we have read" or "we have seen", signaling their collectively created knowledge base. In addition, aside from offering mediation through hashtags and links to other sources that typically accompanied a high epistemic stancetaking, learners took on an authoritative voice that attested to their learning.

The annotation threads in *Willkommenskultur* are also distinct from those in previous texts because of their lack of consistent stance focus across threads. As learners discuss different perspectives in Germany's "Willkommenskultur", six out of ten annotation threads shift their stance focus, even though this divergence does not necessarily correspond to consistent negative alignment. The stance foci of Henry's and Clara's annotations (Table 9) as well as Frank and Graces's annotations (Table 10) illustrate just how much stancetaking can diverge in an annotation thread. While Henry's stance focusses on "fear of refugees because of a lack of interaction", Clara focusses on "suspected physiological origin of fear of strangers".

Table 9. *Willkommenskultur* — Thread #2

Henry	Ich finde den Satz in Klammern sehr schockierend. Es ist auch erwähnenswert, dass die Menschen, die diese irrationalen Ängste haben, wahrscheinlich nie mit geflüchteten Menschen interagiert haben, wie wir in anderen Texten gelesen und gesehen haben. Deswegen ist die Interaktion wichtig, um diese irrationalen Ängste und rassistischen Überzeugen zu kämpfen. #Interaktion
Clara	Wie entsteht diese Angst? Ich wäre neugierig zu erfahren, ob es physiologisch in Menschen drin ist, Fremde zu fürchten? Die Medien und bestimmte Politiker verstärken diese Gefühle sicherlich.

		Stance focus	Alignment	Affect	Investment
Henry	To me the sentence in parenthesis is shocking. It is also noteworthy that the people who have these irrational fears have never interacted with refugees as we have seen and read in other texts. For that reason, interaction is important in order to combat these racist convictions. #interaction	Fear of refugees because of a lack of interaction	N- Initial Post but appeal to commonly read and viewed media	H	H

Table 9. *(continued)*

Clara	How does this fear come about? I would be curious whether it is physiologically within people to fear strangers? The media and certain politicians surely reinforce these feelings.	Suspected physiological origin of fear of strangers	N — No explicit engagement with interlocutor/ Engagement with topic	H	N

And while Frank focusses on "Arbitrary control of identities by majority culture", Grace focusses first on the "disconnection of decision makers from local population" and then on the "need for respect of customs of local population".

Table 10. *Willkommenskultur* — Thread #4

Frank	Wenn ich dies richtig verstanden habe, wollen die Mehrheitsgesellschaft nicht, dass Leute ihnen erklären wer kann und kann nicht Deutsch sein. Sie wollen es wie es "in der Verganenheit war" präservieren. Aber dann, entscheiden sie wer kann und kann nicht Deutschsein!?!?!?!?!?
Grace	Wer ist eigentlich "oben"? Sind es Leute, die Appel und ihre Bürger kennen? Ich denke schon, dass ein gewisses Verständnis für die Stadt und ihre geografische und ideologische Struktur vorhanden sein muss.

		Stance focus	Alignment	Affect	Investment
Frank	If I understood this correctly, the majority culture does not want that people explain to them who can and cannot be German. They want to preserve it as it "was in the past". But then they decide who can and cannot be German!?!?!?!?!?	Arbitrary control of identities by majority culture	N- Initial Post	H	H
Grace	Who exactly is "above"? Is it people who know Appel and its citizens?	Disconnection of decision makers from local population	N — No direct engagement with interlocutor/ topic	H	H
Grace	I do think that a certain understanding for the city and its geographic and ideological structure must be present.	Need of respect for customs of local population	L — No disagreement expressed but strongly implied	N	H

Chapter 3. Critical historical literacy in world languages through digital social reading

While higher investment of epistemic stance and increased complexity and divergence in stance focus are noteworthy, such shifts over time may not be entirely surprising. Assuming that, in week twelve of this critical content-based German class, learners have actively engaged with complex issues in the target language, these communicative changes in their annotations may be an indication of learning. Yet, learners' stance foci lacked synoptic judgement, the key historical thinking habit that emerged in *Undeutsch*. In annotating a xenophobic rant by a townsperson, Clara (Table 9) wondered whether fear of strangers is biologically determined through a "physiological origin" rather than a cultural perspective with deep historical roots. Similarly, Grace (Table 10) contemplated the "need of respect for customs of local population", even though the only customs the townspeople expressed were those of xenophobia. Elsewhere, in annotating a story about a retiree who helps refugees, Grace wonders if it is not old people, then, who are afraid of refugees, and excludes them. And Jack and Brittany agree that only personal encounters with eyewitnesses could lead to empathetic understanding, not reading texts.

Thus, despite much moral outrage professed at the beginning of the semester regarding social injustices and despite having spent a semester immersed in learning about the deep sociocultural and political roots of inequities throughout Germany's history, in this final DSR activity, learners did not draw on essential concepts of change and continuities that are key to a robust multiperspectival assessment of social and cultural phenomena.

Discussion

Community norms emerged early on and held steady throughout the semester, confirming as Donato and Mccormick (1994) noted, "the classroom is a culture with distinctive forms of practice, mediation, and social relation" (p. 454). This also confirms Kiesling et al.'s (2018) results in which stance alignment, as an indicator of collaboration, emerged as the most persistent dimension in stancetaking. Both early establishment of community norms and persistence of stance alignment as collaborative interaction are positive indicators that DSR can mediate interaction for learning.

As our analysis of annotations threads for *Schlüsselereignis, Undeutsch*, and *Willkommenskultur* indicates, learners developed interactional patterns that shifted from personal perspective and reliance on personal background knowledge to developing an identity as a learning community with a collective knowledge base. The emergence of cohesive, co-occurring textual patterns, such as agent-patient or question parallelisms provides further linguistic evidence that this community of learners developed not only social but also linguistic cohesion. This social and linguistic cohesion is evidence of a collective referential system through which social talk is filtered and begins to take on meaning.

We cannot unequivocally conclude that DSR mediates social and linguistic cohesion. However, our study does show that such cohesion develops favorably in DSR. Thus, DSR can be understood as a mediational tool for learning, particularly for world language curricula designed to integrate critical content and language learning.

As indicated by the annotations for all texts but especially by the strong stance focus divergences in *Willkommenskultur,* our study also showed that students did not intuitively adopt habits of historical thinking. While the instructor had posted general guided reading questions in *Undeutsch,* which facilitated interaction with and adoption of complex social and cultural concepts, there was no explicit instructor guidance on historical thinking.

As noted earlier, alignment persistence is an indicator for cooperativeness in interaction (Kiesling et al., 2018). When following the rules of cooperative interaction (Grice's cooperative principle), interactants seek relevant, truthful, and clear information rather than overtly emotional (dis)agreements. Because foreign language learners are not always intelligible to each other or because they prioritize individual written or oral language output rather than collaborative understanding of content, cooperativeness in interaction is a desired but elusive achievement in foreign language instruction. However, such cooperativeness is a precondition for developing and applying historical thinking strategies. We, thus, further analyzed the annotations for linguistic features that may indicate mediation of historical thinking.

Thus, the stance focus shift in learner annotations, from word focus to complex cultural and social phenomena, highlights the potential of DSR for discussion of critical content as well as integrating critical content in world language curricula. The results of our stancetaking analysis also indicated that learners became intelligible to each other and eager to collaborate on textual understandings, a necessary condition for language learners who need to elaborate a common focus, shared understandings, and disciplinary tools of thinking in content-focused courses. The persistence of presentist perspectives, which focus on moral indignation rather than analytic perspectives, indicates the need for supporting learners in critical disciplinary ways of thinking.

Limitations and future directions

This exploratory study examined stancetaking in DSR to better understand how learners come to engage with each other in DSR and what types of engagement facilitate peer-to-peer mediation in exchanges about challenging historical topics. As discussed earlier, our inquiry was prompted by a curricular reform in our department that responds to the MLA's urgent call to implement literacies-oriented curricula to unify the study of language and content, as well as the resulting challenge of how to engage language learners with linguistically and conceptually challenging content. Thus, as researchers and as practitioners, we note the following limitations of our study and future directions.

Our data analysis was limited to learner interactions in DSR. Future studies could complement this type of analysis with participant interviews and feedback on data interpretation to get a deeper ethnographic perspective on what is going on in an interaction. Our analysis was also limited to key texts of the semester and a more extensive study with different kinds of texts may reveal a better understanding of how social affordances transfer to different contexts.

Learners' annotations demonstrated an increase over time in complexity and diversity in stance focus, higher investment of epistemic stance, and a sense of agency as manifested by the authoritative voice that emerged in their annotations. Based on these results, we suggest incorporating DSR as a regular feature in world language curricula, as it can promote a community of learners, who are empowered to create knowledge and cultivate critical disciplinary ways of thinking.

However, continued teacher engagement may be needed to ensure progress to associated learning goals. Here, our results indicate the exchanges around the last text lacked synoptic judgement by learners, suggesting a move away from the historical thinking habit that had emerged earlier with *Undeutsch*. This finding indicates that historical thinking did not become an intuitive and consistent habit for learners. Thus, there is a need to support learners in critical disciplinary ways of thinking.

Teachers should consistently provide mediation in DSR throughout the semester (e.g., glosses, reading questions) to focus learners attention more clearly on essential concepts of change and continuities that are necessary for a multiperspectival assessment of social and cultural phenomena. Learners can prepare for the close reading in DSR by being asked to situate the text. Learners should be asked to take note of the historic significance of texts (who, what, when why); to research its context (when, where) and note any continuities and changes, before reading the text in DSR. After these steps, learners should be better equipped to complete close reading in DSR, in which they identify the claims, evaluate the evidence provided, and reflect on the language itself. In the process, they might ask themselves what are the word choices made by the author? How are they significant? How do they indicate the author's perspective? As a follow-up exercise, learners should corroborate the evidence and their interpretations by looking at other primary and secondary sources. Engaging in this cyclical and iterative process for each text, we would argue, can lead to developing a more intuitive and consistent habit of historical thinking.

References

Adams, B., & Wilson, N. (2020). Building community in asynchronous online higher education courses through collaborative annotation. *Journal of Educational Technology Systems*, 49(2), 250–261.

Agha, A. (2007). *Language and social relations*. Cambridge University Press.

Allen, H., & Paesani, K. (2010). Exploring the feasibility of a pedagogy of multiliteracies in introductory foreign language courses. *L2 Journal*, 2(1), 119–142.

Bakhtin, M. M. (1986). The problem of speech genres. In M. Holquist & C. Emerson (Eds.), *Speech genres and other late essays* (V. W. McGee, Trans.) (pp. 60-102). University of Texas Press.

Barton, K. (2001). A sociocultural perspective on children's understanding of historical change: Comparative findings from Northern Ireland and the United States. *American Educational Research Journal*, 38(4), 881–913.

Blyth, C. (2014). Exploring the affordances of digital social reading for L2 literacy: The case of eComma. In J. Pettes Guikema & L. Williams (Eds.), *Digital literacies in foreign and second language education* (pp. 201–226). Calico.

Chen, C. M., & Chen, F. Y. (2014). Enhancing digital reading performance with a collaborative reading annotation system. *Computers & Education*, 77, 67-81.

Chen, I. J., & Chen, W. C. (2016). Perceived usefulness of a strategy-based peer annotation system for improving academic reading comprehension. *Journal of Interactive Learning Research*, 27(1), 27-51.

Chen, C., Chen, L., & Horng, W. (2021). A collaborative reading annotation system with formative assessment and feedback mechanisms to promote digital reading performance. *Interactive Learning Environments*, 29(5), 848–865.

Cole, D., & Pullen, D. (2009). *Multiliteracies in motion: Current theory and practice*. Routledge.

Cope, B., & Kalantzis, M. (2009) 'Multiliteracies': New literacies, new learning. *Pedagogies: An International Journal*, 4(3), 164–195.

Donato, R., & MacCormick, D. (1994). A sociocultural perspective on language learning strategies: The role of mediation. *The Modern Language Journal*, 78(4), 453–464.

Du Bois, J. (2007). The stance triangle. In R. Englebretson (Ed.), *Stancetaking in discourse: Subjectivity, evaluation, and interaction* (pp. 139–182). John Benjamins.

El-Tayeb, F. (2016). *Undeutsch. Die Konstruktion des Anderen inderpostmigrantischen Gesellschaft*. Transcript Verlag.

Chapter 3. Critical historical literacy in world languages through digital social reading 71

Eryilmaz, E., Chiu, M., Thoms, B., Mary, J., & Kim, R. (2014). Design and evaluation of instructor-based and peer-oriented attention guidance functionalities in an open source anchored discussion system. *Computers & Education*, 71, 303–321.

Fairclough, N. (1999). Global capitalism and critical awareness of language. *Language Awareness*, 8(2), 71–83.

Gao, F. (2013). A case study of using a social annotation tool to support collaboratively learning. *The Internet and Higher Education*, 17, 76-83.

Geisler, M., Kramsch, C., McGinnis, S., Patrikis, P., Pratt, M., Ryding, K., & Saussy, H. (2007). Foreign languages and higher education: New structures for a changed world, MLA Ad Hoc Committee on Foreign Languages. *Profession* 2007, 234–245. https://www.jstor.org/stable/25595871

Gergely, G., & Csibra, G. (2007). The social construction of the cultural mind: Imitative learning as a mechanism of human pedagogy. In P. Hauf & F. Försterling (Eds.), *Making minds. The shaping of human minds through social context* (pp. 241–257). John Benjamins.

Goffman, E. (1981). *Forms of talk*. University of Pennsylvania Press.

Grice, H. (1975). Logic and conversation. In P. Cole & J. Morgan (Eds.), *Studies in syntax and semantics 3: Speech acts* (pp. 41–58). Academic Press.

Jaffe, A. (2009). Introduction: The sociolinguistics of stance. In A. Jaffe (Ed.), *Stance: Sociolinguistic perspectives* (pp. 3–28). Oxford University Press.

Jakobson, R. (1960). Closing statement: Linguistics and poetics. In T. Sebeok (Ed.) *Style in Language* (pp. 350–377). The MIT Press.

Jan, J., Chen, C., & Huang, P. (2016). Enhancement of digital reading performance by using a novel web-based collaborative reading annotation system with two quality annotation filtering mechanisms. *International Journal of Human-computer Studies*, 86, 81–93.

Jay, L., & Reisman, A. (2019). Teaching change and continuity with historical analogies. *Social Studies Research and Practice*, 14(1), 98–104.

Johnson, K. E. (2009). Second language teacher education: A sociocultural perspective. Routledge.

Johnstone, B. (1994). Repetition in discourse : interdisciplinary perspectives. Ablex Pub. Co.

Johnstone, B. (2007). Linking identity and dialect through stancetaking. In R. Englebretson (Ed.), *Stancetaking in discourse: Subjectivity, evaluation, interaction* (pp. 49–67). John Benjamins.

Kärkkäinen, E. (2006). Stance taking in conversation: From subjectivity to intersubjectivity. *Text & Talk*, 26(6), 699–731.

Kiesling, S. (2009). Style as stance: Stance as the explanation for patterns of sociolinguistic variation. In A. Jaffe (Ed.). *Stance: Sociolinguistic perspectives* (pp. 171–195). Oxford Academic.

Kiesling, S. (2022). Stance and stancetaking. *Annual Review of Linguistics*, 8, 409–429.

Kiesling, S., Pavalanathan, U., Fitzpatrick, J., Han, X., & Eisenstein, J. (2018). Interactional stancetaking in online forums. *Computational Linguistics*, 44(4), 683–718.

Kubota, R. (2012). Memories of war: Exploring victim-victimizer perspectives in critical content-based instruction in Japanese. *L2 Journal*, 4(1), 37–57.

Kubota, R. (2016). Critical content-based instruction in the foreign language classroom: Critical issues for implementation. In L. Cammarata (Ed.), *Content-based foreign language teaching: Curriculum and pedagogy for developing advanced thinking and literacy skills* (pp. 192–211). Routledge.

Lantolf, J. (2006). Sociocultural theory and l2: State of the art. *Studies in Second Language Acquisition*, 28(1), 67–109.

Lantolf, J., Thorne, S., & Poehner, M. (2014). Sociocultural theory and second language development. In B. Vanpatten & J. Williams (Eds.), *Theories in second language acquisition: An introduction* (pp. 207–226). Routledge.

Law, J., Barny, D., & Poulin, R. (2020). Patterns of peer interaction in multimodal L2 digital social reading. *Language Learning & Technology*, 24(2), 70–85. http://hdl.handle.net /10125/44726

Lempert, M. (2008). The poetics of stance: Text-metricality, epistemicity, interaction. *Language in Society*, 37(4), 569–592.

Lévesque, S. (2008). *Historical thinking: Educating students for the 21st century*. University of Toronto Press.

Lévesque, S. (2011). What it means to think historically. In P. Clark (Ed.), *New possibilities for the past: Shaping history education in Canada*. University of British Columbia Press.

Lévesque, S., & Clark, P. (2018). Historical thinking: Definitions and educational applications. *The Wiley international handbook of history teaching and learning*, 117-148.

Lin, L. (1994). Language of and in the classroom: Constructing the patterns of social life. *Linguistics and Education*, 5, 367–409.

Lomicka, L., & Lord, G. (2018). Ten years after the MLA report: What has changed in foreign language departments? *ADFL Bulletin*, 44(2), 116–120.

New London Group. (1996). A pedagogy of multiliteracies: Designing social futures. *Harvard Educational Review*, 66(1), 60–92.

Paesani, K., & Menke, M. (2023). Literacies in language education: A guide for teachers and teacher educators. Georgetown University Press.

Paesani, K. W., Allen, H. W., & Dupuy, B., (2016). A multiliteracies framework for collegiate foreign language teaching. Pearson.

Pienemann, M. (1998). *Language processing and second language development: Processability theory*. John Benjamins.

Plevinski, J., Weible, J., & DeSchryver, M. (2017). *Anchored annotation to support collaborative knowledge construction*. International Society of the Learning Sciences.

Reisman, A. (2015). Entering the historical problem space: Whole-class text-based discussion in history class. *Teachers College Record*, 117(2), 1–44.

Seixas, P. (2017). A model of historical thinking. *Educational Philosophy and Theory*, 49(6), 593–605.

Silverstein, M. (1998). The improvisational performance of culture in realtime discursive practice. In R. K. Sawyer (Ed.), *Creativity in performance* (pp. 265–312). Ablex.

Tannen, D. (1987). Repetition in conversation: Toward a poetics of talk. *Language*, 63(3), 574–605.

Tannen, D. (1989). Talking voices : repetition, dialogue, and imagery in conversational discourse. Cambridge University Press.

Chapter 3. Critical historical literacy in world languages through digital social reading 73

Thoms, J., & Poole, F. (2018). Exploring digital literacy practices via L2 social reading. *L2 Journal*, 10(2), pp. 36–61.

Thoms, J., Sung, K., & Poole, F. (2017). Investigating the linguistic and pedagogical affordances of an L2 open reading environment via eComma: An exploratory study in a Chinese language course. *System*, 69, pp. 38–53.

Tocaimaza-Hatch, C., & Bloom, M. (2019). Promoting intercultural thinking and reflection through U.S. history. *Foreign Language Annals*, 52(3), 507–528.

Tomasello, M. (1999). The cultural origins of human cognition. Harvard University Press.

Urban, G. (1991). Grammatical parallelism and thought. In J. Wilce (Ed.), *A discourse-centered approach to culture: Native South American myths and rituals* (pp. 29–57). University of Texas Press.

van der Pol, J., Admiraal, W., & Simons, P. (2006). The affordance of anchored discussion for the collaborative processing of academic texts. *Computer-Supported Collaborative Learning*, 1, 339–357.

Yang, X., Yu, S., & Sun, Z. (2013). The effect of collaborative annotation on Chinese reading level in primary schools in China. *British Journal of Educational Technology*, 44(1), 95-111.

Yeh, H. C., Hung, H. T., & Chiang, Y. H. (2017). The use of online annotations in reading instruction and its impact on students' reading progress and processes. *ReCALL*, 29(1), 22-38.

Vygotsky, L. (1986). *Thought and language*. The MIT Press.

CHAPTER 4

Incorporating mindfulness into multiliteracies pedagogy
Contemplative digital social reading and writing

Carl Blyth
The University of Texas at Austin

This chapter describes the distinctive state of mind of *Mindfulness* (also referred to as Contemplation) and argues for its inclusion in Multiliteracies pedagogy (Cope & Kalantzis, 2015). *Contemplative literacy practices* encourage instructors and learners to focus on the present moment, thereby deepening our understanding of reading and writing as processes. More specifically, the chapter reports on a Multiliteracies-inspired college-level course entitled "Narrating the Multilingual Self" during which L2 learners of French were guided to tell their "multilingual life story" (Edwards, 2019). Based on the premise that learners become the autobiographical narratives they construct about themselves, the course explored the diverse, intersectional experiences of French-speaking multilinguals. Following Barbezat and Bush (2014), contemplative reading and writing activities were employed to heighten the learners' awareness of their own multilingual subjectivities and identities. In contrast to traditional digital social reading (DSR) assignments, contemplative forms of literacy oblige learners to "slow things down" by annotating, reading aloud and reflecting on the meanings and feelings engendered by texts. Similarly, contemplative digital writing (DSW) activities include freewriting, journaling, and annotating to promote greater self-awareness of meaning-making as a personal, creative act.

> Writing is my deepest Zen practice.
> Natalie Goldberg, *Writing Down the Bones* (2016, p. 9)

Introduction

In her book *Writing down the bones*, the well-known creative writing guru Natalie Goldberg explains how she deepens her writing pedagogy with techniques borrowed from Zen meditation. According to Goldberg, Zen practice goes well

https://doi.org/10.1075/aals.21.04bly
© 2024 John Benjamins Publishing Company

beyond the typical advice given to would-be writers. For example, writing teachers often advise their students to "show, don't tell," a phrase meant to exhort novice writers to avoid explanation in favor of narration. However, Goldberg contends that showing rather than telling is about more than sophisticated style or clever technique. Rather, according to Zen principles, it is about becoming aware of "first thoughts," that is, the mind's authentic emotional reactions to lived experiences.

> First thoughts are the mind reflecting experiences — as close as a human being can get in words to the sunset, the birth, the Bobby pin, the crocus. We can't always stay with first thoughts, but it is good to know about them. They can easily teach us how to step out of the way and use words like a mirror to reflect the pictures. (Goldberg, 2016, p. 8)

As an advocate of contemplative approaches to writing pedagogy, Goldberg encourages her students to access their "first thoughts" through mindfulness, a practice that calls for quieting the mind, anchoring oneself in the present moment, beholding an object with sustained attention, and noticing but not judging one's thoughts and feelings as they arise (Kabat-Zinn, 2005).

In this chapter, I give a first-person account of my attempt to enrich my Multiliteracies pedagogy with contemplative practices like those suggested by Goldberg to enhance my students' literacy skills in an upper-division French course entitled "Narrating the Multilingual Self." The course focused on the lived experiences of multilingual Francophones, including L2 French learners. One of my main goals for the course was to add a contemplative dimension to the Learning-by-Design approach (L-by-D). The creators of L-by-D frame literacy instruction in epistemological terms as "the things you do to know" and cite activities that emphasize four different "knowledge processes": Experiencing, Conceptualizing, Analyzing, and Applying (Cope & Kalantzis, 2015). As an L2 French instructor with an interest in second language literacy, I was drawn to L-by-D, especially the framing of knowledge as action. However, over the years, I became increasingly concerned that L-by-D, like most Western approaches to education, privileges objectivity, rationality and generalization as the primary means of creating knowledge (Miller, 2014; Zajonc, 2014). I wondered how I might include a greater emphasis on subjectivity, emotionality and particularity in my teaching. In addition, I wanted my students to gain a greater awareness of L2 reading and writing as fully embodied practices. Barbezat and Bush (2014, p. 19) claim that contemplative practices "are not intended to replace other effective means of learning. Rather, they are powerful complements for instruction across the curriculum."

In search of "powerful complements" to my instructional practices, I began to explore the affordances of contemplation as a different form of textual thinking to those commonly described in the educational literature such as analysis and application (Anderson & Krathwohl, 2001; Barbezat & Bush, 2014; Gunnlaugson et al., 2014). For example, according to Bloom's Taxonomy, discrete cognitive processes are arranged in a hierarchy from lower-level thinking skills (e.g., remembering, understanding, applying) to higher-level skills (e.g., analyzing, evaluating, creating) (Anderson & Krathwohl, 2001). In contrast, contemplation, also referred to as mindfulness, is best viewed as a meta-cognitive state that can co-occur with any type of cognitive activity at any level. In a nutshell, mindfulness involves a non-judgmental attention directed toward one's present thoughts and feelings. It also implies a consideration of an external object such as a written text from multiple perspectives (decentering) that often leads to personal insights. Therefore, the four knowledge actions identified by L-by-D pedagogy may be performed in either a contemplative or non-contemplative manner. In summary, contemplation/mindfulness is not a knowledge action per se, but rather *how* one performs a knowledge action.

According to Davidson and Dahl (2016), *"The boundary that defines what falls within the category of contemplative practices is somewhat hazy, but from a general perspective, we can say that this form of training emphasizes self-awareness, self-regulation, and/or self-inquiry to enact a process of psychological transformation. These practices thus involve some form of mental training, even when they also involve physical movement or dialogue-based exercises. Although contextualized differently among the traditions that use them, contemplative practices are typically viewed as practical methods to bring about a state of enduring well-being or inner flourishing."* Much like a Zen novice who ponders a koan to better understand the limitations of their logical reasoning, second language students may practice textual contemplation by focusing for extended periods of time on a single phrase or brief passage, embracing its contradictions, and noticing one's own cognitive and affective reactions during the process. Moreover, advocates of mindfulness reject the Cartesian separation of emotion and cognition as based on an erroneous view of the human mind (Damasio, 1994). For example, rather than describing reading in purely cognitive terms, Barbezat and Bush (2014, p.14) employ embodied metaphors such as "sinking into a text" to capture what contemplative literacy feels like. In short, contemplation is qualitatively different from other forms of textual thinking typically described in Multiliteracies Pedagogy.

In addition to my dissatisfaction with the perceived cognitive biases of Multiliteracies pedagogy in higher education, I was also worried about my students' growing levels of distraction, isolation, and burnout in the aftermath of the COVID-19 pandemic. As reported in many recent news accounts, the pandemic unleashed a "mental health tsunami" on college campuses where students grappled with unprecedented levels of anxiety and depression (McGee, 2022;

Zimmerman, 2022). In response, many institutions of higher education, including my own, began wellness programs that included tele-counseling services, online support groups, and peer mentoring sessions. However, students were not the only ones adversely affected by the pandemic. Recent studies confirm that the mental health of faculty worsened as a result of the sudden shift to remote instruction, the continued fear of infection, and the difficulties balancing public health concerns and educational priorities (Pandya & Lodha, 2022). For these reasons, I adopted contemplative techniques to help my students and me reduce our elevated levels of anxiety.

This chapter begins with a brief review of the research on contemplative practices in educational settings, including foreign and second language classrooms. Next, I describe the content and pedagogy of my upper-division French course on "multilingual life writing." An autobiographical genre, multilingual life writing typically includes examples of translanguaging that call attention to how lives and identities are shaped by multiple languages in different ways (Edwards, 2019). In an effort to heighten my students' awareness of their first thoughts during reading and writing activities, as suggested by Goldberg (2016), I employed digital tools to facilitate a more deliberative process (Barbezat & Bush, 2014). In addition, I kept a "teaching journal" to record my own first thoughts throughout the semester. As such, this essay constitutes an example of autoethnography, a form of qualitative research commonly employed in arts-based studies (Adams et al., 2015). After describing the course content, I discuss how I supplemented my usual, non-contemplative activities with Digital Social Reading and Writing (DSRW) activities that emphasized mindfulness. In addition, I describe what students did during contemplative DSRW activities and how they responded to these pedagogical innovations. I end the chapter by summarizing the lessons that I learned from my pedagogical innovation and calling for the inclusion of mindfulness in Multiliteracies pedagogy (Cope & Kalantzis, 2015).

L2 mindfulness studies

Although thousands of years old, mindfulness practices have only recently been the subject of empirical research. According to Morgan and Katz (2021), researchers in Positive Psychology (Peterson, 2006) have been conducting experimental studies on the effects of mindfulness for nearly two decades. Similarly, Zeilhofer (2023) asserts that published research on "mindfulness interventions" in the field of educational psychology have increased rapidly. However, Zeilhofer cautions that most of the mindfulness studies do not focus on language learning per se, but rather on general topics such as reducing classroom anxiety and improving learner perceptions of self-regulation. Thus, despite the growth of mindfulness research in general, it remains relatively unexplored by second language specialists (Koçali & Asik, 2022; Morgan & Katz, 2021; Scida & Jones, 2017; Zeilhofer, 2023).

Focusing on studies of mindfulness and language learning, Koçali and Asik (2022) conducted a systematic review of academic research databases (e.g., Google Scholar, ERIC) and found only 19 published studies based on ESL and EFL contexts. The authors note that most of these L2 studies do not focus on linguistic outcomes per se, but rather on the reduction of "foreign language classroom anxiety" (Horwitz et al., 1986). Furthermore, of the few studies that do investigate linguistic outcomes, the construct of achievement is operationalized in terms of course grades, a general measure that lacks linguistic granularity (e.g., Zeilhofer, 2023). Finally, mindfulness studies conducted in second language contexts employ a similar methodology — a brief meditation session in the L1 at the start of class. Unfortunately, this kind of intervention frames mindfulness as something that learners and teachers should do *before* second language instruction begins. In summary, a review of the L2 research literature indicates that there are no studies that investigate contemplative practices in the target language *as an integral part of L2 instruction*. As such, contemplative digital social reading and writing appear to be new research topics in L2 pedagogy.

A French course on multilingual life writing

The new French course was inspired by three focal concepts — the "multilingual subject" (Kramsch, 2009), "multilingual life writing" (Edward, 2019), and "perezhivanie," a concept from Vygotskyan sociocultural theory that refers to the dialectic between emotion and cognition in acts of human sense-making (Vygotsky, 1994). According to Kramsch (2009), the term "multilingual subject" refers "to a learner's experience of the subjective aspects of language and the transformations he or she is undergoing in the process of acquiring it (p. 17)" Kramsch (2009) draws on a wide variety of autobiographical texts written by prominent multilingual authors to illustrate the symbiotic relationships between a writer's multilingualism, subjectivity, and identity. In similar fashion, Edwards (2019) adopts the cover term 'life writing' to facilitate the exploration of different autobiographical genres such as testimonies, documentaries, and narratives, including written, oral, and multimodal narratives. Situating her book *Multilingual life writing by French and francophone women* within the new field of Translingual French Studies, Edwards (2019) claims that life writing "draws attention to the practice of reading and interpretation and to the position of the writer, the reader, and the critic" (p.3). Edwards argues that writers employ multilingual writing as a critical practice to explore the varied contributions that different languages make to their lives.

The class comprised eight seniors and two sophomores, all "double majors" specializing in French and another discipline (e.g., Biochemistry, Business Administration, International Relations, Middle Eastern Studies and Psychology). In addition, nine students had spent an extended time in a French-speaking country either during a study-abroad experience or a family vacation. Importantly, all identified as bilingual or multilingual. In fact, five students were English-Spanish bilinguals with extended family networks in the US and Mexico, as well as Central and South America. Based on their oral and written performances, I estimated that most of the students had attained an Advanced-Low level of linguistic proficiency in French. According to the ACTFL proficiency guidelines for French, readers at the Advanced-Low proficiency level can fully understand paragraph-length texts when dealing with a current event of general interest (ACTFL Proficiency Guidelines-French). They can also comprehend the main ideas as well as supporting details of both past and present narration. However, reading comprehension at this level is often troubled by unconventional narrative texts that interrupt the chronology of plotline events with frequent flashbacks and flashforwards. In summary, the course was designed for French majors with a relatively advanced language proficiency who identified as multilinguals.

Based on the focal concepts of the multilingual subject, multilingual life writing, and perezhivanie, I created a reading list that combined both conventional and unconventional narrative texts — language memoirs, poems, songs, interviews, podcasts and films — that emphasized the emotional lives of French-speaking multilinguals (see Appendix for Course Description, Syllabus and Reading List). As numerous anthropologists, narratologists, and psychologists have pointed out, the act of self-narration helps humans make sense of their experiences and, as a consequence, is central to their identity development (Bamberg et al., 2007; Bruner, 2004; McAdams, 1990, 2013; Vygotsky, 1994). Anthropological linguists Ochs and Capps (2002) note that narrators often retell their "life stories" as part of everyday conversations in hopes of gaining greater understanding of their experiences. In my description of the course, I emphasized the act of self-narration and its role in the construction of a multilingual identity by citing the work of psychologist Jerome Bruner who argued that "in the end, we become the autobiographical narratives by which we 'tell about' our lives" (2004: 694). Bruner's quotation implies that the telling of one's life story is a consequential act that affects how the narrator subsequently organizes memories and perceives future events.

Russian psychologist Lev Vygotsky made a similar point in his discussion of *perezhivanie*, a central concept in sociocultural theory that refers to how emotionally charged experiences trigger affective and cognitive responses in the individual which in turn lead to ontological changes. Lantolf and Swain (2020) describe the Vygotskyan concept of perezhivanie and demonstrate its relevance for second language acquisition (SLA). The authors cite numerous examples in the SLA literature of L2 learners who experience strong emotions such as joy and excitement during communicative success or embarrassment and frustration during communicative failure (e.g., Lantolf & Genung, 2002; Lotherington, 2007). These kinds of emotionally charged events have been found to affect learners' motivation and linguistic development (Mok, 2015; Pavlenko, 2014; Poehner & Swain, 2016; Swain, 2013). Thus, as the instructor of a course focused on narrating the multilingual self, I wanted to help my students recall their language-related perezhivaniya (the plural form of perezhivanie) and unpack their thoughts and feelings surrounding those events. My hope was that by writing autobiographical accounts of their perezhivaniya, my students would gain insight into how such events had shaped them as L2 learners and incipient multilinguals.

To help my students remember their language learning highlights and lowlights, I began the course with a powerful essay written in English by the African American writer and journalist Ta-Nehisi Coates entitled "Acting French" (Coates, 2014). Published in The Atlantic magazine, the essay recounts the "childlike amazement" that the 37-year-old Coates feels upon traveling to Paris, his first trip abroad. Realizing how little he knows about life outside his American bubble, Coates decides to enroll in a summer intensive French class in L'école française at Middlebury College in Vermont. At Middlebury, Coates soon discovers that he also knows precious little about how to learn a foreign language compared to the "young masters," the phrase he uses to describe his much younger and more academically proficient peers. In his essay, Coates captures not only the universal joys and frustrations of language learning, but also his personal struggles with the foreignness of Middlebury's scholastic culture. A talented essayist and narrator, Coates explores his language-learning journey at Middlebury to better understand the "borders of race and class" in the American educational system and in the second language classroom.

When I taught the course for the first time in 2021, I had felt confident that after reading several language memoirs such as the one by Coates that my students would be able to recall similar events from their own lives with ease and clarity. Following L-by-D principles, I had planned many targeted activities meant to guide my students in the discovery of the "Available Designs" employed by multilingual francophone writers so that the students could recycle those designs in their own creative writing. In addition, I had developed activities to help my students refine multiple drafts of their narratives, each activity targeting a specific narrative element such as the use of dialogue or descriptive detail. However, I had not anticipated that my students would have difficulty recalling specific language-related perezhivaniya. How could they write their personal L2 narratives if they couldn't even recover the original events?

In addition to having trouble remembering their lived experiences, my students seemed to struggle to verbalize their emotional experiences in the L2. Was it for lack of vocabulary or was it due to something deeper? Citing research by Pavlenko (2014) in their discussion of the concept of perezhivanie, Lantolf and Swain (2020, p.96) note that emotional experiences present special difficulties for L2 learners who typically lack an affective connection to their L2. To draw attention to how this disconnect impacts learner discourse, Pavlenko coined the expression "feeling-for-speaking" based on Slobin's (1996) "thinking-for-speaking" concept. The term "feeling-for-speaking" emphasizes that emotionality, including the semantics of emotion words and the pragmatics of emotional expression in interaction, is deeply connected to how we are socialized in our primary cultures. In essence, to speak cogently about emotions in French, you must know how

Francophones understand and express their own "French" feelings. Thus, Pavlenko hypothesizes that L2 learners will likely encounter difficulties when verbalizing their feelings in the target language because their own feelings are always closely bound to their L1s. Moreover, as Dewaele (2010) points out, since the evaluation of emotions (i.e., perezhivanie) is closely connected to the L1 rather than the L2, the target-language discourse of many L2 learners may exhibit a lack of affect. Based on the research on emotion and multilingualism as well as my students' struggles to remember and express their emotions in the L2, it became clear that I would need to address these important issues.

When I taught the course again in 2022, I decided to include contemplative techniques embedded in *Experiencing* activities in hopes of prodding my students' emotional memories. Zapata (2022) describes *Experiencing* activities as a kind of advanced organizer whose main purpose is to connect the L2 students' knowledge of familiar content and genres based on their lifeworlds ("the known") with less familiar content and genres based on academic fields and foreign cultures ("the unknown"). Following Cope and Kalantzis (2015), Zapata gives many examples of *Experiencing* activities that oblige students to retrieve specific pieces of information and reflect on familiar and unfamiliar meanings. For instance, Zapata (2022) outlines an initial pedagogical sequence in a unit meant to prepare students to interview an expert from the target culture. Zapata begins the unit with Experiencing-the-known exercises that activate the students' schemata of the topic ("the known"):

> The L2 instructor introduces the topic of focus, eliciting students' previous knowledge and personal experiences. For example, the instructor can use newspaper headlines, word clouds, or photos to trigger ideas and activate schemata. Once learners are situated within the topic, the teacher provides information about the expert with whom students will be interacting. The instructor also presents the driving question, project calendar, division of labor, outcomes, and expected results. Students are divided into groups, and they are asked to create five or six questions for the expert. (p. 96)

In general, I found such *Experiencing* activities to work well for activating the students' schemata based on easily retrievable events and facts. However, I became convinced that I needed to try something new to help my students unpack their own emotional reactions to the course readings. Put differently, instead of focusing solely on critical thinking to access retrievable knowledge, I decided to focus more on "critical feeling" (Reber, 2016) to uncover forgotten or inaccessible memories.

A contemplative approach to digital social reading (DSR)

To illustrate and organize the diversity of contemplative practices, the Center for Contemplative Mind in Society (CMind, 2021) created an image of a tree as shown in Figure 1. Note that the tree is rooted in communion, connection and awareness, the three major goals of contemplation. From there, the tree branches into different categories of practices. The most relevant categories of contemplative practices for my course were "stillness," "generative," and "creative."

I employed specific digital social reading (DSR) activities to promote a more contemplative approach to textual thinking. Admittedly, combining contemplation with digital tools seems counter-intuitive. For example, many language specialists equate the idea of "digital literacy" with the opposite of contemplation, namely, distraction, hyperactivity, and stupefaction (Bauerlein, 2008, 2011, 2022). Along similar lines, science writer Nicolas Carr (2020) refers to online cognitive activity as "the shallows," a pejorative term that characterizes digital meaning-making as facile and superficial. However, reading scholar Hayles (2012) counters the pejoration of digital practices by reminding educators that literacy is best viewed as a set of historically situated practices. Hayles contends that critiques of digital literacy practices tend to equate reading with the close reading of printed texts. Such a view fails to acknowledge the importance of newer types of computer-mediated semiotic activity such as hyper-reading and machine reading. Despite Hayles' insightful and balanced analysis, digital tools tend to place ever greater value on speed and efficiency. In contrast, contemplation invites the reader

Chapter 4. Incorporating mindfulness into multiliteracies pedagogy

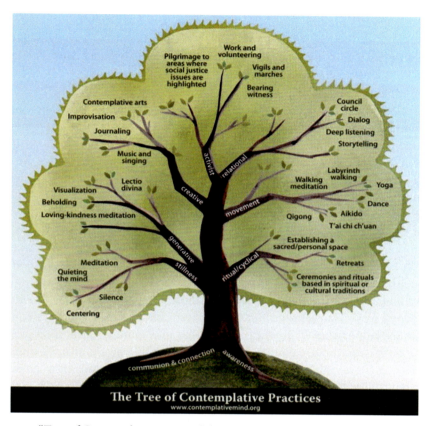

Figure 1. "Tree of Contemplative Practice" (Center for Contemplative Mind in Society. Reprinted with permission. CC-BY-SA 4.0)

(and writer) to slow things down. In other words, lingering over a text during a reading or writing activity can be seen as a valuable way to become more aware of "first thoughts" as argued by Goldberg (2016). In the following sections, I outline my contemplative approach and describe my new classroom-based practices.

Framing the classroom as a contemplative space

My course coincided with the post-pandemic years when colleges and universities were slowly returning to face-to-face teaching. This chapter is based on the second iteration of the course taught in 2022. Despite my students' palpable excitement at being back in the classroom, they seemed disconnected from me and each other, their faces hidden by laptops and smartphones. As a result, I was obliged to spend several minutes at the beginning of each class getting my students' full attention. I was convinced that mindfulness techniques at the start of each class would improve this dynamic. According to the experts whom I consulted at my university, instructors should undertake their own mindfulness training before attempting to bring contemplative techniques into the classroom. Therefore, several months before the semester started, I began my own meditative practice to become better acquainted with the difficulties encountered by learners new to meditation.

On the first day of class, I arrived early to meditate in preparation for the start of a new semester. My journal entry for the day was focused on my anxieties concerning my students' reactions to my planned mindfulness activities. I feared that my students would interpret my adoption of mindfulness as evidence of a religious agenda. To counteract this unwanted perception, I played part of a video produced by my university's Mental Health Services about the importance of mindfulness for student wellness ("Intro to Mindfulness"). Based on the video, I encouraged my students to try out several mindfulness practices that would help frame our classroom as a more contemplative space, including an exercise developed by Dr. Jan Chozen Bays, a physician and Zen teacher. Bays demonstrates the importance of entering new spaces in a mindful fashion by pausing at the door's threshold, taking a breath, and becoming aware of one's thoughts and feeling (Bays, 2011). Following Bays' advice, I asked my students to enter our classroom accordingly. Next, I asked my students to take their seats and immediately perform a one-minute breathing exercise meant to focus them on the present moment. Finally, I challenged my students to turn off their devices and use the time before class to prepare for the lesson.

#AnnotatedSyllabus

After discussing these simple mindfulness techniques for starting class in the right frame of mind, I turned my attention to the course description and syllabus. However, rather than reviewing and explaining the syllabus, I asked the students to read and annotate the document online in preparation for a group discussion. My goal was to demonstrate the basics of digital social annotation to my students and to justify its frequent use during class. To begin, I directed my students to the "Collaborations" page of our LMS course site where I had prepared a Google doc of the syllabus. In his blog #AnnotatedSyllabus, digital media scholar Remi Kalir points out that the social annotation of a syllabus conveys three specific messages: "that course documents are not static artifacts, that something authored by an instructor is not unwelcoming of feedback, and that student voice is both appreciated and necessary for a shared endeavor (Kalir, 2022, Strategies for Syllabus Annotation)." As shown in Figure 2, a screenshot of my #AnnotatedSyllabus Google doc, I prefaced the syllabus with a series of ground rules to guide the students' annotation behavior. I also emphasized that the syllabus activity would continue at intervals throughout the semester to promote an on-going conversation about the course. To guide their initial annotations, I seeded the text with leading questions. I was pleased when the students immediately began writing thoughtful comments about the proposed syllabus.

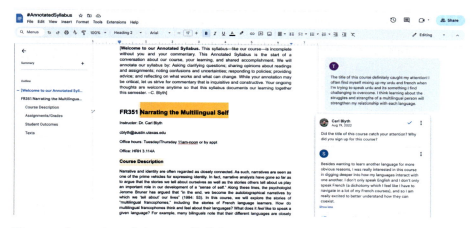

Figure 2. Screenshot of #AnnotatedSyllabus activity

When the students had finished the task, I projected the newly annotated text on the screen in the front of the room and asked my students to explain in more detail their annotations. Did their annotations indicate that parts of the syllabus were more ambiguous than others? Did their annotations call for greater specificity? Did their annotations index certain emotions? Kalir and Garcia (2021) contend that the analysis of one's own annotation activity is helpful for promoting a greater awareness of one's meta-cognitive processes. I was surprised to discover that the students had much to say about all parts of the syllabus. I had intentionally left the "course outcomes" section blank to prompt my students to articulate their personal goals. As shown in Figure 3, this empty section generated extensive commentary. For instance, one student wrote that his personal goal for the course was "to figure out where French fits within my multicultural and multilingual identity as an immigrant and polyglot…" In summary, the #AnnotatedSyllabus activity was not intended as a contemplative practice per se. Rather, the goal of the activity was to help my students quickly grasp the fundamentals of digital social annotation — what it is and what we would do with it during the semester.

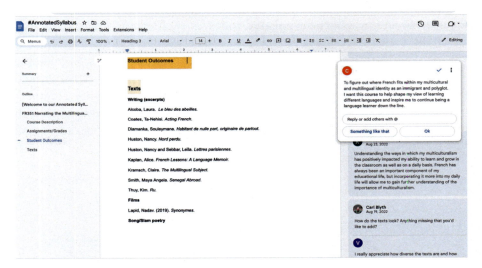

Figure 3. Screenshot of #AnnotatedSyllabus comments about "student outcomes"

Contemplative reading activities

Barbezat and Bush (2014, p. 113) define contemplative reading as "a process of quiet reflection, which requires mindful attentiveness, letting go of distracting thoughts and opinions to be fully in the moment with the text." The authors note that contemplative reading is historically related to the exegesis of sacred texts such as the monastic Christian practice called *lectio divina*. Adapted from early Judaism as a system for reading the Hebrew Bible, *lectio divina* recognized four levels of meaning: literal, metaphorical, moral and mystical. In the sixth century, when reading was essentially limited to religious scriptures, European monks formalized reading as the practice of four sequenced "knowledge-actions": *lectio* (reading and then understanding the basic meaning of the text), *meditatio* (reflecting and contextualizing), *oratio* (listening to one's inner voice), and *contemplatio* (being still and meeting God in the text). In today's secular classrooms, contemplative reading refers to a set of heterogeneous practices meant to guide readers beyond literal meaning towards a calm awareness of deeper meanings. Whatever the precise methods employed, contemplative reading aims to slow down the interpretive process and narrow the focus to a small stretch of text, such as a few sentences of prose.

In 2021 when I taught the course for the first time, I asked my students to annotate the readings with glosses of unknown words and comments about difficult passages using Hypothesis, a digital annotation tool (DAT). According to the literature on DSR, one of the major affordances of DATs is that they turn reading into a collaborative activity during which participants help each other co-construct meaning (Blyth, 2014). However, my students had paid little attention to each other's annotations and had rarely commented on each other's opinions or ideas, likely due to the asynchronous format of the assignment. The literature on social annotation indicates that my experience is not anomalous. In a study of the DAT eComma, Law, Barny and Poulin (2020) found that 215 students enrolled in beginning French classes at a large public university rarely used the tool in a collaborative fashion during asynchronous assignments. Thus, I wondered how I might use DATs to promote a more contemplative and social approach to reading.

When I taught the course again in 2022, I mixed synchronous and asynchronous uses of social annotation in several ways. As an asynchronous homework activity, the students were required to annotate narrative texts written by students from the previous course. More accessible than very brief excerpts from texts written by well-known francophone authors, L2 French texts allowed my students to spend less time on unfamiliar vocabulary and more time on the writer's rhetorical choices. The next day in class, I led a teacher-fronted discussion based on the students' asynchronous annotations. During one of these lessons, a colleague came to observe my class as part of my annual teaching evaluation. The day's lesson was based on an L2 text entitled "Séjour de Papi" ("Granddad's visit"). My colleague described my annotation-based lesson as follows:

> Carl announced an outline for the "Séjour de Papi" discussion and explained how the text related to the day's overall lesson. Students had annotated the text before class to share their ideas. Carl revealed that the student who wrote this text had previously written numerous drafts over the course of the semester and had annotated his own text to explain his stylistic choices. I thought that this was a brilliant way of emphasizing the work that goes into improving a written text and helping the students see themselves as writers. Carl then asked students some questions about the text based on comments that they had made in their annotations. The students responded voluntarily and seemed to be very engaged with the style and ideas presented in the text. Then Carl asked the students to read the text aloud as a class. Carl commented on certain features of the text as they read and corrected pronunciation. I observed that students were reading the text with great attention to inflection and tone. This struck me as quite noteworthy because it showed that the students were aware of authorial voice and interpretive effects. Next, Carl began a discussion on narrative structure using a French website called *Alloprof*. After his overview of the structural elements required for storytelling, Carl asked students to work in pairs to identify the narrative segments of "Séjour de Papi.

Missing from my colleague's description was my instructional focus on "Available Designs." For instance, the goal of the pair work was to focus the students on the Available Designs of the narrative text. Following the pair group activity, I created three small groups and challenged them to identify and articulate the text's "agencements possibles" (translation by Beatrice Dupuy). Again, I asked the groups to write their "agencements possibles" on the Google doc itself and to pinpoint where the specific designs appeared in the text. After a few minutes, I asked each group to present their Available Designs to the class. Once the Available Designs had been named, defined, and exemplified, I asked the students to add this information to yet another shared Google doc that served as a curated list of Available Designs as shown in Figure 4. This list was updated following every annotation activity. Note that the Available Designs represent a heterogenous group of devices: codeswitching, verbatim dialogue, slang, interior rhymes, proverbs, juxtaposition of images, syntactic repetition, etc. The final list included 30 Available Designs with examples culled from the course readings.

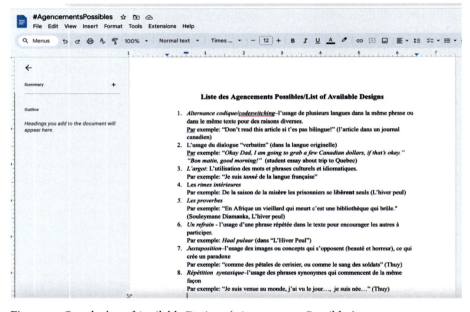

Figure 4. Google doc of Available Designs (#AgencementsPossibles)

In addition to the asynchronous, non-contemplative uses of annotation, I also created in-class, synchronous, contemplative annotation activities focused on very brief excerpts from texts written by well-known francophone authors. By employing very short texts (no more than a paragraph), I gave students plenty of time to linger over the text and to annotate their thoughts and feelings. To set a contemplative mood for this activity, I had several students read the entire text aloud followed by a few moments of silence. Then, I asked my students to spend the next ten minutes annotating the text in a slow and deliberate fashion. When the shared Google doc had been liberally annotated, I asked each student to share one of their annotations with the class. Students were told to listen attentively but not to comment.

The practice of "contemplative annotation" is exemplified by my students' "slow reading" of the first page of Kim Thuy's immigrant novel *Ru* as shown in Figure 5 (Thuy, 2009:11). The novel tells the story of Thuy's life during the Vietnam War and her eventual immigration to Quebec. The excerpt is composed of three sentences, each set off as an indented paragraph. An analysis of the chronology of the annotations shows a clear progression. Students begin the exercise by translating, that is, annotating unfamiliar vocabulary and cultural referents (e.g., "the Year of the Monkey"). Next, the students note Thuy's style, such as her fondness for juxtaposed images (See Appendix B for full text and translation). In the last stage, when most of the literal and non-literal meanings have been annotated, the students become more introspective and annotate the text with their own subjective thoughts and feelings. It is this final stage in which the students appear to be reading the text in a contemplative manner. In Figure 5, we see that student S perceives the pronunciation of the grapheme -ch- in the French past participle *déchiré* ("ripped") as a violent sound, an example of sound symbolism (See Kramsch, 2009, Chapter 1). Her annotation draws attention to her iconic interpretation of the sound, an act that indexes her symbolic competence as a multilingual subject ("in speaking it out loud it sounds violent"). Kramsch (2009:37) gives a similar example of a learner who interprets the German grapheme ß in the word Streß ("stress") as intensifying the word's denotational meaning, an example of "hyperstress." It appears that listening to the text read aloud by their classmates followed by an extended silence allowed my students the reflective space to finally notice their subjective reactions to the text.

From this annotation activity, my students added two new Available Designs to the curated list seen in Figure 3 above — Juxtaposition and Syntactic Repetition. Juxtaposition is exemplified by citing Thuy's phrase "...comme des pétales de cerisier, ou comme le sang de deux millions de soldats..." ("like the blossoms of the cherry tree or like the blood of two million soldiers"). According to the student who curated this Available Design, the author positions beauty and horror side by side thereby creating a paradox (How can something be both beautiful and horrific at the same time?). The students also noticed Thuy's use of phrasal triplets; the excerpt contains three sentences about Thuy's birth that repeat the same first-person sentential frame (e.g., *Je suis venue au monde, J'ai vu le jour, Je suis née* ("I came into the world," "I saw the light of day," "I was born"). In summary, based on a short text, a slowed down reading process, and extended moments of silence, my students were able to identify important stylistic elements of Thuy's writing – the use of syntactic repetition to juxtapose images, sounds, and smells in startling ways. In addition, by slowing down the reading process, students were able to unpack layers of textual meaning in a more deliberate fashion: first, the denotational meanings of the words, next, the impact of stylistic devices, and third, the subjective reactions to the text's language and to the process of reading itself.

Figure 5. Annotated excerpt from Kim Thuy's novel Ru (Thuy, 2009:11)

A contemplative approach to digital social writing (DSW)

In addition to a heavy reading load, the course carried a "writing flag," a special designation for an undergraduate course in which at least a third of the final grade is based on student writing. A writing flag lets students know to expect a substantial paper requiring detailed feedback and extensive revisions. To meet these requirements, I devised two writing assignments that counted for much of the class grade: (1) a 5-page personal narrative written in French about a turning point in one's multilingual life journey and (2) a 5-page analysis written in English of an oral interview of a multilingual French speaker. These two assignments were meant to give students a chance to practice different written genres: a narrative genre and an expository genre.

Freewriting, translanguaging, and perezhivanie

To create an open platform for all course writing assignments, I asked each student to share a Google doc with the entire class. This shared document promoted a richer creative writing process that included the contemplative exercises of freewriting, translanguaging and reflective journaling. In particular, the shared Google doc proved useful for giving and receiving feedback on multiple drafts of the students' personal narratives. Students were encouraged to employ translanguaging in drafts to help them remember narrative events and to access their "first thoughts" of the events that were likely encoded in their native or dominant languages. In language pedagogy, the term translanguaging usually refers to the strategic use of more than one language within a single lesson (Garcia & Wei, 2014; Wei, 2017). The term was first coined in Welsh as *trawsieithu* in the 1980s by Cen Williams in his unpublished thesis on innovative methods in bilingual education (Lewis et al., 2012). According to Cenoz and Gorter (2020), Williams used the term to describe the use of two languages in the same lesson, a method at odds with the field's received wisdom of the day that called for the separation of languages by class, time, or day (Cenoz & Gorter, 2020). Today, the term *translanguaging* is viewed as an extension of the monolingual concept of *languaging* originally described by Swain (2000, 2006) as the cognitive process of negotiating and producing meaningful, comprehensible output in the target language as part of learners' collaborative dialogue.

A few weeks into the semester, most students adopted freewriting to compose their first drafts. Freewriting is a technique in which authors write their thoughts quickly and continuously, without worrying about form, style, or even grammar. Alongside brainstorming, freewriting is typically used early in the writing process to collect and manifest one's thoughts. Freewriting was not employed to produce narratives per se, but rather descriptions of narrative events in the L1. Nevertheless, L1 freewriting allowed the students to recover their memories and feelings surrounding lived events with more clarity and facility than would have been possible if they had written in their L2. In my comments on their initial drafts, I praised their "good beginnings" but called for more details to flesh out their narratives. In subsequent drafts, students intentionally employed translanguaging as an Available Design following the many examples gleaned from their readings. For instance, mimicking the student narrator of Séjour de Papi, many students used their L1s to represent their interior monologue. Some students overtly played with translations in their languages to help them unlock their multilingual subjectivities. Many of these translations were redundant and did not serve any particular narrative function. As French gradually became the default language in subsequent drafts, these translations tended to disappear. By their final drafts, most of the students had not only recovered the narrative events but had accessed their "first thoughts" of the events allowing them to narrate with appropriate levels of emotionality.

A good example of this entire 12-week process was a narrative entitled "Cher moi" ("Dear Me"), a moving story written by the student who had shared on the first day that his goal for the course was "to figure out where French fits within my multicultural and multilingual identity as an immigrant and polyglot." The narrative was a twist on an Available Design that the student had discovered reading "Lettres Parisiennes," a work based on the correspondence between two multilingual Francophones — the Algerian-born French writer Leïla Sebbar and the Canadian-born French writer Nancy Huston (Sebbar & Huston, 1986). To tell his multilingual life story, the student created a narrator who was an older, wiser version of himself. The older version of himself recounts his lived experiences to his younger self. In his first draft, the student explained how his Spanish-English bilingual upbringing had led to a sense of linguistic insecurity. Because he had often moved between the United States and Central America, the student's bilingual competence did not match that of his monolingual peers. In the second draft, the student described in Spanish the moment when his eighth-grade teacher in Guatemala tells him that his reading proficiency in Spanish requires remediation. He is promptly sent to a room by himself and given children's literature to read for the rest of the year. As recounted in an early draft, the moment is one of great shame and embarrassment. In subsequent drafts, the student recounts similar events in the American educational system when he is sent to ESL classes by a well-intentioned teacher who finds his English proficiency too foreign or too heavily influenced by Spanish. The narrator's movement between countries is indexed by his choice of narrative language — Spanish to report events in Guatemala and English for events in the United States. In the final version of the story, the student adopts the epistolary technique of telling the story to his younger self through a letter. In addition, the student settles on French as the default narrative language with translanguaging used specifically to index different emotions tied to his two languages.

Writers annotating their own texts

Throughout the semester, I asked my students to annotate their emerging narratives with comments about their feelings during the creative writing process, yet another use of social digital annotation to connect textual production to critical feeling. The author of "Cher moi" adopted this technique and used it frequently throughout the semester as a way of regulating his feelings about his struggles to produce a coherent narrative in French. In his final evaluation of the course, the student described his realization that the course was as much about his own life as it was about the lives of the writers studied in class. And in keeping with the epistolary design uncovered during his reading, he composed his final course evaluation as a letter to a future student who might be thinking of enrolling in the class: "The sooner you realize that this class is about you, the better you will be able to tell your story." Similarly, many students annotated the final versions of their narratives as advice addressed to future students about what to expect when writing one's multilingual life story.

Lessons learned

My attempt to enrich Multiliteracies pedagogy with contemplative practices taught me three major lessons — that contemplative reading is qualitatively different from close reading; that the efficacy of digital annotation tools (DATs) depends largely on the features of the text and the assignment; and that by slowing down my instructional practices, I could improve my students' wellbeing as well as their L2 literacy.

Contemplative reading vs. close reading

When I taught the new course for the first time in 2021, I wrongly assumed that contemplative reading was similar to close reading. While both focus on a small stretch of text, the similarities end there. Close reading, a practice cherished by many humanists and literary scholars, refers to an analytic process during which the reader interrogates the text. The process begins by reading the selected passage and noting anything that strikes the reader as relevant or interesting. Next, the reader makes observations about various elements of the passage, such as diction, voice, tone, and rhetorical devices. These observations are then used to develop a thesis and argument about the passage. The last step in the process is to select examples from the text to support one's argument. Thus, a close reading, referred to in French as *explication de texte*, requires the reader to pay close attention to formal structures of language — vocabulary, syntax, and discourse — that can be marshaled as evidence in the construction of a coherent interpretation. In other words, an *explication de texte* requires the reader to search the text for meaning. In contrast, contemplative reading requires the reader to wait for meaning to be revealed in a slow and unhurried process that feels less agentive and effortful than close reading. Advocates of contemplative reading capture this phenomenological difference with metaphorical language: Close reading requires the reader to go to the text, whereas contemplative reading requires the text to come to the reader.

The efficacy of digital annotation tools (DATS)

As noted, my students did not seem to pay much attention to each other's annotations while using a DAT when I first taught the course in 2021. In retrospect, this does not seem to be the fault of the DAT, but rather how I had asked my students to use the tool. When I taught the class for the first time, I asked students to annotate PDFs of relatively long literary passages written in French. In retrospect, I believe that the length and difficulty of the texts did not allow my students enough time to read their peers' contributions. Moreover, the asynchronous nature of the assignment impeded collaboration and sharing.

When I taught the course again in 2022, I chose shorter and easier texts for assignments that allowed my students to finish reading with time left over to explore their peer's comments. Moreover, I integrated annotation into contemplative activities based on short passages that the students read aloud followed by a moment of silence. Once the students had read the text aloud and had sat together with the text as a class, I asked them to annotate the shared Google doc on their laptops. Next, working in pairs, the students drew conclusions based on their aggregated annotations. Finally, working in small groups, the students articulated the Available Designs they had discovered during their annotation activities. This type of collaborative meaning-making was greatly facilitated using Google docs that not only allowed for comments and annotations, but also allowed the group to compose written summaries of discovered Available Designs as shown in Figure 3.

Designing slow literacy

L-by-D is distinguished by its innovative metalanguage that emphasizes design as both product and process. Central to this approach is the idea of Designing as a semiotic process during which Available Designs become Redesigned when they are deployed in the creation of a new text. What if we were to extend this type of design thinking to the creation of literacy instruction that simultaneously raises awareness of Designs of Meaning while reducing the stress and anxiety currently engulfing our classrooms? Contemplation does just that. Contemplation helps us discover textual meanings while improving our mental health. It accomplishes these goals by forcing us to slow down thereby giving us the time and space to gain a more holistic perspective on literacy education. For these reasons, I believe that mindfulness deserves a greater role in Multiliteracies pedagogy.

Conclusion

My interest in integrating mindfulness into my Multiliteracies-inspired French course had two main origins. After years in higher education, I strongly desired a more holistic approach to teaching and learning in response to the current mental health crisis on college campuses. In addition, I was looking for new strategies to help my students gain greater awareness of their own semiotic biases. In particular, I wanted to improve their understanding of the dialectic between cognition and emotion in their own multilingual development. As I became better acquainted with mindfulness and contemplative pedagogy, I grew more convinced that contemplation deserved a more prominent role in my teaching. In general, I found that contemplative practices, including contemplative digital social annotation, deepened my students' awareness of their own thoughts and feelings during textual interpretation and production. That said, many students continued to struggle with their creative writing. On the final course evaluation, one student summed up what they had learned: "My best advice, knowing what I know now, is that you just need to write, write, write. Write it out. Waiting for the right ideas doesn't create good writing. Writing creates good writing." My student's observation could not be more Zen. For like mindfulness itself, literacy is fundamentally a practice.

References

ACTFL Proficiency Guidelines (French). (2012). Retrieved on 3 August 2023 from https://www .actfl.org/educator-resources/actfl-proficiency-guidelines/french

Adams, T., Jones, S., & Ellis, C. (2015) *Autoethnography*. Oxford University Press.

Anderson, L., & Krathwohl, D. (2001). A taxonomy for learning, teaching, and assessing: A revision of Bloom's taxonomy of educational objectives. Longman.

Bamberg, M., DeFina, A., & Schiffrin, D. (Eds.) (2007). *Selves and identities in narrative and discourse*. John Benjamins.

Barbezat, D. & Bush, M. (2014). *Contemplative practices in higher education: Powerful methods to transform teaching and learning*. Jossey-Bass.

Bauerlein, M. (2008). *The dumbest generation: How the digital age stupefies young Americans and jeopardizes our futures*. Penguin.

Bauerlein, M. (2011). *The digital divide: Arguments for and against Facebook, Google, texting and age of social networking*. Penguin.

Bauerlein, M. (2022). *The dumbest generation grows up: From stupefied youth to dangerous adults*. Penguin.

Bays, J. (2011). *How to train a wild elephant and other adventures in mindfulness*. Shambala.

Blyth. C. (2014). Exploring the affordances of digital social reading for L2 literacy: The case of eComma. In J. P. Guikema & L. Williams (Eds.), *Digital literacies in foreign and second language education* (Vol. 12, pp. 201–226). Calico.

Bruner, J. (2004). *Life as narrative*. Social Research, 71(3), 691–710.

Carr, N. (2020). *The shallows: What the internet is doing to our brains*. Norton.

Cenoz, J., & Gorter, D. (2020). Pedagogical translanguaging: An introduction. *System*, 92, 102269.

CMind. (2021). The tree of contemplative practices [Illustration]. The Center for Contemplative Mind in Society. Retrieved on 7 August 2023 from https://www.contemplativemind.org/practices/tree

Coates, T. (2014). Acting French. *The Atlantic*. Retrieved on 7 August 2023 from https://www.theatlantic.com/education/archive/2014/08/acting-french/375743/

Cope, B., & Kalantzis, M. (2015). The things you do to know: An introduction to multiliteracies pedagogy. In B. Cope & M. Kalantzis (Eds.), *A pedagogy of multiliteracies: Learning by design* (pp. 1–36). Palgrave Macmillan.

Damasio, A. (1994). *Descartes' error: Emotion, reason, and the human brain*. Penguin.

Davidson, R. and Dahl, C. (2017). Varieties of contemplative practices. *JAMA Psychiatry*, 74(2), 121-123.

Dewaele, J.-M. (2010). *Emotions in multiple languages*. Palgrave Macmillan.

Edwards, N. (2019). *Multilingual life writing by French and francophone women: Translingual selves*. Routledge.

Garcia, O., & Wei, L. (2014). *Translanguaging: Language, bilingualism and education*. Palgrave Macmillan.

Goldberg, N. (2016). *Writing down the bones: Freeing the writer within*. Shambala.

Gunnlaugson, O., Sarath, E., Scott, C., & Bai, H. (Eds). (2014). *Contemplative learning and inquiry across disciplines*. SUNY Press.

Hayles, N. K. (2012). How we think: Digital media and contemporary technogenesis. University of Chicago Press.

Horwitz, E., Horwitz, M., & Cope, J. (1986). Foreign-language classroom anxiety. *Modern Language Journal*, 70(2), 125–132.

"Intro to Mindfulness." An online video produced by University of Texas at Austin Mental Health Services. Retrieved 14 March 2023 from https://www.healthyhorns.utexas.edu/mindfulness-about.html

Kabat-Zinn, J. (2005). *Coming to our senses: Healing ourselves and the world through mindfulness*. Hyperion.

Kalir, R. (2022). #AnnotatedSyllabus. Retrieved 14 March 2023 from https://remikalir.com/annotatedsyllabus/

Kalir, R., & García, A. (2021). *Annotation*. The MIT Press.

Koçali, Z., & Asik, A. (2022). A systematic review of mindfulness studies in ESL and EFL contexts. *I-manager's Journal on Educational Psychology*, 15(3), 47–61.

Kramsch, C. (2009). *The multilingual subject*. Oxford University Press.

Lantolf, J., & Genung, P. (2002) I'd rather switch than fight: An activity theoretic study of power, success and failure in a foreign language classroom. In C. Kramsch (Ed.), *Language acquisition and language socialization: Ecological perspectives* (pp. 175–196). Continuum.

Lantolf, J., & Swain, M. (2020). Perezhivanie: The cognitive-emotional dialectic within the social situation of development. In A. Al-Hoorie & P. MacIntyre (Eds.), *Contemporary motivation theory: Sixty years since Gardner and Lambert* (1959) (pp. 80–105). Multilingual Matters.

Law, J., Barny, D., & Poulin, R. (2020). Patterns of peer interaction in multimodal L2 digital social reading. *Language Learning & Technology*, 24(2), 70–85.

Lewis, G., Jones, B., & Baker, C. (2012). Translanguaging: Origins and development from school to street and beyond. *Educational Research and Evaluation*, 18(7), 641–654.

Lotherington, H. (2007). Diary of an edu-tourist in Costa Rica: An autoethnographical account of learning Spanish. *TESL Canada Journal*, 24, 109–131.

McAdams, D. (1990). Unity and purpose in human lives: The emergence of identity as a life story. In A.I. Rabin, R.A. Zucker, R.A. Emmons, & S. Frank (Eds.), *Studying persons and lives* (pp. 148–200). Springer.

McAdams, D. (2013). *The redemptive self: Stories Americans live by*. Oxford University Press.

McGee, K. (2022, January 19). Texas college students confront anxiety, apathy as another pandemic semester begins. *The Texas Tribune*. Retrieved 14 March 2023 from https://www.texastribune.org/2022/01/19/texas-coronavirus-pandemic-college-mental-health/

Miller, J. (2014). Contemplation: The soul's way of knowing. In O. Gunnlaugson, E.W. Sarath, C. Scott, & H. Bai (Eds), *Contemplative learning and inquiry across disciplines* (pp. 15–29). SUNY Press.

Mok, N. (2015). Toward an understanding of perezhivanie for sociocultural SLA research. *Language and Sociocultural Theory*, 2(2), 139–160.

Morgan, W., & Katz, J. (2021). Mindfulness meditation and foreign language classroom anxiety: Findings from a randomized control trial. *Foreign Language Annals*, 54, 389–409.

Ochs, E., & Capps, L. (2002). *Living narrative: Creating lives in everyday storytelling*. Harvard University Press.

Pandya, A., & Lodha, P. (2022). Mental health consequences of COVID-19 pandemic among college students and coping approaches adapted by higher education institutions. *Social Science and Medicine, Social Health*, Vol. 2.

Pavlenko, A. (2014). *The bilingual mind and what it tells us about language and thought*. Cambridge University Press.

Peterson, C. (2006). *A primer in positive psychology*. Oxford University Press.

Poehner, M., & Swain, M. (2016). L2 development as cognitive-emotive process. *Language and Sociocultural Theory*, 3(2), 219–241.

Reber, R. (2016). *Critical feeling: How to use feelings strategically*. Cambridge University Press.

Scida, E., & Jones, J. (2017). The impact of contemplative practices on foreign language anxiety and learning. *Studies in Second Language Learning and Teaching*, 7(4), 573–599.

Sébbar, L., & Huston, N. (1986). *Lettres parisiennes: Autopsie de l'exil*. Barrault.

Slobin, D. (1996). From "thought and language" to "thinking for speaking." In J. Gumperz & S. Levinson (Eds.), *Rethinking linguistic relativity* (pp. 70–96). Cambridge University Press.

Swain, M. (2000). The output hypothesis and beyond: Mediating acquisition through collaborative dialogue. In J. P. Lantolf (Ed.), *Sociocultural theory and second language learning* (pp. 97–114). Oxford University Press

Swain, M. (2006). Languaging, agency and collaboration in advanced second language learning. In H. Byrnes (Ed.), *Advanced language learning: The contributions of Halliday and Vygotsky* (pp. 95–108). Continuum.

Swain, M. (2013). The inseparability of cognition and emotion in second language learning. *Language Teaching, 46,* 195–207.

Thuy, K. (2009). *Ru.* Libre Expression.

Thuy, K. (2012). *Ru* (English translation by Sheila Fischman). Bloomsbury.

Vygotsky, L. S. (1994). The problem of the environment. In R. van der Veer & J. Valsiner (Eds.) *The Vygotsky reader* (pp. 338–354). Blackwell.

Wei, L. (2017). Translanguaging as a practical theory of language. *Applied Linguistics, 39*(1), 9–30.

Zajonc, A. (2014). Contemplative pedagogy in higher education: Toward a more reflective academy. In O. Gunnlaugson, E. W. Sarath, C. Scott, & H. Bai (Eds.), *Contemplative learning and inquiry across disciplines* (pp. 69–80). SUNY Press.

Zapata, G. (2022). *Learning-by-design and second language teaching: Theory, research, and practice.* Routledge.

Zeilhofer, L. (2023). Mindfulness in the foreign language classroom: Influence on academic achievement and awareness. *Language Teaching Research, 27*(1), 96–114.

Zimmerman, E. (2022, October 6). Meeting the mental health challenge at school and at home. *New York Times.* Retrieved 14 March 2023 from https://www.nytimes.com/2022/10/06 /education/learning/students-mental-health.html

Appendix A

Course description

Narratives are seen as one of the prime vehicles for expressing identity. In fact, narrative analysts have gone so far as to argue that the stories we tell about ourselves as well as the stories others tell about us play an important role in our development of a "sense of self." Along these lines, the psychologist Jerome Bruner has argued that "in the end, we become the autobiographical narratives by which we 'tell about' our lives" (1994:53). In this course, we will explore the stories of "multilingual francophones," including the stories of language learners. How do multilingual francophones think and feel about their languages? What does it *feel* like to speak a given language? For example, many multilinguals note that their different languages are closely tied to their cultural identities or different linguistic selves. What exactly does the French language symbolize for different multilingual speakers? For immigrants to a francophone country, French may represent a struggle to find one's place in an alien society. Dialect speakers often recount feelings of linguistic insecurity as well as ethnic pride when speaking their dialect. And what about classroom learners of French? What does the French language mean to them? Do they experience language learning as an expansion or a fragmentation of the self? In this course, students will read and analyze excerpts from language memoirs, as well as poems, songs, interviews, podcasts and films that focus on the experiences of French-speaking multilinguals. Finally, students in this course will have the opportunity to reflect on their own multilingual experiences. In summary, this course seeks to explore the concept of *multilingual subjectivity* through the analysis of *multilingual life writings* (Edwards, 2019) such as written and spoken narratives, slam poetry, song, film, and ethnographic interviews.

The course will adopt a Multiliteracies approach to foster better "textual thinking and feeling." Basically, Multiliteracies goes beyond "mere literacy" by emphasizing multimodality and the interaction of multiple languages during textual production and interpretation. We will think about texts through various collaborative activities such as social annotation, contemplative readings and other experimental pedagogical techniques.

Grading

– Participation	10%
– Discussions/Annotations	10%
– Podcast	10%
– Récit personnel	20%
– Récit brouillons (6 x 5%)	30%
– Entretien oral	10%
– Entretien écrit (un rapport)	10%

Assignments

1. *Discussions/Annotations*
   Posted discussions on Canvas due by Friday afternoon. The topics are essentially what we discuss in class as based on the texts. You should aim to write a paragraph that summarizes your personal opinions and feelings. Did the text move you? Did you relate to the narrator or the characters? Why or why not? Annotations are assignments that require you to mark up (annotate) a text. We will discuss your annotations in class the following day. Annotation is an important textual practice for exchanging thoughts and feelings that arise during the reading process. For example, the syllabus is a text and you will probably have thoughts and feelings about it, right? So let's begin this course by annotating the syllabus! To help us annotate, we will use Google docs.

2. *Podcast autobiographie*
   A 5-minute podcast about your life as a *French language learner*. The structure and focus are up to you, but the content must be autobiographical. In essence, the podcast should detail your experiences as a learner of French. What does the learning of French mean to you? What is the impact of language learning on your life? How has French affected you?

3. *Récit personnel*

A 5-page example of "multilingual life writing," that is, a narrative about what it means to be a multilingual/multicultural person. The narrative should focus on a lived event or series of events in your life. As a final, culminating assignment, you should try to incorporate as many "Available Designs" to bring your narrative to life (e.g., descriptive detail, metaphor, dialogue, voice, etc.). An "Available Design" refers to a particular semiotic (meaning-making) convention that authors employ in their texts. You will be asked to start a Google doc *rédaction* very early in the semester. The travaux pratiques assignments should feed into your récit personnel.

4. *Entretrien*

   You will interview a multilingual francophone about their languages/cultures and you will analyze/interpret your interview "data" in a written report (5 pages).

5. Travaux pratiques/brouillons écrits

   As we read different authors who narrate their multilingual experience, we will pay close attention to their writing. The travaux pratiques are opportunities for you to incorporate various literary elements into your own writing. The goal is for you to play with the "Available Designs" of other writers so that you can make them part of your own repertoire. (approx. 400 words).

Student outcomes

In this course, you will...

– gain insight into how multilingualism has shaped and continues to shape who you are and how you communicate;
– become more familiar with the language attitudes and ideologies in the French-speaking world;
– improve your ability to communicate with other speakers of French in speech and in writing;
– become more familiar with French dialects (e.g., acadien, québécois, cadien, etc.) and registers (e.g., familier, soutenu, académique, etc);
– acquire a richer vocabulary and more complex syntax in French;
– improve your metalinguistic skills (skills needed to discuss linguistic phenomena);
– improve your storytelling skills in French.

Texts

Writing (excerpts)

Alcoba, Laura. *Le bleu des abeilles.*
Coates, Ta-Nehisi. *Acting French.*
Diamanka, Souleymane. *Habitant de nulle part, originaire de partout.*
Huston, Nancy. *Nord perdu.*
Huston, Nancy and Sebbar, Leïla. *Lettres parisiennes.*
Kaplan, Alice. *French Lessons: A Language Memoir.*
Kramsch, Claire. *The Multilingual Subject.*
Smith, Maya Angela. *Senegal Abroad.*

Thuy, Kim. *Ru.*
Stories written by former students in this class (given with their permission)

Films

Lapid, Nadav. (2019). *Synonymes.*

Song/Slam poetry

Diamanka, Souleymane. *L'Hiver peul* (album)

Podcasts

Miscellaneous podcasts

Appendix B

(Excerpt from Ru by Kim Thuy)

Je suis venue au monde pendant l'offensive de Têt, aux premiers jours de la nouvelle année du Singe, lorsque les longues chaînes de pétards accrochées devant les maisons explosaient en polyphonie avec le son des mitraillettes.

J'ai vu le jour à Saigon, là où les débris des pétards éclatés en mille miettes coloraient le sol de rouge comme des pétales de cerisier, ou comme le sang des deux millions de soldats déployés, éparpillés dans les villes et les villages d'un Vietnam déchiré en deux.

Je suis née à l'ombre de ces cieux ornés de feux d'artifice, décorés de guirlandes lumineuses, traversés de roquettes et de fusées. (Thuy, 2009: 11)

I came into the world during the Tet Offensive, in the early days of the Year of the Monkey, when the long chains of firecrackers draped in front of houses exploded polyphonically with the sound of machine guns.

I saw the light of day in Saigon, where firecrackers fragmented into a thousand shreds, coloured the ground red like the petals of cherry blossoms or like the blood of two million soldiers deployed and scattered throughout the villages and cities of a Vietnam that had been ripped in two.

I was born in the shadow of skies adorned with fireworks, decorated with garlands of light, shot through with rockets and missiles. (Thuy, 2012: 1)

SECTION II

Texts, tasks, and teachers

CHAPTER 5

Addressing text difficulty in novice L2 digital social reading

James Law[1], David Barny[2] & Rachel Dorsey[2]
[1] Brigham Young University | [2] The University of Texas at Austin

Data from L2 digital social reading (DSR) can reveal textual features that increase literary discussion, with text difficulty shown to be a key inhibiting factor. Using DSR, 200 beginning university French students annotated lyrics to six songs of varying difficulty, with words beyond students' expected proficiency levels glossed in English. No inverse relationship was found between four measures of text difficulty and the use of literary affordances, suggesting that glossing effectively allows beginning French learners to engage in literary discussion of texts through DSR beyond their current proficiency level. Analysis of other textual features leads to recommendations that teachers of beginning L2 learners hoping to maximize literary discussion should prioritize multimedia texts with cultural specificity and should embrace texts of higher difficulty provided that glosses are added as needed.

Introduction

From a multiliteracies perspective, second-language (L2) reading that focuses only on decoding a text is insufficient (The New London Group, 1996, p.64). Multiliteracies pedagogy engages readers in an "active, transformative process" of meaning making through the critical analysis of texts (Cope & Kalantzis, 2009, p.175). Digital social reading (DSR) supports this kind of reading pedagogy in two ways. First, it facilitates a social context in which learners gain knowledge from peers (Blyth, 2014). Drawing on sociocultural theory, this is crucial to the establishment of situated practice wherein learning emerges from interaction with peers and experts (Vygotsky, 1978; van Compernolle, 2014; Cope & Kalantzis, 2015). Second, it provides data for instructors on how learners experience the central element of a reading task, the text itself. DSR annotations can reveal which kinds of texts, and which parts of texts, are most engaging for a particular audience (Pianzola et al., 2020).

https://doi.org/10.1075/aals.21.05law
© 2024 John Benjamins Publishing Company

Thoms and Poole (2018) identified a significant point of concern at the intersection of these two aspects of DSR: as the difficulty of an L2 text increases, the extent to which learners take advantage of the affordances of DSR for analyzing the literary features of the text decreases. In their study, they found that when reading more difficult texts with a DSR tool, learners focused their annotations on linguistic decoding (e.g., translating words, commenting on language forms), rather than on the kind of expansive critical analysis that is the goal within a multiliteracies approach. The authors suggest that instructors may want to provide definitions (i.e., glossing) of difficult words in order to overcome this problem and maximize literary discussion (ibid., p. 54).

Glossing of difficult words in L2 texts has been shown to improve vocabulary learning and global comprehension in some cases, especially with more difficult texts (Jacobs et al., 1994; Yoshii, 2006; Ko, 2012; Jung, 2016; Ouyang et al., 2020; Hosseini Alast & Baleghizadeh, 2021). This suggests that glossing may help to overcome the dampening effect of text difficulty on analysis of literary features in a DSR context by effectively making difficult texts easier.

This study explores this possibility by engaging adult learners of L2 French in DSR of six glossed texts of varying difficulty. Learner annotations of these texts are coded according to their focus on literary, linguistic, or social affordances.

Our first research question asks whether the use of literary affordances in DSR annotations is still impacted by text difficulty even when glosses are provided. The results suggest that glossing is effective in a DSR context, overcoming the potential effect of text difficulty on the use of literary affordances.

A secondary qualitative research question asks what other textual features impact the use of literary affordances in DSR annotations if the difficulty factor is neutralized. The familiarity of the topic, the richness of the input (e.g., multimedia texts), and the accessibility of rhetorical devices are explored as relevant factors.

Affordances in digital social reading

Gibson (1979) first defined *affordances* in his ecological theory of visual perception as "what [the environment] offers the animal, what it provides or furnishes, either good or ill" (Gibson, 1979, p. 127). Affordances constitute perceived characteristics of the environment of an organism that render further actions possible for that organism. They are bound to the organism's agency, making actions possible without directly triggering them. Affordances are relational since they are not entirely created by the perceiving organism nor do they fully exist outside of the organism's perception; they emerge from the organism's interaction with its environment. Van Lier (2000) illustrates this notion with a leaf in the forest, which can offer the affordance of *food* to a caterpillar, *shade* to a spider, and *medicine* to a shaman, even though the leaf's intrinsic properties do not change. When applied to a learning context, Gibson's ecological theory of perception breaks away from traditional cognitive approaches that frame learning as the processing of objective input by the learner. In an ecological approach, the learner's interaction with their environment is paramount.

Van Lier (1996, 2000, 2004) applied the affordance construct to L2 acquisition, connecting it to a Vygotskyan sociocultural approach of situated language learning. To van Lier (2000, 2004), meaning potentials, action potentials, and thus opportunities for language use can emerge from speakers' interaction with their semiotic environment. His proposed ecological linguistics consists in the study of language as relations (i.e. actions) rather than as mere objects of study (i.e. words, sentences, rules). Thus, language is not simply treated as input received by passive learners, an approach often referred to as the "conduit metaphor" (Reddy, 1979). Rather, language learners actively participate in meaning-making actions within their environment in which they pick up some of the semiotic budget, that is, "opportunities for meaningful action that the situation affords" (van Lier, 2000, p.252). In language learning, this semiotic budget is not only embedded in L2 texts, but it may also emerge from interactions with peers around the texts (van Lier, 2004).

Against the background of this ecological and sociocultural framework, the affordances of DSR for language learning (versus traditional solo reading of printed texts) are apparent. DSR transforms the individual practices of reading printed texts into collective, social practices (Blyth, 2014). This creates new opportunities for interactive meaning making between readers and texts, expanding the semiotic budget. Although the transition within education from printed to digital texts has often been motivated by financial or practical considerations (Reynolds, 2011; Raibe & Denoyelles, 2017; Cardbaugh, 2020), this transition has allowed innovative reading practices that require a digital format, such as DSR, to expand in language classes (Chen, 2020).

While research exploring the potential learning outcomes of DSR has certainly gained momentum in recent years (see Zhu et al., 2020 for a systematic review), and while studies categorizing the affordances of digital tools for L2 learning are increasing (Darhower, 2009; Jin, 2018; Rama et al., 2012), research implementing the ecological lens of affordances to analyze DSR remains rare. Such studies generally approach affordances by directly analyzing the texts or the medium with which the learner interacts. For example, O'Brien and Voss (2011) highlighted that DSR maintains the affordances of printed texts (marking, annotating) while also affording social exchange and collaboration. Blyth (2014) collected the testimonies of four L2 university teachers at various levels who implemented the DSR platform eComma in their class. Teachers' perceived affordances of DSR were summarized in five points: (i) DSR provides a zone of proximal development (Vygotsky, 1978) for less expert readers, (ii) DSR distributes the cognitive load among readers, (iii) DSR blends several reading activities into one, (iv) DSR allows for the observable aggregation of reading behavior, and (v) DSR incorporates a vast diversity of digital reading types.

Such reports of instructors and learners' perceived affordances provide insight on the potential of DSR for L2 learning. Observation and categorization of the affordances in actual DSR annotations reveals more precisely how affordances emerge in reading. Observing L2 Spanish learners using HyLighter, Thoms and Poole (2017, 2018) operationalized affordances using a three-part typology: linguistic, literary, and social. Linguistic affordances were used in annotations addressing grammatical or lexical information in the text. Literary affordances related to the poetic and rhetorical dimensions of the text. Social affordances pertained to topics other than the text itself, and to participant interactions (e.g. opinions, personal references, agreement, disagreement). Thoms and Poole (2018) found that text difficulty influences the types of affordances learners recruit in their annotations. Increased lexical diversity (type-token ratio) resulted in fewer literary affordances, while an increased proportion of frequent words produced higher rates of linguistic affordances. Furthermore, the use of social and literary affordances increased over time. Michelson, Abdennebi, and Michelson (2023) compared affordances of face-to-face and digital group reading activities for L2 French, finding that in the DSR condition, learners stayed more focused on the text with less off-topic social interaction.

However, the affordances used in DSR are not always consistent. Law et al. (2020) used the same typology to analyze French L2 learners' annotation of songs as multimedia texts (lyrics, music, video) with eComma. In this study, annotation patterns were found to be self-reinforcing within each of 11 course sections: some participants favored social behaviors like asking and answering questions among peers, while others produced short, repetitive statements. These results support the notion that affordances emerge from the unique relationship that individuals establish with their environment: the text, but also the medium through which it is delivered, and other users.

Despite the highly individualized nature of affordances, some variables in the texts themselves make them more prone to certain types of affordances. Instructors surveyed in Law et al. (2020), based on their own perception of the DSR annotations and the subsequent in-class discussions with students, observed that the topic of the text may impact the level of social engagement with the text, while the integration of alternate media like videos may foster interpretation of the text and enhance the subsequent discussion. These observations highlight the potential influence of text selection on the affordances readers exploit in DSR.

Text difficulty in digital social reading

Text difficulty or text readability has been defined as the accessibility of text to the reader (Fulcher, 1997). This construct has been argued to play an important role in L2 learning, as texts that are far beyond a student's current linguistic proficiency may be demotivating and ultimately damaging to their language acquisition journey (ibid.). Within sociocultural theory, input that is beyond the proficiency level of the learner and unsupported by appropriate scaffolding is seen as unproductive (Amerian & Mehri, 2014). For this reason, text difficulty is a crucial factor when considering how students engage with the texts presented in this current study investigating L2 DSR.

In previous studies on L2 acquisition, text difficulty has been operationalized in a variety of ways relating to sentence complexity, vocabulary, organization of the text, style, subject matter content, and predictability. Traditional readability formulae based on vocabulary and grammatical complexity are perhaps the most widespread methods (Greenfield, 2004). Vocabulary complexity can be measured using the average word length (in syllables or characters) or using frequency, as learners are more likely to be familiar with high frequency words due to increased exposure. Grammatical difficulty is often measured using the average number of words per sentence as a proxy for syntactic complexity.

Some well-known readability formulae include the Flesch formula (Flesch, 1948) and Chall and Dale's (1995) formula, which consider the number of syllables per 100 words as well as the average number of words per sentence. Despite having been found to robustly predict reading time (Haberlandt & Graesser, 1985; Just & Carpenter, 1980) these formulae are limited, as they use word and sentence length as proxies for lexical and syntactic complexity. Another possible issue with these formulae is that they have been developed in the context of first language reading acquisition in English classrooms and thus may not be able to generalize to languages that differ greatly from English grammatical structures. Fulcher (1997) instead used "expert judgments" to determine text difficulty based on linguistic, contextual, conceptual structures, as well as the reader — writer relationship. However, this method has limitations based on unavoidable biases that experts may bring into their analyses.

When considering text difficulty in second language acquisition studies, this construct has been similarly measured by accounting for the ratio of words to sentences within a given text. The number of propositions per text has also been one way of determining text difficulty (Bernhardt, 2011), but this method is heavily influenced by the text's genre. For example, Bernhardt (2011) discusses how an expository text would be deemed as more complex in comparison to other text genres simply as an artifact of its high content load (p.132). Furthermore, more complex algorithms have been derived by using word n-grams as a way of determining lexical diversity (Crossley et al., 2019). Unavoidably, each of these operationalizations come with its own limitations. The field is beginning to move away from fixed formulae to account for text complexity by shifting to natural language processing systems trained on large corpora, which they argue greatly reduce these limitations (Crossley et al., 2022).

In the present study, we followed Thoms and Poole (2018) in adopting the same three measures of text difficulty. This ensures comparability with this closely related study and avoids over-reliance on any single measure. The first two measures involve vocabulary complexity. These are K1/1000, which measures use of frequent vs. infrequent words, and TTR (type-token ratio), which measures the diversity of vocabulary within a text. The third measure (PDR — professor difficulty rating) is a count of cultural references and figurative devices requiring interpretation, as determined by instructors. Given the literary qualities of the song lyrics used in this study, similar to the poetry used in Thoms and Poole's (2018) study, we see value in this measure which ties difficulty to literary and cultural notions of task complexity, as recommended by Fulcher (1997). We also introduce a fourth measure not used by Thoms and Poole (2018), the number of glosses, that is indirectly tied to text difficulty. These four measures are presented in more detail in section 5.

Data

Data employed in this study were obtained from 200 students across 11 sections of an introductory French course at a university in the southwestern United States. Students, who were recruited and consented in person, were primarily L1 English speakers with no prior French language experience. Data were obtained from student assignments in which students were instructed to both read and engage with the lyrics from six songs by using the open-access Digital Annotation Tool (DAT) eComma developed by the Center for Open Educational Resources and Language Learning. This tool allows for its users to make both tags and comments; tags allow learners to label recurring trends throughout the text, while the comment function is meant to introduce novel ideas or questions regarding an element. Students were required to leave five comments or tags as part of their graded assignment but were encouraged to contribute further if they so desired.

Comments could be in English or French to allow these novice learners to express themselves fully, and most comments (98%) were written in English.

These six songs were previously established during the curriculum development process and thus were not selected by the researchers in the present study according to the text difficulty levels discussed in Section 5. Their relevance was primarily thematic, aligning with the vocabulary and grammar being taught in each module. However, all songs were selected with beginner learners in mind, and their difficulty levels are intended to minimally increase as the students progress throughout the semester.

Songs were presented as text along with a link to the music and a music video where available. Learners were instructed to listen to the song (and watch the music video, if applicable) before opening the glossed lyrics in eComma. Figure 1 shows the eComma environment with glossed lyrics on the left and comments on the right. Each comment is attached to a particular word or section of the text. By selecting a comment, a user can see this part of the text highlighted. The written text was presented with bracketed glosses for words, short expressions, and some cultural references which the students were not expected to know at their current level so as to provide crucial scaffolding to these novice learners.[1] Glosses (short translations in English) were written by the course supervisor, with glossing provided for words necessary for understanding the text which students would not have encountered up to that point in the curriculum, and which were not cognates with English.

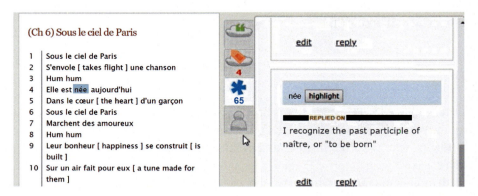

Figure 1. The eComma environment

---

1. The glosses used are provided in the Appendix. Full lyrics for all six songs can be found at www.genius.com.

The first song, "Sénegal Fast Food" by Amadou and Mariam, treats the subject of globalization and is marked for its simplicity due to the maintenance of the present tense and employment of anglicisms and transparent cognates between French and English. The second song, "Ma Louisianne" by Zachary Richard, narrates a folkloric account of Cajun history with frequent repetition but some unfamiliar dialectal constructions. Next, "Comme d'habitude" by Claude François describes a loveless relationship, introducing some literary devices, particularly metaphors, that can challenge students more than the previous songs. "Les cornichons" by Nino Ferrer recounts the story of a family picnic, and consequently is narrated with long lists of food vocabulary, rendering this a rather transparent song for the students to decode but not necessarily to interpret. "Sous le ciel de Paris" by Yves Montand comes next in the course, romanticizing Paris and increasing the complexity with the implementation of compound verb tenses, metaphors, and a variety of more abstract concepts. Finally, we end with "Le bal masqué" by La Compagnie Créole, a Zouk song that details the characters one might encounter at Carnival. Here, students encounter a variety of characters who likely fall outside of the typical American college student's purview in terms of cultural, literary, and historical references, rendering this song referentially complex.

Although these DSR assignments were part of all student coursework, we only include the 5,067 comments from those 200 participants who had provided informed consent in the recruitment process.

Methods

Two rounds of coding were completed. During the first, two of the researchers labeled each comment according to the primary affordance employed. According to the classification used by Thoms and Poole (2018), comments could employ literary, linguistic, or social affordances. Literary affordances employ rhetorical devices or interpretations of the text or build off another participant's interpretations of the texts. Linguistic affordances address grammatical or lexical aspects of the text. Social affordances were applied to any comment that consisted primarily of an expression of opinion, references to personal subjects, any agreement/ disagreement, compliments, or miscellaneous topics digressing from the text. If multiple affordances were present within a single comment, the researchers coded this comment according to the affordance they interpreted as most prominent.

Any comments that were found to be unclear in the first round of tagging were noted and determined in a second round of tagging by the third researcher. In the first round of tagging, raters found the same primary affordance type for

4,543 (90%) of the comments, disagreeing on 180 (4%). One or both raters found the primary affordance type unclear for 344 (7%) of the comments. Of these unclear or disputed tokens, the third rater then resolved all but two. These two were unclear due to insufficient length and were discarded, leaving a total of 5,065 tokens included in the final analysis.

Text difficulty was measured in four ways introduced above. The first measure, K1/1000, indicates the percentage of words found in the text that are among the 1000 most frequent word families in the target language. We used the MultilingProfiler tool by the National Centre for Excellence for Language Pedagogy[2] to perform this analysis for French (Finlayson et al., 2022). This tool was selected because it provides automatic word family lemmatization and draws from a large, balanced corpus (Lonsdale & Le Bras, 2009).

The second difficulty measure was type-token ratio (TTR). The number of unique words in each text was divided by the total number of words within the text. This is meant as a measure of lexical diversity where a higher TTR would be indicative of a higher text difficulty. We used the tool SiNLP,[3] selected for its ease of use, to perform this analysis (Crossley et al., 2014). K1/1000 and TTR were calculated using the versions of the texts without glosses.

A professor difficulty rating (PDR) was employed where the three researchers, all university French instructors, analyzed the six texts and identified each uniquely occurring rhetorical device, cultural reference and historical reference appearing in each text. The counts of these features made by each researcher were averaged to determine this measure. This replicates the measure used by Thoms and Poole (2018) in terms of textual criteria, although the raters are not literature professors.

The final measure is a simple count of glosses in each text, an indirect measure that was obviously not used by Thoms and Poole (2018) because their texts were not glossed. The glosses do not directly correspond to any one operationalization of difficulty. In some cases, glosses were added to clarify cultural references or figurative language (measured by PDR). Other glosses were added to define unfamiliar words (measured by K1/1000, and less directly by TTR). In principle, the most difficult texts as judged by the course supervisor received the most glosses. However, once glosses are added, it could be argued that the texts with the most glosses are the easiest to read, because they provide more assistance to the reader. In either case, the number of glosses provided with each text is a factor that should be accounted for. Ratings for each song are provided in Table 1.

---

2. https://www.multilingprofiler.net/

3. https://www.linguisticanalysistools.org/sinlp.html

Chapter 5. Addressing text difficulty in novice L2 digital social reading

Table 1. Text difficulties according to four measures

Song	K1/1000	TTR	PDR	Glosses
1. Sénégal Fast Food	53.0%	.517	12	10
2. Ma Louisianne	72.3%	.772	2.5	7
3. Comme d'habitude	71.0%	.467	3.5	31
4. Les cornichons	52.0%	.491	1.5	7
5. Sous le ciel de Paris	52.4%	.613	13.5	28
6. Le bal masqué	49.3%	.452	9.5	0

The second research question asks what other textual features besides difficulty impact the use of literary affordances in DSR annotations. For this question, we adopt a qualitative, inductive approach, moving backwards from the results to possible factors. That is, we first observe which texts saw the most literary affordances in reader annotations. Then we examine those texts and their annotations, comparing them to the texts with the least literary affordances, to identify relevant textual differences. A relevant feature will be one which separates texts with high and low levels of literary affordances, and which is evident in the content of annotations across many participants.

Results

The first research question asks whether the use of literary affordances in DSR annotations is still impacted by text difficulty even when glosses are provided. Before presenting the results on the relationship between text difficulty and the use of literary affordances, it is worth considering the relationship among the four difficulty measures. K1/1000 reflects the percentage of words in a text that are among the 1000 most frequent in the language. For this measure, a higher value suggests lower reading difficulty. For the other three measures, a higher value suggests higher reading difficulty. Each of these measures assesses a different textual quality that can contribute to reading difficulty: the use of (in)frequent words, the diversity of words used and amount of repetition, the use of cultural references and figurative language, and the use of language judged to be beyond the level of the learners by the course supervisor.

The four measures do not provide a consensus on the relative difficulty of the six texts. As shown in Table 2, the measure that most closely matches the order of presentation throughout the course is K1/1000. For this measure, the three texts presented in the first half of the course all rank as lower difficulty than the three texts presented in the second half of the course, and the final text, *Le bal masqué*, is the most difficult. The other measures show more divergence. Notably, TTR measures *Le bal masqué* as the least difficult and *Ma Louisianne* as the most difficult, an inversion of K1/1000. This is likely due to the length and amount of repetition in these texts. The lyrics of *Le bal masqué* are quite long with many repeated expressions across verses and the chorus, while those of *Ma Louisianne* are the shortest in the set. This shows a weakness in the use of TTR to measure the reading difficulty of song lyrics, where repetition can be common, because these can have an inflated denominator (the token count).

Table 2. Relative text difficulty based on each measure

Relative difficulty	Order in course	K1/1000	TTR	PDR	Glosses
Least difficult	1. SFF	ML	LBM	LC	LBM
	2. ML	CDH	CDH	ML	ML
	3. CDH	SFF	LC	CDH	LC
	4. LC	SCP	SFF	LBM	SFF
	5. SCP	LC	SCP	SFF	SCP
Most difficult	6. LBM	LBM	ML	SCP	CDH

Abbreviations used: SFF = Sénégal Fast Food, ML = Ma Louisianne, CDH = Comme d'habitude, LC = Les cornichons, SCP = Sous le ciel de Paris, LBM = Le bal masqué

Rather than calling into question the validity of these measures, the divergence in relative difficulty rankings of these texts highlights the complex nature of reading difficulty as a construct. Any one measure cannot capture the full set of properties that determine an L2 text's difficulty. Using a combination of measures is necessary, and while the four selected measures are only a sample of possible operationalizations, together they provide a more comprehensive assessment of difficulty.

Using R version 4.2.2 (R Core Team, 2022) and the lme4 package (Bates et al., 2015), we created a linear regression model for the proportion of literary affordances with the four difficulty measures as predictor variables. None of the measures predicts the amount of literary affordances used in comments, adjusted $R^2 = -0.4229$, $F_{(4,1)} = 0.6285$, $p > 0.05$. That is, even though K1/1000, TTR, PDR, and the number of glosses provide different rankings of the relative difficulty of the six texts, none of these rankings corresponds to the ranking of texts in terms of the percentage of annotations using literary affordances. This evidence supports the hypothesis that glossing is effective in erasing the negative impact of text difficulty on the use of literary affordances in DSR. The interpretation with respect to the first research question is that glosses "level the playing field" so that all else being equal, readers of glossed texts that are more or less difficult make use of literary affordances at the same rate.

The second research question is qualitative and asks what other textual features impact the use of literary affordances in DSR annotations if the difficulty factor is neutralized through glossing. Although difficulty as operationalized for these texts did not significantly affect the affordances used, the annotations produced by learners were not uniform across the texts. We can therefore rank and group the texts in terms of the proportion of literary affordances found in their annotations. This allows us to compare texts and identify features that may have contributed to the difference.

Table 3 presents the affordances used in annotations of each text, in descending order from the text with the highest proportion of literary affordances ("Ma Louisianne" by Zachary Richard) to the one with the lowest ("Sous le ciel de Paris" by Yves Montand).

Table 3. Affordances used in annotations of each text

Song	Affordances		
	Literary	Linguistic	Social
2. Ma Louisianne	450 (54%)	287 (34%)	97 (12%)
1. Sénégal Fast Food	445 (52%)	287 (34%)	120 (14%)
3. Comme d'habitude	393 (46%)	391 (46%)	70 (8%)
6. Le bal masqué	344 (40%)	377 (44%)	145 (17%)
4. Les cornichons	328 (39%)	360 (43%)	155 (18%)
5. Sous le ciel de Paris	305 (37%)	397 (49%)	114 (14%)

We can roughly group the texts into three categories based on the affordances used: those where literary affordances predominate ("Ma Louisianne" and "Sénégal Fast Food"), one for which literary and linguistic affordances are nearly equal ("Comme d'habitude"), and those where linguistic affordances predominate ("Le bal masqué", "Les cornichons", and "Sous le ciel de Paris"). The use of social affordances is low compared to the other types and we do not give it special attention in our analysis. We can consider the textual features of these three groupings of songs beyond the difficulty measures already considered in order to identify what factors may play a role in the difference.

Our analysis identifies two major textual features that promote increased use of literary affordances: unfamiliar cultural concepts and multimodality. We also identify a feature that we expected would promote increased literary affordances, but which actually did not: figurative language. Below we explain precisely what is meant by each of these features, our evidence for these results, and our account of why these effects are observed.

One factor that separates the two songs with the most literary affordances from the others is apparent from the titles. "Ma Louisianne" and "Sénégal Fast Food" both represent non-European francophone cultures, in terms of topic as well as national origin of the artists. In contrast, "Sous le ciel de Paris" takes the city of Paris as its topic, while the others do not focus on any particular place in their lyrics. France and particularly its capital enjoy a special status as the cultural center of the French-speaking world and as one of the top global tourist destinations. In the southwestern United States where this study was conducted, the majority of students in beginning university French courses express more familiarity with Paris (through travel or media) than with other majority French-speaking places, based on the experience of the authors who have all taught in this context. While Louisiana is not particularly far from the study's location and some students have ties to the state, details of its Cajun culture and history are often unfamiliar to these students. We therefore suspect that one reason for the higher use of literary affordances while reading "Ma Louisianne" and "Sénégal Fast Food" could be student curiosity about the cultures represented by those texts.

Some examples from these songs of the annotations that use literary affordances will illustrate this point.

(1) ("Ma Louisianne") *Cajuns were in Louisiana before the Americans. This further supports the idea of Zachary Richard trying to instill pride and preservation in the Cajun culture.*
(annotated lyric: *On était [We were] en Louisianne avant les Américains* 'We were in Louisiana before the Americans')

(2) ("Ma Louisianne") *He is speaking ironically here. He is commenting about how the Cajuns were treated badly for seemingly no reason other than their heritage*
(annotated lyric: *Pour le grand crime d'être Cadien.* 'for the great crime of being Cajun')

(3) ("Sénégal Fast Food") *Perhaps the closest many of these people will ever get to experiencing the outside world is through the fast-food chains that open in their country.*
(annotated lyric: *C'est au Manhattan fast-food Dakar Sénégal!* 'It's at the Manhattan fast food Dakar Senegal')

(4) ("Sénégal Fast Food") *Maybe these are the things people in his society view/ idolize as "paradise."*
(annotated lyric: *Quelle heure est-il au Paradis?* 'What time is it in Paradise?')

Each of these comments analyzes a particular lyric and connects it to a broader theme of the text. The themes of "Ma Louisianne" that receive attention here are Cajun pride (1) and the mid-18th century Expulsion of the Acadians (2). In (3) and (4), "Sénégal Fast Food"'s themes of globalization and its impact on West African societies are highlighted.

"Sous le ciel de Paris" similarly offers themes grounded in a particular place and culture, notably the idea of Paris as the city of love, and these themes are addressed in its annotations. However, comments on these themes are much fewer than those for "Ma Louisianne" and "Sénégal Fast Food" like the ones seen above, with 37% literary affordances compared to 54% and 52%. A reasonable explanation for the difference is that the idea of Paris as the city of love is less novel and therefore less noteworthy for most participants than the more unfamiliar cultural ideas found in "Ma Louisianne" and "Sénégal Fast Food".

Another factor that may explain the elevated use of literary affordances with "Sénégal Fast Food" is the accompanying music video. Participants were asked to listen to the songs along with reading and annotating the lyrics. In the case of "Comme d'habitude" and "Le bal masqué", this included a video of a live performance by the artist. In the case of "Sénégal Fast Food", this included a music video that shows the story of a man trying to immigrate from Dakar to France. 28 annotations made explicit reference to this music video, and many others draw on ideas from the video without explicitly citing it. An example of one such annotation is given in (5).

(5) ("Sénégal Fast Food) I was confused about this line in the song, but once watching the video it gave me the idea that maybe the man that traveled to Paris had an idea of what it would be like based on movies he'd seen. Once he got there he saw the hardships he would face.

This comment refers to a repeated lyric about "cinéma Le Paris," a movie theater in Dakar. With only the text to draw from, this lyric's meaning can be confusing, as evidenced by a number of annotations asking about it. However, this commenter and others noticed that the music video shows this movie theater juxtaposed with other scenes of life in Dakar. By assuming a literary unity between the video and the text, participants not only identified a referent for the unclear lyric but made their own meaning around the text. For instance, there is no representation in either the lyrics or the video of a man watching movies about Paris, but this is a creation of this commenter, drawn from inferences found in multiple modes, that gives more meaning to the text.

This example illustrates Kress' (2000) observation that it is impossible to understand a multimodal text without considering all of its modes together. Multiliteracies pedagogy acknowledges that multimodal texts are not simply parallel:

a music video expresses meanings that could not be expressed satisfactorily in lyrics alone (Cope & Kalantzis, 2009, p. 180). Because each mode offers its own meanings, misunderstandings can occur when readers privilege one mode over another, such as the visual over the textual (Jewitt, 2005). However, our participants found an affordance in multimodality, making meaning through the integration of the text's different modes.

For the third and final textual factor, we expected that texts with a denser concentration of figurative imagery and other salient literary devices might be annotated in ways that exploit these literary affordances to a greater degree. However, this turns out not to be the case in our study. The "Professor difficulty rating" described above as a measure of text difficulty directly counts the number of rhetorical devices and cultural-historical references that might be seen by students as abstract or unfamiliar. This measure on its own shows no relationship with the use of literary affordances. "Sous le ciel de Paris" has the highest average score on this measure, 13.5, but the lowest proportion of literary affordances. "Sénégal Fast Food" has the next highest professor difficulty rating, 12, and has one of the highest proportions of annotations using literary affordances. "Ma Louisianne", which has the highest proportion of literary affordances, has a professor difficulty rating of 2.5, among the lowest.

In fact, annotations rarely show evidence of literary analysis of figurative devices. For example, the few rhetorical devices and allusions identified for "Ma Louisianne" include a single instance of personification of nature (*Le ciel et la terre ont beaucoup à nous montrer* 'The sky and the earth have much to show us') which received a few annotations translating the words but no comments on the literary device. "Sous le ciel de Paris" is rich in metaphors personifying the Parisian sky, but this fact only receives a handful of comments, not enough to outweigh the annotations focused on linguistic affordances.

Glossing does not appear to increase the commentary on such literary devices. For instance, the lyric *Quand elle lui sourit* from "Sous le ciel de Paris" was presented to readers with the gloss [When she {the island} smiles at him {the sky}], not only translating the key word *sourit* 'smiles' but also identifying the antecedents of each pronoun. This line receives just a few comments pointing out the metaphor, and none that explore it more deeply. Because of the presence of the gloss, the reason for the limited commentary does not seem to be lack of understanding of the figurative language. Instead, it seems as though many learners at this level are not equipped to give meaningful commentary on these kinds of literary devices. While they may understand the intended meaning of the metaphor, they do not have the vocabulary (in their L1) or the training in literary analysis to say much about it. Annotations using literary affordances tended to appear on references to history or culture within lyrics (such as those in "Ma Louisianne" discussed earlier), and less so on figurative devices. Therefore, these learners appear to be better equipped to give commentary on literary content grounded in something concrete rather than something abstract.

The texts with relatively many literary affordances in their annotations differ in a number of ways from those with relatively few. By comparing these texts and examining the content of their annotations, we were able to identify the most significant textual differences as the familiarity of the referenced cultural concepts and the multimodality of the texts. We were also able to support the counterintuitive result that figurative language did not serve as a rich literary affordance for these participants.

Discussion

For the quantitative purposes of this study, text difficulty was operationalized in four ways, discussed above in section 3. According to these measures, text difficulty did not significantly impact the use of literary affordances in reader annotations. This differs from the finding of Thoms and Poole (2018) that increased lexical diversity leads to fewer literary affordances used. We explain this result with reference to the glosses provided with the texts, which were designed to make difficult texts accessible for first-year students. The results suggest that glossing does effectively increase the use of literary affordances in annotations by attenuating the dampening effect of difficulty. We do still observe differences between texts with respect to the use of affordances, but we attribute these to features besides difficulty that can be observed qualitatively.

It should be noted that there was no control group within this study; glosses were provided to all participants. We acknowledge this limitation as part of the demands for fairness in graded assignments across sections of the course. Although we can make informal comparisons with other studies, particularly Thoms and Poole (2018) in which fewer annotations with literary affordances were used on more difficult, unglossed texts, the impact of glossing in DSR is far from settled.

One of the textual features that counterintuitively did not increase the use of literary affordances was the presence of figurative language. We found that even when such language was entirely glossed in English, many figurative devices received few comments containing literary analysis. This reinforces the central notion of the ecological theory of learning, namely that it is the interaction between organism and environment, not the environment itself, that produces affordances (Gibson, 1979; van Lier, 2000, 2004). A text with a high level of literary quality or complexity does not necessarily provide literary affordances to readers who are unprepared or untrained to interact with those literary aspects of the text.

These findings lead us to reflect on the progression advocated within multiliteracies frameworks from Situated Practice to Transformed Practice (The New London Group, 1996). As a starting point, learners should be situated and immersed within an environment of rich L2 exposure from peers, instructors, and texts. However, immersion is not sufficient. Learners require overt instruction and critical framing in order to transform their practice into one by which they can analyze texts critically and participate in the L2 environment as informed agents (ibid., p. 88). In other words, learners must be taught tools of literary analysis alongside the traditional tools of linguistic analysis. Text difficulty is one hurdle for learners to overcome in order to analyze L2 literary texts (Thoms & Poole, 2018). However, even when learners are given support in this area via glosses, they still require overt instruction and critical framing to take full advantage of the literary affordances that some texts offer.

We can connect this insight to the previously discussed observations about culturally unfamiliar texts, multimodal texts, and rhetorical devices. When learners lack distance from a text because of its cultural familiarity, they may struggle to produce much analysis of its ideas. As learners mature in their reading practices, they may be better equipped to analyze texts about familiar ideas and cultures with the same critical eye that they apply to less familiar ones. Learners may struggle to grasp the themes of texts if they are presented only abstractly (as with the lyrics of "Sénégal Fast Food") but will understand those themes better if presented via a narrative (as with the accompanying music video). And just because learners comprehend the intended meaning of metaphors and other rhetorical devices does not mean they will have ideas of what to say about them. If they are given tools of analysis, they may be able to appreciate and discuss these devices in a more meaningful way. Specific pedagogical suggestions will follow in the next section.

All of this underlines the perhaps obvious point that the most important factor in how affordances will be exploited in a DSR context is not any feature of the text including its difficulty or the presence of glosses, but the learners themselves. The students of Thoms and Poole's (2018) Hispanic poetry course had a very different level of preparation for literary analysis than the first-year beginning French students of our study. Even when glosses are provided for all unfamiliar words, learners participating in DSR may still rely mostly on linguistic affordances in their annotations if they are not equipped to take advantage of the kinds of literary affordances provided by the text.

Conclusion

We have provided evidence that glossing difficult words and phrases in the L1 is effective in overcoming the text difficulty barrier to exploiting literary affordances in L2 DSR. We have also examined other textual features that might inhibit or enhance the use of literary affordances among beginning learners in this context. We now turn to some practical suggestions for instructors and curriculum designers who wish to use these findings to inform their use of L2 texts in beginning foreign language classrooms, with or without DSR tools.

The most important practical implication of this paper is that difficult texts can be made accessible for beginning learners through glossing. The first song encountered by students in this course, "Sénégal Fast Food", was assigned only a couple of weeks after their first introduction to French. Given the level of difficulty of the text at that stage (without glossing), we would expect readers to focus their attention on deciphering its linguistic content. However, DSR evidence shows that with glosses added, students are able to draw meaning from the text and discuss its themes, even making connections between textual and audiovisual modes. Instructors wishing to offer even beginning students cultural contact with L2 texts should therefore not hesitate to assign somewhat difficult texts, as long as sufficient glossing is provided.

Next, instructors should be aware of the kinds of textual features that help students engage critically with texts at this level. Unfamiliar cultures, histories, and concepts provide rich material for discussion. On the other hand, familiar cultures may not inspire much discussion without support from the instructor that provides critical framing and analytical distance. For example, an instructor introducing "Sous le ciel de Paris" might first ask students to think critically about the notion of Paris as the city of love, to interrogate why they have that association and not to take it for granted. Learners might then be better able to comment critically on this familiar cultural idea as found in the text.

Instructors might wish to prioritize multimodal texts, such as the music video that accompanies the lyrics to "Sénégal Fast Food". Multimodal texts provide multiple pathways for students to engage with a text's meaning, which can be helpful for beginning learners who may struggle to understand the more abstract parts of a text. If an otherwise appropriate text (e.g., one with a topic relevant to the course) does not have this feature, activities might be considered that help learners to engage with the text via multiple avenues. For instance, learners might sketch the scene described by the song "Les cornichons" using stick figures. These sketches could then be linked or embedded in annotations on the text, allowing learners to compare their sketched interpretations and focusing their attention on the narrative and literary quality of the text over its linguistic content.

Finally, instructors should bear in mind that making sense of the linguistic content of a text is only the first step in engaging critically with its figurative or rhetorical elements. In addition to providing glosses as needed, instructors presenting a text rich in a device such as personification might ask students before reading to explain what personification is. Then students might be encouraged while reading to identify instances of personification and think about the author's purpose in using this device.

These suggestions can be summarized in two main ideas. First, instructors selecting texts for the beginning level should prioritize those with features that have been shown to provide literary affordances for these learners: multimodality and unfamiliar cultural concepts. Second, they should prepare texts for reading by adding glossing as needed and prepare learners for reading by presenting scaffolding for critical analysis of familiar concepts and figurative devices.

Our suggestions arise from our analysis of DSR annotations produced by a particular set of beginning learners of French working with a particular kind of text (song lyrics) on a particular digital platform (eComma). While we believe our findings regarding text difficulty, glossing, and other textual features are generalizable to L2 reading more broadly, there is much more to discover by repeating this method in other L2 reading contexts. Our most important conclusion is that DSR is a useful tool for identifying and assessing the affordances of particular texts with particular populations of learners. Careful analysis of DSR annotations can guide text selection and modification and can inform pre-reading tasks to provide scaffolding for learners. We encourage the use of DSR as a tool to these ends at all levels of L2 reading.

References

Amerian, M., & Mehri, E. (2014). Scaffolding in sociocultural theory: Definition, steps, features, conditions, tools, and effective considerations. *Scientific Journal of Review* 3(7), 756–765.

Bates, D., Maechler, M., Bolker, B., & Walker, S. (2015). Fitting linear mixed-effects models using lme4. *Journal of Statistical Software*, 67(1), 1–48.

Bernhardt, E. (2011). *Understanding advanced second-language reading*. Routledge.

Blyth, C. (2014). Exploring the affordances of digital social reading for L2 literacy: The case of eComma. In J. P. Guikema & L. Williams (Eds.), *Digital literacies in foreign and second language education* (pp. 201–226). Calico.

Carbaugh, B. (2020). The decline of college textbook publishing: Cengage learning and McGraw-Hill. *The American Economist*, 65(2), 284–299.

Chall, J., & Dale, E. (1995). *Readability revisited: The new Dale-Chall readability formula*. Brookline Books.

Chen, I.-C. J. (2020). Integrating literature circles to facilitate reading comprehension on Facebook groups: Questioning and learning perceptions. *Taiwan Journal of TESOL*, 17(2), 119–146.

Cope, B., & Kalantzis, M. (2009). "Multiliteracies": New literacies, new learning. *Pedagogies: An International Journal*, 4, 164–195.

Cope, B., & Kalantzis, M. (2015). The things you do to know: An introduction to the pedagogy of multiliteracies. In B. Cope & M. Kalantzis (Eds.), *A pedagogy of multiliteracies* (pp. 1–36). Palgrave Macmillan.

Crossley, S., Allen, L., Kyle, K., & McNamara, D. (2014). Analyzing discourse processing using a simple natural language processing tool (SiNLP). *Discourse Processes*, 51, 511–534.

Crossley, S., Skalicky, S., & Dascalu, M. (2019). Moving beyond classic readability formulas: New methods and new models. *Journal of Research in Reading*, 42(3–4), 541–561.

Crossley, S., Heintz, A., Choi, J. S., Batchelor, J., Karimi, M., & Malatinszky, A. (2022). A large-scaled corpus for assessing text readability. *Behavior Research Methods*, 55, 491–507.

Darhower, M. (2009). The role of linguistic affordances in telecollaborative chat. *CALICO Journal*, 26(1), 48–69.

Finlayson, N., Marsden, E., & Anthony, L. (2022). *MultilingProfiler* (Version 3) [Computer software]. University of York. Retrieved on 10 September 2022 from https://www .multilingprofiler.net/

Flesch, R. (1948). A new readability yardstick. *Journal of Applied Psychology*, 32, 221–233.

Fulcher, G. (1997). Text difficulty and accessibility: Reading formulae and expert judgement. *System*, 25(4), 497–513.

Gibson, J. (1979). *The ecological approach to visual perception*. Houghton Mifflin.

Greenfield, J. (2004). Readability formulas for EFL. *JALT Journal*, 26, 5–24.

Haberlandt, K., & Graesser, A. (1985). Component processes in text comprehension and some of their interactions. *Journal of Experimental Psychology: General*, 114(3), 357–374.

Hosseini Alast, S., & Baleghizadeh, S. (2021). The interplay of glossing with text difficulty and comprehension levels. *Language Teaching Research*, 28(3).

Jacobs, G., Dufon, P., & Hong, F. (1994). L1 and L2 vocabulary glosses in L2 reading passages: Their effectiveness for increasing comprehension and vocabulary knowledge. *Journal of Research in Reading*, 17(1), 19–28.

Jewitt, C. (2005). Multimodality, "reading", and "writing" for the 21st Century. *Discourse: Studies in the Cultural Politics of Education*, 26(3). 315–331.

Jin, L. (2018). Digital affordances on WeChat: Learning Chinese as a second language. *Computer Assisted Language Learning*, 31(1–2), 27–52.

Jung, J. (2016). Effects of glosses on learning of L2 grammar and vocabulary. *Language Teaching Research*, 20(1), 92–112.

Just, M., & Carpenter, P. (1980). A theory of reading: From eye fixations to comprehension. *Psychological Review*, 87, 329–354.

Ko, M. (2012). Glossing and second language vocabulary learning. *TESOL Quarterly*, 46(1), 56–79.

Kress, G. (2000). Multimodality: Challenges to thinking about language. *TESOL Quarterly*, 34(2). 337–340.

Law, J., Barny, D., & Poulin, R. (2020). Patterns of peer interaction in multimodal L2 digital social reading. *Language Learning and Technology*, 24(2), 70–85. .

Lonsdale, D., & Le Bras, Y. (2009). *A frequency dictionary of French: Core vocabulary for learners*. Routledge.

Michelson, K., Abdennebi, M., & Michelson, C. (2023). Text-centered "talk" in foreign language classrooms: Comparing the affordances of face-to-face and digital social annotated reading. *Foreign Language Annals*, 56(3), 600–623.

O'Brien, D., & Voss, S. (2011). Reading multimodally: What is afforded? *Journal of Adolescent & Adult Literacy*, 55(1), 75–78.

Ouyang, J., Huang, L., & Jiang, J. (2020). The effects of glossing on incidental vocabulary learning during second language reading: Based on an eye-tracking study. *Journal of Research in Reading*, 43(4), 496–515.

Pianzola, F., Rebora, S., & Lauer, G. (2020). Wattpad as a resource for literary studies. Quantitative and qualitative examples of the importance of digital social reading and readers' comments in the margins. *PLOS ONE*, 15(1), Article e0226708.

R Core Team (2022). *R: A language and environment for statistical computing* [Computer software]. R Foundation for Statistical Computing. Retrieved on 17 February 2023 from https://www.R-project.org/

Raibe, J., & Denoyelles, A. (2017, October 9). Exploring the use of e-textbooks in higher education: A multiyear study. *Educause Review*. Retrieved on 6 June 2024 from https://er.educause.edu/articles/2017/10/exploring-the-use-of-e-textbooks-in-higher-education-a-multiyear-study

Rama, P., Black, R., van Es, E., & Warschauer, M. (2012) Affordances for second language learning in World of Warcraft. *ReCALL*, 24(3), 322–338.

Reddy, M. (1979). The conduit metaphor: A case of frame conflict in our language about language. In A. Ortony (Ed.), *Metaphor and thought* (pp. 164–201). Cambridge University Press.

Reynolds, R. (2011). Trends influencing the growth of digital textbooks in US higher education. *Publishing Research Quarterly*, 27(2), 178–187.

The New London Group. (1996). A pedagogy of multiliteracies: Designing social futures. *Harvard Educational Review*, 66(1), 60–93.

Thoms, J., & Poole, F. (2017). Investigating linguistic, literary, and social affordances of L2 collaborative reading. *Language Learning & Technology*, 21(2), 139–156.

Thoms, J., & Poole, F. (2018). Exploring digital literacy practices via L2 social reading. *L2 Journal*, 10(2), 36–61.

van Compernolle, R.A. (2014). *Sociocultural theory and L2 instructional pragmatics*. Multilingual Matters.

van Lier, L. (1996). *Interaction in the language curriculum: Awareness, autonomy and authenticity*. Routledge.

van Lier, L. (2000). From input to affordance: Social-interactive learning from an ecological perspective. In J.P. Lantolf (Ed.), *Sociocultural theory and second language learning* (pp. 245–259). Oxford University Press.

van Lier, L. (2004). *The ecology and semiotics of language learning: A sociocultural perspective*. Springer.

Vygotsky, L. (1978). *Mind in society: The development of higher psychological processes*, M. Cole, V. John-Steiner, S. Scribner, & E. Souberman (Eds.). Harvard University Press.

Yoshii, M. (2006). L1 and L2 glosses: Their effects on incidental vocabulary learning. *Language Learning and Technology* 10(3), 85–101.

Zhu, X., Chen, B., Avadhanam, R., Shui, H., & Zhang, R. (2020). Reading and connecting: Using social annotation in online classes. *Information and Learning Sciences*, 121(5/6), 261–271.

Appendix

1. "Sénégal Fast Food" glosses (Full lyrics at https://genius.com/Amadou-and-mariam-senegal-fast-food-lyrics)
   je serais parti [I'll be gone]
   je me marie [I'm getting married]
   j'ai confiance [I am confident]
   Ascenseur [elevator]
   Refrain [chorus]
   Bambara [Malian dialect]
   y'attends [I'm waiting]
   la frontière? [border]
   Entre les murs se faufiler… [squeezing between the walls]
   Bambara [Malian dialect]
2. "Ma Louisianne" glosses (Full lyrics at https://genius.com/Zachary-richard-ma-louisianne -lyrics)
   Oublie voir pas [Never forget]
   On était [We were]
   On sera [We will be]
   après ils seront partis [they have left].
   étaient chassés [were chased]
   ils ont trouvé [they found]
   Les manières [customs]
3. "Comme d'habitude" glosses (Full lyrics at https://genius.com/Claude-francois-comme-dhabitude-lyrics)
   je te bouscule [I lightly bump you]
   Sur toi je remonte le drap [I cover you up with the sheet]
   J'ai peur que tu aies froid [I'm afraid that you're cold]
   Ma main [my hand]
   Presque malgré moi [Almost in spite of myself]
   tu me tournes le dos [you turn your back to me]
   la chambre [bedroom]
   Tout seul [All alone]
   je bois [I drink]
   Sans bruit [Without a noise]
   J'ai froid, je relève mon col [I'm cold, I turn up my collar]
   Toute la journée [All day long]

faire semblant [pretend]
sourire [to smile]
rire [to laugh]
vivre [to live]
s'en ira [will go away]
je reviendrai [will come back]
tu seras sortie [will have left]
pas encore rentrée [not home yet]
j'irai [future simple: aller]
Dans ce grand lit froid [in this big, cold bed]
Mes larmes, je les cacherai [My tears, I'll hide them]
Même la nuit [Even at night]
Tu rentreras [You'll come home]
Je t'attendrai [I'll wait for you]
Tu me souriras [You'll smile at me]
Tu te déshabilleras [future simple: se déshabiller]
Tu te coucheras [future simple: se coucher]
On s'embrassera [future simple: s'embrasser]
on fera semblant [we'll pretend]

4. "Les cornichons" glosses (Full lyrics at https://genius.com/Nino-ferrer-les-cornichons-lyrics)
Un tire-bouchon [corkscrew]
On n'avait rien oublié [we didn't forget anything]
Elle avait travaillé [she had worked]
sans s'arrêter [without stopping]
Les ouvre-boîtes [can openers]
la pluie [rain]
les parapluies [umbrellas]

5. "Sous le ciel de Paris" glosses (Full lyrics at https://genius.com/Yves-montand-sous-le-ciel-de-paris-lyrics)
S'envole [takes flight]
le cœur [the heart]
bonheur [happiness]
se construit [is built]
un air fait pour eux [a tune made for them]
le pont de Bercy [the Bercy bridge]
assis [sitting]
quelques badauds [some onlookers]
Puis [Then]
par milliers [by the thousands]
Jusqu'au [Until]
L'hymne d'un peuple [the anthem of a people]
épris [taken with or smitten]
couve [hatches/develops]
Paname [nickname for Paris]
Tout peut s'arranger [Anything can happen]
rayons [rays]

L'espoir fleurit [Hope blooms]
pour lui [for himself]
Depuis vingt siècles [for twenty centuries]
Quand elle lui sourit [When she {the island} smiles at him {the sky}}]
habit [outfit]
C'est qu'il [It's because]
amants [lovers]
Il fait gronder sur nous [He makes rumble over us]
Son tonnerre éclatant [his resounding thunder]
Pour se faire pardonner [To make it up to them]
un arc en ciel [a rainbow]

6. (No glosses were presented to participants for the final song, "Le Bal masqué". Lyrics available at https://genius.com/La-compagnie-creole-le-bal-masque-lyrics)

CHAPTER 6

Digital social reading annotations as evidence of L2 proficiency

Frederick J. Poole & Joshua J. Thoms
Michigan State University | Utah State University

In this chapter, we put forth an exploratory approach for using digital social reading (DSR) tools and activities to develop and implement performance-based assessments. We argue that by planning tasks for assessment purposes within an assessment for learning framework, second language (L2) educators can systematically collect formative data to make better evaluations of student proficiency levels. In addition, we demonstrate how DSR tools can facilitate this approach to classroom-based assessments. Drawing on data collected from two earlier studies in Chinese L2 classrooms, we demonstrate how engagement with DSR tools can provide evidence of reading proficiency at different levels. We also provide recommendations for designing DSR tasks using the evidence-centered design framework (Yin & Mislevy, 2021) and illustrate how these tasks can be expanded into Integrated Performance Assessments that evaluate other modes of communication, in addition to interpretive reading.

Introduction

In the last two decades, there has been an increased emphasis on proficiency-oriented approaches, which has promoted more of a focus on meaning and communication of messages in the world language classroom in contrast to a focus on explicit grammar instruction (Adair-Hauck et al., 2006; Ritz & Sherf, 2023). However, scholars have noted that while instructional approaches have begun to shift, assessment practices often remain the same (Giraldo, 2019; Kaplan, 2016). Past studies have shown that while language teachers report using more communicative approaches, their assessments still focus heavily on grammar and vocabulary knowledge (e.g., Cheng et al., 2004; Frodden et al., 2004). Performance-based assessments have been argued as a better alternative to align proficiency-based instructional practices with assessments (Kissau & Adams, 2016; Shrum & Glisan, 2010). A performance-based approach to assessment identifies a real-world task

https://doi.org/10.1075/aals.21.06poo
© 2024 John Benjamins Publishing Company

to be completed with the target language. Evaluation of the performance is then made using criteria derived from language standards associated with the real-world task (Purpura, 2016).

Aligning assessments with instructional practice is important as it may lead to positive washback, which occurs when students and/or teachers adjust their study and/or teaching and curricular practices in ways that are conducive to learning (Brown & Abeywickrama, 2019). The Integrated Performance Assessment (IPA), a type of performance assessment that involves the three communicative modes (i.e., interpretive, interpersonal, and presentational), is often promoted as an effective way to align assessments to proficiency-oriented instructional practices and promote positive washback (e.g., Darhower & Smith-Sherwood, 2021; Martel, 2019). While IPAs have helped to promote proficiency-oriented practices in the classroom, some studies have explored their shortcomings. Notably, there is the perception that IPAs are too time-consuming to implement and difficult to design (e.g., Kaplan, 2016; Kissau et al., 2012). Therefore, while this shift towards proficiency-oriented pedagogy and assessment in the world language classroom is undoubtedly encouraging, exploring practical approaches to performance-based assessments is vital to support and sustain this positive trend.

In this chapter, we set out to demonstrate how digital social reading (DSR) via digital annotation tools (DATs) can be leveraged to design and implement performance-based assessments. In the following literature review, we first provide an overview of terminology of second language (L2) assessments to establish a common framework for thinking about assessment issues. Next, we review research that provides suggestions for aligning assessments with world language standards. We then explore research on DSR and make an argument for its use as an assessment tool. Following the literature review, we use data collected from two prior studies in Chinese L2 classrooms to illustrate how engagement with DSR tools might elicit evidence of reading proficiency at the novice, intermediate, and advanced levels. We then provide suggestions for designing DSR tasks using the evidence-centered design framework (Yin & Mislevy, 2021). Finally, we conclude the chapter by demonstrating how such DSR tasks can be expanded into IPAs that assess other communicative modes besides interpretive reading.

Literature review

L2 assessment issues

According to Purpura (2016) "language assessment is a broad term referring to a systematic procedure for eliciting test and non-test data (e.g., a teacher checklist of student performance) for the purpose of making inferences or claims about certain language-related characteristics of an individual" (p. 191). Assessments include both large, professionally developed standardized tests as well as context-specific/classroom-based assessments. In this chapter, we focus specifically on classroom-based assessments. Classroom-based assessments come in many forms; they are used for diagnostic purposes (e.g., placement tests), to track learner progress, measure mastery of skills and knowledge (i.e., achievement), and/or to make decisions about teaching effectiveness (Purpura, 2016). However, likely the most important characteristic of classroom-based assessments is that they are created by teachers for their specific needs.

When addressing the need to improve classroom-based assessments, researchers and educators have either suggested that assessment experts should design and validate assessments for language teachers or that language teachers should be trained in assessment literacy to create localized assessments for their context (Poehner & Inbar-Lourie, 2020). This debate centers on the quality and practicality of designing and implementing language assessments across multiple contexts. While assessment experts may be able to design more valid and reliable assessments, there is a question about the practicality of creating and implementing assessments that address the individualized needs of teachers across the same school district, much less the same state. In contrast, while language teachers are more familiar with their own and their students' assessment needs, creating valid assessments that measure what learners can do with their language (e.g., proficiency-oriented assessments) rather than what they know about the language (i.e., grammar- or lexical-focused assessments) is both challenging and time-consuming for individual teachers who already have a full workload (Kaplan, 2016; Kissau et al., 2012). Given that scholars have argued that assessments should be a starting point for designing curriculum, and thus have a more central role in L2 instruction (Wiggins & McTighe, 2012), it is unsurprising that there has been a recent surge of research focusing on teacher assessment literacy (e.g., Coombe et al., 2020; Giraldo, 2019; Harding & Kremmel, 2016).

As a result of time constraints, language teachers often report using multiple choice quizzes that target explicit grammar and/or vocabulary knowledge to assess language progress in the classroom (Giraldo, 2019). Whether it be expert- or teacher-designed assessments, time constraints are likely associated with the assessment of learning (AoL) approach, which evaluates performance after a learning activity (Schellekens et al., 2021). These assessments have also been called summative assessments. By separating assessment from the learning process, and subsequently isolating the learner from external support (e.g., mediation from a teacher), the intuitive belief is that such assessments provide more valid evidence of learners' 'true linguistic ability', because the learner is completing assessments independent of support. It has been argued that the AoL paradigm is problematic because educators often try to measure a complex construct (e.g., language proficiency) with one assessment, at one point in time (see Clarke-Midura & Dede, 2010 and York, 2023 for discussion). This one-snapshot assessment approach seemingly reduces the amount of time spent on assessment and better captures a learner's proficiency level. In lieu of this approach, we argue that educators should be collecting data at multiple points in multiple contexts to get a better understanding of the L2 construct being measured. However, within an AoL perspective, more assessments mean less instructional time.

As a complement to the AoL approach, the assessment for learning (AfL) approach — also often referred to as formative assessment — explores assessment approaches that are embedded into students' everyday learning practices (Klenowski, 2009). It is important to note here that the difference between formative and summative assessment is better characterized by the function of the assessment. In other words, if an assessment is used to improve teaching and learning (e.g., successfully reteach a unit that students performed poorly on), then it can be said to be a formative assessment (William & Black, 1996). This inevitably blurs the line between formative and summative assessment as an L2 assessment could function as both. Given that this chapter discusses the design of assessments rather than how assessments are used by educators, we opt for assessment for learning as a paradigm for thinking about, designing, and evaluating formative assessments.

In the AfL approach, teachers actively monitor learners' performance on in-class activities, make evaluations, and provide feedback in a timely manner so as to be readily implementable during ongoing learning (i.e., before summative assessments or before it is 'too late'). These assessments are argued to focus on improving learning and teaching by providing learners feedback as they engage with in-class tasks (Ketabi & Ketabi, 2014; Schellekens et al., 2021). AfL or formative assessments can be either informal (e.g., teacher providing corrective feedback in the classroom) or formal (e.g., planned in-class tasks to assess a skill/knowledge) (Cizek et al., 2019). Given that these assessments are embedded into everyday classroom practices, collecting multiple data points becomes possible because such assessments do not take away from instructional time. However, data collection and analysis must be systematic and linked to language standards. Otherwise, teacher bias and/or errors may impact overall assessment evaluations (Bennet, 2019).

While an AfL approach appears promising in terms of addressing the practical realities of the L2 classroom, Brown (2019) casts doubt on the ability of teachers to assess learners and provide "on-the-spot" feedback within the context of a classroom effectively and reliably (p.3). Instead, he argues that AfL is simply effective teaching, rather than an approach to assessment. In this critique, Brown seemingly focuses on informal implementations of AfL/formative assessments. In this paper, we acknowledge the shortcomings of AfL highlighted by Brown (2019) but argue that AfL can be more systematic and produce meaningful inferences by using the evidence-centered design framework (Yin & Mislevy, 2021) to establish connections between planned in-class tasks (e.g., formal AfL), elicited behaviors, and targeted standards. In the following section, we explore the alignment of assessments to world language standards.

Aligning assessments to standards

Aligning assessments to standards in world language education is argued to be valuable because it can increase the validity of an assessment, facilitate interpretation of learner performance(s), and provide teachers and learners with a clear understanding of linguistic ability (Cox et al., 2018). Although aligning assessments to language standards cannot replace test validation, it does offer a starting point for teachers designing in-class assessments (Papageorgiou, 2016). Further, scholars have questioned the necessity of in-class assessments undergoing the same validity and reliability requirements associated with research-based assessment tools (Bennett, 2019). Additionally, by aligning assessments with standards that target performance-based indicators, educators can promote positive washback and encourage teachers and students to focus on strategies that improve language development rather than rote memorization.

In this paper, we align our assessment to the ACTFL standards. Before illustrating what alignment to the ACTFL standards looks like, it is first important to discuss what standards are, as the characteristics of educational standards often vary across context and purpose. Maxwell (2009) argues that standards are typically characterized as either: content standards, performance standards, or developmental standards. Content standards are often used to ensure "comprehensive coverage of important concepts and skills" (Maxwell, 2009, p. 274). ACTFL's World Readiness Standards (WRS), which include the 5C's: Communication, Cultures, Connections, Comparisons, and Communities, are an example of content standards (see Figure 1 for an example). While the WRS remind teachers that teaching and learning languages is multifaceted, they do little in terms of guiding educators on when and what to assess.

> Communication 1.2: Learners understand, interpret, and analyze what is heard, read, or viewed on a variety of topics.

Figure 1. WRS example: Communication 1.2

Performance standards provide benchmarks for language learning outcomes. They usually include a description of performance at various levels. These are the ACTFL Proficiency Guidelines (ACTFL, 2012) and/or more recently the Proficiency Benchmarks (ACTFL, 2017) in the form of can-do statements. Proficiency in these frameworks is separated into novice, intermediate, advanced, and superior levels. The first three of these levels are each further sub-divided into low, mid, and high. The ACTFL Proficiency Benchmarks further characterize proficiency across the three communicative modes: interpretive, interpersonal, and presentational (see Figure 2 for an example).

> Intermediate–Interpretive: I can understand the main idea and some pieces of information on familiar topics from sentences and series of connected sentences within texts that are spoken, written, or signed.

Figure 2. Proficiency Benchmark example

The Proficiency Benchmarks provide a clear expectation for what learners should be able to achieve at different proficiency levels. Finally, development standards are similar to performance standards except they give more discrete details and indicators of proficiency across the proficiency levels. ACTFL provides this through performance indicators found in Proficiency Benchmarks and/or through Performance Descriptors. While content and performance standards can provide general guides to ensure coverage and accountability at the macro level, we argue that developmental standards provide a more actionable guide for creating classroom-based/teacher-created assessments. Further, the proficiency indicators provide examples to illustrate what proficiency looks like in specific contexts (see Table 1).

As noted previously, traditional assessment paradigms typically focus on measuring explicit knowledge about a language (e.g., grammar and vocabulary) rather than what learners can do with their target language. Within this paradigm, educators attempt to make inferences about a learner's overall language proficiency based on a collection of individual constructs associated with the language learner's knowledge of the language. In contrast, when we align assessments to ACTFL standards (in our case, the Proficiency Indicators), we are advocating that teachers design performance-based assessments. Performance-based assessments ask learners to complete tasks that they are familiar with (Cox & Malone, 2018). This approach acknowledges that most language learning happens within the classroom and thus attempts to assess performance based on tasks that learners have experienced previously in the classroom. In a classroom where the assessment is aligned with proficiency-based instruction, learners are given tasks

Table 1. ACTFL Proficiency Indicators of interpretive skills at intermediate range

	Proficiency Indicators	Examples
Intermediate low	I can identify the topic and related information from simple sentences in short informational texts.	I can understand some information on job postings.
Intermediate mid	I can understand the main idea and key information in short straightforward informational texts.	I can understand the basic requirements for a career as described on a brochure.
Intermediate high	I can usually follow the main message in various time frames in straightforward, and sometimes descriptive, paragraph-length informational texts.	I can understand information provided in a travel guide about an historical site.

*Full Document here: https://www.actfl.org/uploads/files/general/Resources-Publications/Intermediate-Can-Do-Statements.pdf

associated with a target proficiency level (e.g., intermediate), perform those tasks repeatedly (in different contexts) until they can be performed spontaneously, and then demonstrate mastery of the skill via performance-based assessments (Darhower & Smith-Sherwood, 2021). It is important to note that performance and proficiency are distinct concepts in language assessment. While performance focuses on what learners can do with the language in controlled and supported environments (e.g., the classroom), proficiency assesses a learner's ability to use the language in a variety of spontaneous real-life contexts. In the context of this chapter, we will explore how student annotations within DSR environments provide evidence for students *performing* at different *proficiency* levels. In the next section, we briefly review past research on DSR and then make an argument for its use in assessment.

Digital social reading

Digital social reading (DSR) is a pedagogical approach that affords technology-mediated collaborative reading (Pianzola, 2021). That is, DSR involves texts being read through a digital annotation tool (DAT) that allows two or more readers to highlight the same virtual copy of a text and analyze it via synchronous or asynchronous threaded discussions tied to specific passages. While many DATs allow for the digitization and collaborative reading of literary texts (e.g., eComma, Classroom Salon, eMargin), others (e.g., Perusall) allow for the incorporation of a wider array of "texts" (broadly defined), such as digital pictures and paintings,

PDFs, and videos. DSR tools allow users (including L2 learners) to interactively comment on and interact with each other via their uploaded comments, images, emojis, and hyperlinks in discussion threads on apps and websites like Perusall.

To date, much of the research on DSR in L2 contexts has focused on how learners co-construct meaning in various L2 environments (e.g., Blyth, 2014; Law et al., 2020; Thoms & Poole, 2018; Thoms, et al., 2017) while also analyzing the emergence of various literary, linguistic, and social affordances in learners' digital interactions in these virtual spaces (e.g., Thoms & Poole, 2017). Other work has looked at how DSR might result in new forms of interaction with texts and peers, for example, through multimodal communication (e.g., Solmaz, 2020; Zapata & Morales, 2018). Some have also researched how DSR might assist L2 teacher professional development efforts (Burhan-Horasanlı, 2022; Michelson & Dupuy, 2018).

While the affordances of DSR in L2 learning and teaching contexts continue to be explored, there remains a lack of literature on how DSR might facilitate the assessment of learners' reading and writing abilities and/or overall emerging digital literacy practices. DSR tools allow students to engage with L2 texts in meaningful ways both in and outside of the classroom. Furthermore, such engagements can be easily tracked and followed by the instructor, thus potentially facilitating timely evaluations of students' reading abilities. In sum, this chapter offers an exploratory approach to using DSR to assess the reading proficiency of L2 learners of Chinese with an aim to expand the research foci of DSR-related work as it relates to the aforementioned L2 assessment issues.

Methods

Participants

The data used in this study comes from data sets from two previous studies. One (Thoms et al., 2017) involved using eComma in a second-semester university-level Chinese L2 classroom. The eleven participants in that study ranged in age from 18 to 67 years old (median 20). All the students in the study were native English speakers except for one, who indicated that she was born in Taiwan and spent four years there where she developed some Chinese literacy skills early in her life. In addition to the first study mentioned, this current chapter also draws on data from a project carried out in 2019 when four university-level students were enrolled in a fifth semester 'Introduction to Modern Chinese Literature and Film' course. All four students were native English speakers.

Procedures

Data from both studies involved students freely using digital annotation tools (i.e., eComma in the lower-level Chinese classroom and Classroom Salon in the upper-level Chinese class) to comment on various readings written in Chinese. For an overview of both digital annotation tools referenced in this paper, see the following websites: https://ecomma.coerll.utexas.edu/; http://www.classroomsalon.com/. It's important to note here that the original screenshots for both of the aforementioned students are no longer available. In the data samples below, we input the data from the two studies into a generic digital annotation tool for illustrative purposes.

The second-semester students used eComma when reading two texts used by the university-level Chinese program; we explain the topics of the readings below. For the upper-level Chinese literature and film course, students were presented with five texts that represented various genres (again, see next section for details). In both studies, students weren't asked to comment on specific aspects of the text. Rather, after training each class how to use their specific DAT via a practice/tool orientation session, students in each class freely commented on different aspects of the texts by highlighting certain passages and making comments for other students to see, posing questions related to language matters and/ or meaning-based inquiries, and simply engaging with other students in a social manner while engaged in DSR. The sample data that we provide in this study comes from a mixture of students from both classes to better illustrate the varying proficiency levels of students. The researchers archived students' comments made in the DSR environment and identified three learners at the novice, intermediate, and advanced levels to explore how their annotations were representative of their reading levels. We selected the three participants based on students who contributed actively to the DSR environment. Those with more posts provided more evidence of their proficiency level. Additionally, we were looking for students who performed clearly at each of the three levels (novice, intermediate, and advanced) for illustrative purposes.

Sample responses at multiple proficiency levels

Novice example — Heather

In this first example, we explore comments made by Heather (pseudonym), who was a student in the second-semester Chinese language course. Heather was asked to make three annotations and respond to at least two classmates on two different texts. One of the texts was a fictional account of a person's daily routine and discussed vocabulary and phrases that were familiar to the learner (e.g., I shower at X

Chapter 6. Digital social reading annotations as evidence of L2 proficiency   137

time). The second text was non-fiction and discusses differences between American and Chinese birthday celebrations. The fictional text was written for Chinese learners and the non-fiction text was originally an authentic blog post that was adapted for Chinese learners.

In this first example, Heather recognizes the word 是 (is/are) but does not recognize the sentence structure (Figure 3). In the sentence "这一天我常常是七点起床 -*On this day (Wednesday) I usually get up at 7:00 a.m.*", 是 (is/are) is not used as a simple be-verb, rather it is used to emphasize details about events occurring regularly in the past. Heather demonstrates recognition of familiar words and understanding of simple sentence meaning by identifying an exception to the rule that she has learned.

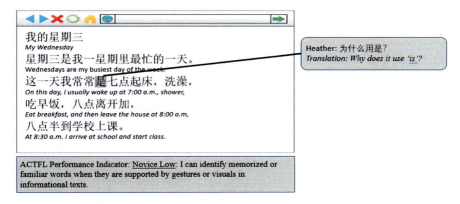

Figure 3. Novice low — Fiction

In the next example (Figure 4), Heather demonstrates that she can rely on the context of the story to guess unknown words. Here, she highlights the word for 离开 (leave) in Chinese, and notes that she understands that it means 'to leave' but wants to check her comprehension. This demonstrates that not only does this text have some unfamiliar vocabulary for Heather, but also that she is not relying on a dictionary to complete this task. More importantly, it shows that Heather is demonstrating comprehension of other parts of this text to inference the meaning of unknown words.

Finally, in Figure 5, Heather provides an example of a novice-high reading skill by illustrating that she can understand simple sentences and identify isolated facts from them. Here, she highlights an excerpt that suggests that Chinese people have been influenced by western culture. She demonstrates understanding by flipping this around and asking her classmates if they think American culture should be influenced by Chinese culture.

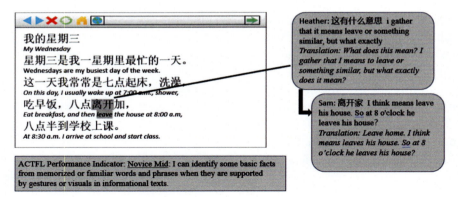

Figure 4. Novice mid — Fiction

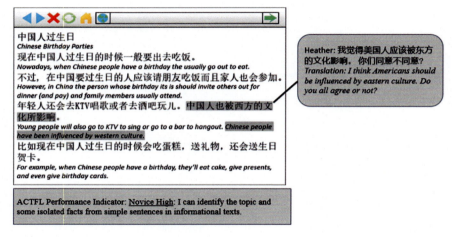

Figure 5. Novice high — Non-fiction

To determine Heather's proficiency level, we must consider that she is reading novice-level texts. These three annotations made by Heather provide early evidence that she is reading at a novice level. In the first excerpt, she identifies frequent vocabulary. In the second example, she provides a direct translation to part of a sentence. In the last example, she demonstrates comprehension by prompting her classmates to answer a question on the topic. However, to make a better argument, we would need to do two things. First, we need additional data demonstrating a wider variety of skills and collected over time to confirm Heather's proficiency level. Secondly, we would need to establish a ceiling (e.g., what Heather is not able to accomplish consistently). Given that both texts are for novice learners because they were adapted and contain familiar vocabulary and phrases for the learners, Heather was not given a chance to perform at the intermediate level. Integrating more authentic texts with a variety of potential tasks would elicit evidence that provides a more holistic understanding of her reading proficiency level.

Intermediate example — Kelly

Our next two examples come from the fifth-semester Chinese literature class. In this class, students were asked to read a combination of authentic non-fictional and fictional texts. The non-fictional texts in all the examples below include a newspaper article that discusses the impact of income disparity on students' decision to attend the university in rural China. The fictional texts are a mix of poems, song lyrics, and excerpts from a novel. All of these texts would be considered appropriate for advanced readers of the target language. Thus, we will focus on how students engage with the text. It is important to recall that completing intermediate tasks with advanced texts does not suffice as evidence for advanced reading proficiencies. Rather, it demonstrates emerging advance reading skills (Clifford & Cox, 2013).

Kelly (pseudonym) admitted to struggling with many of the readings in this project and noted spending more time completing the tasks than other students. In several annotations, Kelly states that she looked up individual words and understood their meaning, but still could not understand what the words meant together. One of Kelly's coping mechanisms in this project was to highlight familiar words, phrases, and concepts in the reading and then discuss them using her own background knowledge.

For example, in Figure 6, when commenting on a song lyric in which the author expresses his love for his partner, Kelly notes the general importance of snow in literature (i.e., not specific to Chinese literature). Rather than try to explore the significance of describing the author's lover as being able to bring on seasonal changes, Kelly describes how snow is relevant for her own local context in her state. This is a key feature of intermediate-high learners; they tend to rely heavily on their own cultural and background knowledge to make sense of authentic materials. In ACTFL's Proficiency benchmarks (ACTFL, 2017), when discussing the investigation of cultural products for intercultural communication, the key difference between intermediate and advanced learners is that intermediate learners can make comparisons or more simply stated, spot commonalities or differences, while advanced learners can 'explain' differences and how they relate to perspectives. Thus in the example above, Heather identifies a commonality, but does not attempt to explain how the literary feature relates to a target culture perspective.

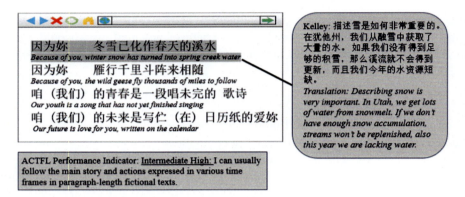

Figure 6. Intermediate high — Fiction

In another reading (a love poem), there's an abstract line that states that the author is a compilation of multiple versions of himself, all of whom were wanting to sleep with his lover. There are multiple ways to interpret this line, but Kelly takes a literal interpretation, focusing on "奔跑" which means to run or sprint (see Figure 7). She mistakenly believes that this line suggests that the author is literally running home to meet his lover. This is a reasonable assumption to make given the theme of the poem and thus shows that Kelly understands the general idea of the poem, and is therefore reading it quite literally, but is missing some of the details and subsequently not reading the text metaphorically. Again, this demonstrates further evidence that Kelly is reading at an intermediate high level but is showing emerging advanced reading skills. Similar, to the example above, a key distinction between intermediate and advanced learners is the ability to explain how authentic texts relate to cultural perspectives, which ultimately means that learners are able to identify abstract or metaphorical meaning within a text.

Finally, in the non-fiction text (see Figure 8), Kelly highlights a section that notes that Chinese people are unhappy with the income disparity due to its unfair origins. She shows comprehension of this text by posing her opinions on the topic and suggesting that China is not doing enough to combat this problem.

In these examples, Heather is engaging with advanced-level texts. However, much of her interactions or tasks would be considered at the intermediate level. Rather than critically evaluating the text, Heather relies primarily on her own background experiences to comment on and discuss the readings. Thus, while she shows comprehension of more advanced texts at a superficial level, she does not demonstrate understanding from different cultural viewpoints. Similar to the assessment of Heather's reading level, to make a clearer determination of Kelly's reading abilities, we would need to collect more examples of Kelly's interaction with texts and tasks at varying reading levels.

Chapter 6. Digital social reading annotations as evidence of L2 proficiency

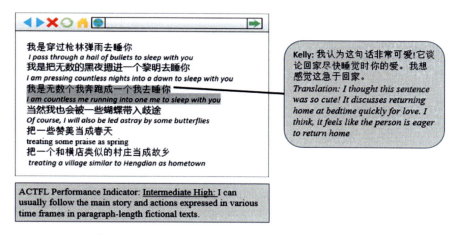

Figure 7. Intermediate high — Fiction

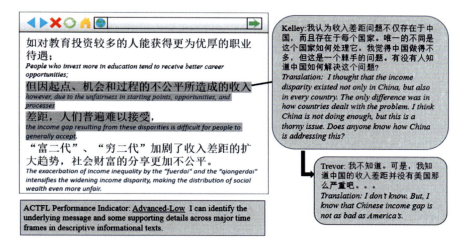

Figure 8. Advanced low — Non-fiction

Advanced example — Trevor

In the final example, Trevor, who is also in the fifth-semester Chinese literature course, reads the same texts as Kelly. In the first example (see Figure 9), Trevor (pseudonym) highlights a section that suggests a university degree will not change one's future. Trevor demonstrates comprehension of this and then expands on the idea by posing questions about the consequences of the ideas suggested in the reading.

The next example is excerpted from a novel. This is a very difficult passage given that it contains several less common vocabulary words, idiomatic expres-

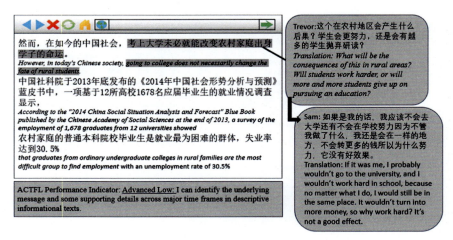

Figure 9. Advanced low — Non-fiction

sions, and cultural references. Trevor highlights a four-character phrase that can be literally translated as "clear insults, hidden praise." In the text, there are two women who are seemingly discussing their grandchildren's failings but doing so in a way that makes their grandchildren seem even better. Trevor demonstrates understanding of several lines after this four-character phrase when he tries to guess the meaning of this excerpt. In doing so, he notes the insults that were used but fails to connect them properly to this idiom when he suggests that the idiom has a derogatory meaning. This demonstrates that Trevor understands many of the main ideas and details of the text but is missing some of the subtler cultural implications of the idiom.

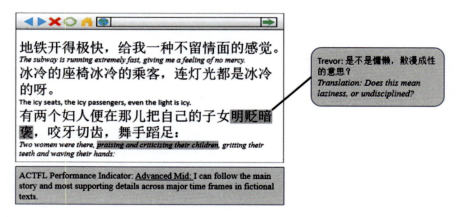

Figure 10. Advanced mid — Fiction

The next example comes from a poem that is at the advanced level. The poem describes a man walking through the streets of Shanghai. It includes several metaphors comparing the city to the ocean and presents a very chaotic scene. However, the protagonist is portrayed as navigating this chaotic scene with much ease. This use of metaphors, idiomatic phrases, cultural references, and complex imagery makes this an advanced level text. Trevor demonstrates understanding of the poem at both the literal and metaphorical level in several annotations. He notes that the poem is quite refreshing and that it demonstrates self-confidence (See Figure 11). This is in contrast to his classmates who focus mainly on the chaotic nature of the poem. Recall that Kelly chose to discuss the importance of snow in her own context, rather than explore interpretations of the poem. Thus, a key difference between advanced readers and intermediate readers is that advanced readers attempt to infer meaning from unfamiliar and abstract topics. However, it is important to note, that these differences may also be a result of literacy skills rather than proficiency levels. In other words, Trevor may have more experience reading and interpreting literary texts in his first language (L1) than other learners in this study. The implications for this will be further explored in the discussion below.

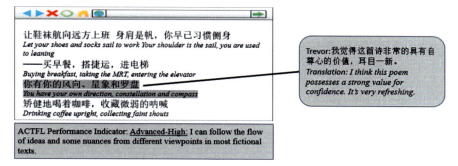

Figure 11. Advanced high — Fiction

In all three examples, Trevor's annotations demonstrate understanding of advanced-level texts by musing about consequences of claims made in the text, interpreting metaphors, and relying on context to guess unknown phrases. As we have noted in these examples, collecting more data over longer periods of time will provide more reliable evaluations for language educators. In the following section, we discuss strategies for eliciting data in which inferences about proficiency can be made.

Limitations

It is important to note that data collected for this chapter was not originally intended for assessment purposes. This must be acknowledged for a few reasons. First, in both data sets, students were not given specific annotation tasks. This is important because without assigning specific tasks, learners may focus more on a particular reading skill while ignoring other skills that may better show their proficiency level. This is especially true if students are reading and being assessed in a literary course and are expected to comment on literary features. Providing explicit tasks and instructions for learners can help educators connect reading annotations to reading performance indicators (i.e., standards).

Secondly, we did not stage the annotations over time to avoid influence from prior students' annotations. In the original studies, we were interested in how DSR provided a social element to reading in the target language. This may be problematic for assessments attempting to determine individual cognitive capacities as the first person who annotates will have a much different experience from the last person who annotates and sees all prior annotations. However, it is important to note that if we take a dynamic assessment perspective (Poehner & Lantolf, 2023) which aligns with assessment for learning practices, we may be less concerned with learners being exposed to their classmates' comments during an assessment. That is, assessing learners in a social environment ultimately lends itself to an expanded view of assessment in which we must consider the context and support learners receive while reading when making inferences about their linguistic proficiency levels. Further, within a DSR environment, we are likely more interested in assessing reading practices or, in the case of more advanced learners, their literary practices. Thus, rather than assess what a learner comprehends or fails to comprehend, we may be more apt to base our assessments on the practices that a learner attempts (or neglects) to engage in (e.g., making inferences, interpretations, and/or challenging ideas).

Finally, there is also a question of the amount of time and external resources used while completing this task. While some students in our prior studies reported using dictionaries, others tried to read assigned texts without additional support. Use of external resources will undoubtedly impact reading fluency and comprehension. We recommend establishing a policy for resource consultation (e.g., dictionary use) on readings as well as a time limit for the completion of reading tasks to promote transparency and understanding of the processes and practices that students engage in while reading. This is not to say that using a dictionary to complete a text should negatively affect a learner's assessment, but rather that understanding when and how a learner uses a dictionary can lead to insights into their literary practices and digital literacies. Finally, as a reminder, our objective in this chapter is not necessarily to validate DSR tools for assessment, but rather demonstrate their potential use for assessment. In the next section, we explore practical steps towards this goal.

Designing for a purpose with the evidence-centered design framework

Discussing procedural policies are practical classroom systems to implement, however, identifying tasks that elicit evidence associated with targeted proficiency levels can be somewhat challenging. Thus, we recommend applying the evidence-centered design (ECD) framework (Bennett, 2019; Yin & Mislevy, 2021) to design assessment tasks. The ECD framework provides a rigorous and systematic model for creating assessments that are aligned with the intended goals. The framework is designed for complex assessments, such as stealth assessments that rely on performance and behavior often in digital environments, as evidence for student competencies. Stealth assessments are assessments that are embedded into activities in digital environments (Shute, 2011). They are similar to assessments used formatively in that they are not separated from the learning process. The ECD framework is a multilayered approach that involves five layers, including domain analysis, domain modeling, conceptual assessment framework, assessment implementation, and assessment delivery. For practical implementation, we will focus on the conceptual assessment framework, which is comprised of three interrelated models, including the competency model, task model, and evidence model. The competency model defines the targeted skill or knowledge domain, the task model focuses on designing tasks that elicit evidence for the competency variables, and the evidence model combines information from both the competency model and task model to create a statistical relationship between the two to provide an actionable interpretation (see Figure 12).

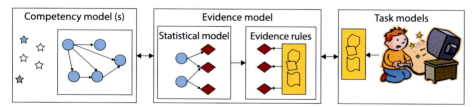

Figure 12. Conceptual assessment framework

Thus, to use DSR tools for assessment purposes, it will be important to first identify our competency variables. We can use Figure 3 which highlights proficiency indicators for each proficiency level. It is important to note that many of the indicators in Figure 3 depend on the characteristics of the text being assigned and subsequently the task associated with the text. After identifying the competency variables, we must establish tasks that elicit evidence of each of those proficiency indicators. To use DSR tools for assessment purposes, we should be focusing on annotation tasks that elicit evidence at our targeted floor levels. Once learners can consistently (i.e., at least 70% of the time) complete tasks at targeted floor levels, we can adjust the tasks to represent new targeted floor levels. Table 2 below provides a list of sample highlighting and annotation tasks at each proficiency level.

Table 2. Sample DSR tasks

Proficiency level	ACTFL Proficiency Indicators	DSR highlight task	DSR annotation task
Novice	Comprehends key words and formulaic phrases that are highly contextualized.	Highlight three vocabulary words from your textbook.	Write the definition for the vocabulary words.
	Comprehends texts ranging in length from lists, to phrases, to simple sentences.	Highlight two items in the list that do not belong.	Describe in the L1 why they do not belong.
	Uses own culture to derive meaning from texts that are read.	The author describes three tasks that they do every morning. Highlight one of the tasks.	Add a comment on whether or not you do this task in the morning as well.
Intermediate	Comprehends main ideas and identifies some supporting details.	Highlight evidence supporting the main idea of this story.	Add a comment about the strength of the evidence.
	Comprehends simple stories, routine correspondence, or short descriptive texts.	Highlight a description of one of the main characters in the story.	Add an annotation describing what additional details about the character you would like to know.
	Uses context clues to comprehend texts.	Highlight three words that you did not know while reading this text.	Use the annotations to guess the meaning. Do not use a dictionary on the first attempt.
Advanced	Makes inferences and derives meaning from context and linguistic features.	This poem presents an optimistic view of humanity's future, highlight evidence of this optimism.	Add a comment about why you think the excerpt is optimistic.

Table 2. *(continued)*

Proficiency level	ACTFL Proficiency Indicators	DSR highlight task	DSR annotation task
	Comprehends specialized and precise vocabulary, and an expanding number of idiomatic expressions.	Highlight three idiomatic phrases that you did not know while reading this text.	Use the annotation to guess the meaning. Do not use a dictionary on the first attempt.
	Uses knowledge of cultural differences between own culture and target culture(s) as well as increasing knowledge of the target culture(s) to interpret texts that are read.	What does the description of the city say about city life in Chinese society in the 1980s? Highlight sections of the poem that support your beliefs.	Describe how the highlighted sections support your opinion about their relationship to Chinese society.

Once we have tasks to elicit evidence for our competency model, the final part involves establishing a statistical relationship between the evidence elicited and our proficiency indicators. For classroom-based assessments, we recommend following Clifford's (2016) suggestion of performing consistently at a proficiency level for 70% — 85% of the time. Thus, if one has five tasks per reading, a simple table could be devised to keep track of students who successfully complete tasks at the targeted proficiency level. This minimizes the amount of time needed for evaluation, but also helps teachers keep track of in-class formative assessments in a systematic way. Over time, the teacher can note when students begin to complete tasks consistently at the 70% success rate, and then adjust task difficulty for the next proficiency level.

In the next section, we illustrate how this assessment could then be tied to an Integrated Performance Assessment to assess all communicative modes.

Integrated performance assessments

As language education has evolved over time, there has been a shift towards aligning curricula and instruction with language proficiency standards that emphasize the three communicative modes of language use: Interpersonal, interpretive, and presentational. In response, the concept of Integrated Performance Assessment (IPA) emerged, which integrates various language skills and competencies within meaningful, real-world tasks (Adair-Hauck et al., 2006). IPAs are comprised of a series of tasks that incorporate the three communicative modes and at least one other standard, such as culture or connections to other disciplines (Troyan et al., 2023). This approach to language assessment has gained support and recognition because it is more authentic and reflective of real-life language use. The integration of language skills within IPAs represents a significant step forward in language education and assessment, offering a more comprehensive and goal-driven approach to language evaluation.

Typically, there is a common theme that connects the tasks assessing the three communicative modes and, while there is not a set sequence, usually learners are first assessed in the interpretive mode, then the interpersonal mode, and finally in the presentational mode. Feedback is given after completion of each of the assessment tasks to ensure that performance in one communicative mode does not impact performance in the following communicative mode. In this way, IPAs align with dynamic assessment approaches (e.g., Poehner & Lantolf, 2023) and AfL frameworks.

For example, in an IPA for a novice learner, an interpretive task may ask students to read an authentic menu and answer a series of comprehension questions. After completing the interpretive mode, students receive feedback on their comprehension questions and may even receive an instructional review of the content (e.g., menu) to support their next task. In the interpersonal mode, students may be asked to use the menu and engage in a role play at the restaurant in which both students have an opportunity to be the server and the customer. Again, feedback is given after the role play (usually facilitated by a rubric). Finally, in the presentational mode, students may be asked to combine knowledge from the menu and the role play to write a short blog post about their experience at this new restaurant. Thus, through an IPA, we can assess student performance on all three communicative modes in an integrated manner.

As previously mentioned, IPAs can be time-consuming, especially when one considers the time needed to provide feedback after each mode. In a best-case scenario, teachers may give an interpretive task on Monday, feedback on Tuesday, the Interpersonal task on Wednesday, feedback on Thursday, and the presentational task on Friday. However, one of the affordances of using DSR tools is the ability to complete some of these tasks outside of the classroom, such as allowing students to complete interpretive tasks via the DSR tool before they come to class. Teachers can then provide feedback and an evaluation of a student's reading ability via the DSR tool before they come to class. Once students are in class, teachers can design assessment tasks around the reading and assessment (e.g., read a classmate's opinion about the poem; how does it compare to yours?). Thus, for the interpersonal task, students may be asked to have a conversation with their classmate about the interpretation of a poem in class. Then, for the final presentational task, students would be asked to write a response to the original poem using their conversation and classmate's annotations. In this way, learners are given tasks that may appear in everyday classes, but due to the digital nature of DSR, much of these tasks can be done outside of the classroom, thus preserving in-class time for high-leverage instructional practices.

Conclusion

In this chapter, we set out to demonstrate how DSR can be leveraged to address assessment issues in the classroom. We provided examples of student annotations in Chinese classrooms via the DSR tool and then illustrated how teachers might design tasks to elicit evidence for students performing at a particular proficiency level. Finally, we discussed how DSR tools could be leveraged to help reduce the burden of delivering IPAs in a classroom setting. We recognize that there may be some pushback against the idea of allowing students to be assessed at home when they are not being observed or monitored by the teacher. This will likely cause concern for those who worry that students who use external resources are spending more time than their classmates on a particular assessment, thus calling into question the validity of the assessment results. We would like to remind those with this belief that grades are simply one way to interpret an assessment and that if grades are not attached to assessment evaluation, students will be less inclined to cheat or disregard task parameters that have been set. If we acknowledge that language learning is non-linear, that individual learner characteristics such as language learning aptitude, first language and additional learned languages can impact the rate of acquisition, then we should be able to acknowledge that grading should not be directly associated with final proficiency achievement, but rather with effort and participation. Aligning grades to effort and participation would likely encourage students to view assessments as evaluative rather than punitive, and as a valuable tool to inform their progress.

References

ACTFL. (2012). ACTFL proficiency guidelines 2012 [Electronic version]. Retrieved on 29 August 2023 from https://www.actfl.org/uploads/files/general /ACTFLProficiencyGuidelines2012.pdf

ACTFL. (2017). NCSSFL-ACTFL can-do statements. ACTFL language connects. Retrieved on 29 August 2023 from https://www.actfl.org/educator-resources/ncssfl-actfl-can-do-statements

Adair-Hauck, B., Glisan, E., Koda, K., Swender, E., & Sandrock, P. (2006). The integrated performance assessment (IPA): Connecting assessment to instruction and learning. *Foreign Language Annals*, 39(3), 359–382.

Bennett, R. (2019). Integrating measurement principles into formative assessment. In H.L. Andrade, R.E. Bennett & G.J. Cizek (Eds.), *Handbook of formative assessment in the disciplines* (1st ed., pp. 20–31). Routledge.

Blyth, C. (2014). Exploring the affordances of digital social reading for L2 literacy: The case of eComma. In J.P. Guikema & L. Williams (Eds.), *Digital literacies in foreign and second language education*. (pp. 201–226). Calico.

Brown, D., & Abeywickrama, P. (2019). *Language assessment: Principles and classroom practices*. Pearson.

Brown, G. T. L. (2019). Is assessment for learning really assessment? *Frontiers in Education*, 4(64), 1–7.

Burhan-Horasanlı, E. (2022). Digital social reading: Exploring multilingual graduate students' academic discourse socialization in online platforms. *Linguistics and Education*, 71, 101099.

Cheng, L., Rogers, T., & Hu, H. (2004). ESL/EFL instructors' classroom assessment practices: purposes, methods, and procedures. *Language Testing*, 21(3) 360–389.

Cizek, G., Andrade, H., & Bennett, R. (2019). Formative assessment: History, definition, and progress. In H. Andrade, G. Cizek, & R. Bennett (Eds.), *The handbook of formative assessment in the disciplines* (pp. 3–19). Routledge.

Clarke-Midura, J., & Dede, C. (2010). Assessment, technology, and change. *Journal of Research on Technology in Education*, 42(3), 309-328.

Clifford, R. (2016). A rationale for criterion-referenced proficiency testing. *Foreign Language Annals*, 49(2), 224–234.

Clifford, R., & Cox, T.L. (2013). Empirical validation of reading proficiency guidelines: Empirical validation of reading proficiency. *Foreign Language Annals*, 46(1), 45–61.

Coombe, C., Vafadar, H., & Mohebbi, H. (2020). Language assessment literacy: What do we need to learn, unlearn, and relearn? *Language Testing in Asia*, 10(1), article 3.

Cox, T., & Malone, M. (2018). A validity argument to support the ACTFL assessment of performance toward proficiency in languages (AAPPL). *Foreign Language Annals*, 51(3), 548–574.

Cox, T., Malone, M., & Winke, P. (2018). Future directions in assessment: Influences of standards and implications for language learning. *Foreign Language Annals*, 51(1), 104–115.

Darhower, M., & Smith-Sherwood, D. (2021). Bridging the language-literature divide via integrated performance assessments in an introductory Hispanic literature course. *Hispania*, 104(3), 395–413.

Frodden, M., Restrepo, M., & Maturana, L. (2004). Analysis of assessment instruments used in foreign language teaching. *Íkala: Revista de Lenguaje y Cultura*, 9(15), 171–201.

Giraldo, F. (2019). Language assessment practices and beliefs: Implications for language assessment literacy. *HOW*, 26(1), 35–61.

Harding, L., & Kremmel, B. (2016). Teacher assessment literacy and professional development. In D. Tsagari & J. Banerjee (Eds.), *Handbook of second language assessment* (pp. 413–428). De Gruyter.

Kaplan, C. (2016). Alignment of world language standards and assessments: A multiple case study: Alignment of world language standards and assessments. *Foreign Language Annals*, 49(3), 502–529.

Ketabi, S., & Ketabi, S. (2014). Classroom and formative assessment in second/foreign language teaching and learning. *Theory and Practice in Language Studies*, 4(2), 435–440.

Kissau, S., & Adams, M. (2016). Instructional decision making and IPAs: Assessing the modes of communication. *Foreign Language Annals*, 49(1), 105–123.

Kissau, S., Algozzine, B., & Yon, M. (2012). Similar but different: The beliefs of foreign language teachers. *Foreign Language Annals*, 45(4), 580–598.

Klenowski, V. (2009). Assessment for learning revisited: An Asia-Pacific perspective. *Assessment in Education: Principles, Policy & Practice*. 16. 263–268.

Law, J., Barny, D., & Poulin, R. (2020). Patterns of peer interaction in multimodal L2 digital social reading. *Language Learning & Technology*, 24(2), 70–85.

Martel, J. (2019). Washback of ACTFL's integrated performance assessment in an intensive summer language program at the tertiary level. Language Education & Assessment, 2(2), 57-69.

Maxwell, G. 2009. Defining standards for the 21st century. In Educational assessment in the 21st century, ed. C.M. Wyatt-Smith and J. Cumming, 263–86. Dordrecht: Springer.

Michelson, K. & Dupuy, B. (2018). Teacher learning under co-construction: Affordances of digital social annotated reading. *Apprentissage des Langues et Systèmes d'Information et de Communication, Alsic*, 21.

Papageorgiou, S. (2016). Aligning language assessments to standards and frameworks. In D. Tsagari & J. Banerjee (Eds.), *Handbook of second language assessment* (pp. 327–340). De Gruyter.

Pianzola, F. (2021). *Digital social reading: Sharing fiction in the 21st Century*. The MIT Press.

Poehner, M. E., & Inbar-Lourie, O. (2020). An epistemology of action for understanding and change in L2 classroom assessment: The case for praxis. In E. M. Poehner, & O. Inbar-Lourie (Eds.), *Toward a reconceptualization of second language classroom assessment: Praxis and researcher-teacher partnership* (pp. 1–20). Springer.

Poehner, M., & Lantolf, J. (2023). Advancing L2 dynamic assessment: Innovations in Chinese contexts. *Language Assessment Quarterly*, 20(1), 1–19.

Purpura, J. (2016). Second and foreign language assessment: Second and foreign language assessment. *The Modern Language Journal*, 100(S1), 190–208.

Ritz, C., & Sherf, N. (2023). Curriculum, instruction, and assessment: A snapshot of world language education in Massachusetts. *Foreign Language Annals*, 56(1), 29–51.

Schellekens, L. H., Bok, H. G., de Jong, L. H., van der Schaaf, M. F., Kremer, W. D., & van der Vleuten, C. P. (2021). A scoping review on the notions of Assessment as Learning (AaL), Assessment for Learning (AfL), and Assessment of Learning (AoL). *Studies in Educational Evaluation*, 71, 101094. 1-15.

Shrum, J. L., & Glisan, E. W. (2010). Teacher's handbook: Contextualized language instruction (4th ed.). Heinle & Heinle.

Shute, V. (2011). Stealth assessment in computer-based games to support learning. *Computer Games and Instruction*, 55(2), 503–524.

Solmaz, O. (2020). Examining the collaborative reading experiences of English Language Learners for online second language socialization. *The Reading Matrix*, 20(1), 20–35.

Thoms, J., & Poole, F. (2017). Investigating linguistic, literary, and social affordances of L2 collaborative reading. *Language Learning & Technology*, 21(2), 139–156.

Thoms, J., & Poole, F. (2018). Exploring digital literacy practices via L2 social reading. *L2 Journal*, 10(2), 36–61.

Thoms, J., Sung, K., & Poole, F. (2017). Investigating the linguistic and pedagogical affordances of an L2 open reading environment via eComma: An exploratory study in a Chinese language course. *System*, 69, 38–53.

Troyan, F., Adair-Hauck, B., & Glisan, E. (2023). *Integrated performance assessment: Twenty years and counting*. ACTFL.

Wiggins, G., & McTighe, J. (2012). The Understanding by Design guide to advanced concepts in creating and reviewing units. Association for Supervision and Curriculum Development.

Wiliam, D., & Black, P. (1996). Meanings and consequences: A basis for distinguishing formative and summative functions of assessment? *British Educational Research Journal*, 22(5), 537–548.

Yin, C., & Mislevy, R. J. (2021). Evidence-centered design in language testing. In G. Fulcher & L. Harding, *The Routledge handbook of language testing* (2nd ed., pp. 289–305). Routledge.

York, J. (2023). Pro-gamer inspired speaking assessment. In S. W. Chong & H. Reinders (Eds.), *Innovation in learning-oriented language assessment* (pp. 257–275). Springer.

Zapata, G., & Morales, M. (2018). The beneficial effects of technology-based social reading in L2 classes. *Lenguas en Contexto*, 9(Supplement), 40–50.

CHAPTER 7

Developing digital social reading in source-based writing

A second language teaching and learning account

Inanç Karagöz & John I. Liontas
Bartin University | University of South Florida

This chapter introduces eight digital social reading tasks to facilitate second language source-based reading and writing (Hirvela & Du, 2013): noticing grammatical structures, applying vocabulary glossing, instigating conversations on reading content, engaging critical thinking on arguments, making inferences, dissecting model texts, reconstructing ideas, and crafting source-based writing. They aim to support learners in acquiring grammatical forms and vocabulary for writing, constructing topical knowledge, and transforming reading-derived knowledge into writing. The tasks are divided into three phases of increasing complexity, which serve as support mechanisms and formative assessment points. Sample prompts are provided for each phase to guide students in showcasing their thinking on the source texts.

Introduction

The emergence of the COVID-19 pandemic has motivated second language (L2) teachers all over the world to rethink the methods, tools, and resources they could potentially use to facilitate collaborative learning online. The very shift to remote instruction undergirded a great many such digital efforts already. Yet how best to incorporate learner-centered tasks that actively involve learners in the meaning-making process while they read online has proven itself most challenging. Indeed, digital social reading (DSR) tools and the theoretical frameworks and pedagogies increasingly associated with them in dialogic learning environments help solidify the ways learners engage with digital texts, the linguistic/semiotic resources applied during meaning construction, and, importantly, the multimodal communication resulting from such dynamic contexts. Source-based reading and writing (Hirvela & Du, 2013), referring to the practice of engaging with and producing texts from various sources, serves as a central focus of our discussion. In such a

https://doi.org/10.1075/aals.21.07kar
© 2024 John Benjamins Publishing Company

practice, authentic materials, such as newspapers, academic articles, and books are the main sources for reading and writing tasks. By doing so, learners are exposed to real-life situations and language use, which can help them improve their linguistic and communicative skills. Moreover, learners could enrich their written work through textual borrowing as they identify authoritative sources, extract information that is pertinent for their arguments, and effectively integrate that information into their own writing while adhering to proper citation and referencing conventions.

In light of this context and a social constructivist pedagogy, we suggest in this chapter eight specific approaches for utilizing DSR tools when involving students in source-based writing tasks that align with their academic language proficiency. We provide an in-depth discussion on the most effective pedagogical approaches for organizing and overseeing learning tasks, taking into account factors such as group size and deadlines. Our aim is to familiarize students with the digital tools in use, encourage mutuality of contributions, and create discussion prompts that align with the intended learning objectives. In the final section of the chapter, we assess the challenges and teaching implications practitioners may encounter, such as DSR location restrictions, time zone differences, students' difficulties in generating new ideas, and limited group participation.

Online collaborative reading in second language teaching and learning

Collaborative reading entails readers engaging with at least one other reader within a social context (Kiili et al., 2012). In the context of online second language learning, learners read texts in the target language within a digital environment, communicate in the target language, and work together toward a common goal to complete a reading task using digital tools that facilitate interaction. The DSR tasks presented in this chapter are designed to foster meaningful interactions among learners, guided by prompts from the instructor that gradually increase in complexity. These prompts are intended to help learners stay on course as they work towards task completion and the associated learning objectives.

Since online collaboration relies on digital tools for communication, offering a brief introduction to computer-mediated communication (CMC) can enhance our understanding of how online collaborative language learning practices may have shifted over time. Early examples of CMC, or rather CMC 1.0, included the use of emails, bulletin boards, chat rooms, and audio conferencing (Chun, 2011). These tools connected individuals' written and spoken output through computers synchronously or asynchronously. The next generation of CMC tools, CMC 2.0, offered social networking capabilities without requiring a local network. Wikis, blogs, virtual worlds, Twitter, Facebook, and Instagram are some examples of CMC 2.0 tools (Chun, 2011). Employing CMC in language learning environments has yielded emotional and performance benefits. Learners have demonstrated reduced anxiety and increased motivation (Beauvois, 1995; Kelm, 1998; Lee, 2010; Meunier, 1998) while also generating increased output (Kern, 1995; Kroonenberg, 1994; Lee, 2010; Salaberry, 2000; Warschauer, 1996) when compared to traditional communication settings.

The purposeful use of CMC notwithstanding, social constructivism is another important theoretical foundation for online collaborative learning that warrants consideration. Simply put, social constructivism is a learning theory built on the precepts of sociocultural theory (Vygotsky, 1978) and cognitive constructivism (Piaget & Inhelder, 1969). Sociocultural theory emphasizes the importance of interactions in the learning process. Vygotsky's concept of the Zone of Proximal Development (ZPD) delineates the gap between what learners can achieve based on their current development level and what they can accomplish with the assistance of more knowledgeable individuals, referred as the More Knowledgeable Others (MKOs). Cognitive constructivism posits that learners construct knowledge by processing information through mental structures shaped by their past experiences. Social constructivism thus asserts that learning occurs when learners actively participate in learning tasks while interacting with both peers and the teacher in dynamic settings. Additionally, learners' historical, social, and cultural backgrounds play a substantial role in shaping and defining the ways in which they collectively construct and reconstruct knowledge using various semiotic and linguistic resources.

Within social constructivist environments, the learner takes a central role in the teaching-learning process. Teachers act as facilitators for learning tasks that enable learners to interact, collaborate, and engage in problem-solving. Simultaneously, teachers offer the necessary support to scaffold learning while progressively enhancing task complexity. Conceptual, (meta)cognitive, procedural, and strategic scaffolds are common support strategies teachers use in source-based learning, particularly in digital environments that facilitate these structures (Hill & Hannafin, 2001). Moreover, learners are acknowledged for their participation in collective scaffolding (Donato, 1994), where they exchange resources to improve their learning and aid each other's comprehension.

Lotman (1988) reinterpreted ZPD for reading instruction, positioning texts as tools for collaborative meaning-making. Learners use their ideas and interactions to collectively understand material and achieve common goals. Klingner et al. (1998) introduced a collaborative strategic reading technique to enhance the reading comprehension of students in small groups. Their technique encompassed various steps, including previewing prior knowledge, predicting passage content, identifying challenging words and concepts, restating the main ideas within a paragraph or section, summarizing, and crafting effective review questions (as detailed in Klingner & Vaughn, 2000). While this technique was not originally designed for online learning, it embodies a collaborative reading approach that can assist learners in meaning-making and gathering content for source-based writing.

In the next section on DSR tasks, we will introduce these strategies and more. We will also briefly touch on the multiliteracies framework, which complements online collaborative reading by emphasizing communication modes, cultural awareness, digital literacy, and critical thinking (New London Group, 1996). Multiliteracies extend beyond traditional literacy, encompassing diverse communication skills needed in our interconnected, fast-changing world. These skills are intended to ready students for interaction within various communication contexts, media, and technologies common in modern society. Furthermore, online collaborative reading requires particular digital literacy proficiencies to help students understand task instructions, navigate digital texts, and collaborate effectively. In addition, critical thinking capabilities are crucial for online collaborative reading. Students must scrutinize and assess information from various sources, discern biases, and formulate well-reasoned arguments. Integrating these skills into online collaborative reading not only improves students' text comprehension but also fosters meaningful discussions among peers. Moreover, emphasizing cultural sensitivity is vital for establishing an inclusive and respectful environment where diverse perspectives are welcomed and valued in online collaborative reading activities (Gay, 2018).

Digital social reading tasks

The DSR tasks presented in this chapter are structured within the framework described below. The first task consideration was to create a social constructivist learning environment. Social constructivism suggests learners can progress beyond their current level by engaging in scaffolded tasks and interacting with more knowledgeable peers. In DSR practices, tools like Hypothesis and Perusall enhance higher-order thinking by enabling highlighting, underlining, and commenting (Thoms & Poole, 2018). This aids learners in expanding their ZPD with the help of strategic scaffolds and more knowledgeable peers, allowing them to exchange interpretations, questions, and opinions synchronously and asynchronously. The DSR tasks are structured into three phases, beginning with easier prompts and advancing to more challenging ones. These phases serve as support structures and allow instructors to monitor learners' development by examining their annotations on the page margins, demonstrating their information processing abilities.

The second task consideration addresses the interplay between L2 reading and writing skills. According to Hirvela (2016), L2 learners find reading tasks beneficial for their writing, as reading offers valuable linguistic and rhetorical input that can be applied in writing. Reading fulfills the dual role of acquiring topic knowledge and enhancing writing comprehension. In the context of academic English learning, Hirvela recommends "a sequence of writing tasks in which students begin with knowledge telling in the form of summary writing and eventually move to the more ambitious knowledge transforming, as reflected in synthesis writing" (p. 36). Thus, it is suggested to start with summary writing and advance to synthesis writing. By extension, the DSR tasks presented in this chapter encompass two models (Hirvela, 2016): the *collaborative model*, which emphasizes collective scaffolding and meaning negotiation, and the *sequential model*, featuring a phased developmental process. They equip learners to integrate information into their writing. Depending on their proficiency levels and learning goals, learners receive guidance through linguistic supports, the utilization of reading for knowledge building, and writerly reading for knowledge transformation (Table 1).

Table 1. DSR tasks for source-based writing

Linguistic scaffolds for lower-proficiency learners	Mining reading for knowledge construction	Writerly reading for knowledge transformation
Noticing grammatical structures	Instigating conversations on reading content	Dissecting model texts
Applying vocabulary glossing	Engaging critical analysis of arguments	Reconstructing ideas
	Making Inferences	Crafting source-Based Writing

The third task consideration involves learners' engagement in DSR tasks, applying collaborative reading strategies to identify main ideas, supporting details, concluding sentences, and summarizing (Lo et al., 2013; Nor et al., 2013; Tseng et al., 2015; Tseng & Yeh, 2018; Yeh et al., 2017). Furthermore, analyzing reading texts can form the basis for a genre-based writing pedagogy (Yang, 2016; Yasuda, 2011), where learners observe specific forms in writing samples (Norris, 2009) before beginning writing tasks. DSR tools facilitate open sharing of analyses and enhance awareness of key textual elements and qualities in exemplary texts. The tasks presented in this chapter include prompts for identifying textual elements and exploring connections between ideas. Annotations render learners' thinking visible to both peers and the teacher, facilitating collective scaffolding and formative assessment.

In this context, we now suggest eight specific ways for utilizing DSR tools to (1) notice grammatical structures, (2) apply vocabulary glossing, (3) instigate conversations on reading content, (4) engage critical thinking on arguments, (5) make inferences, (6) dissect model texts, (7) reconstruct ideas, and (8) craft source-based writing. These eight tasks have been refined through extensive use with second language learners in online collaborative higher education environments. Although we introduce DSR tasks sequentially, teachers can adapt and implement multiple tasks according to the unique needs and language proficiency levels of the learners. Similarly, the extent of guidance and scaffolding included in the lesson plan should be tailored to align with learner interests, cognitive capabilities, and the specific multimodal texts chosen for exploration, discovery, and educational objectives.

The selected texts may encompass webpages, engaging news articles, passages created for language instruction, and scholarly research articles. In addition to written content, these multimedia resources can include photos, graphs, statistical data, figures, or video materials with varying levels of complexity and difficulty. While it is possible to apply these tasks and prompts in traditional face-to-face settings, the utilization of DSR tools enhances the visibility of learners' thoughts to some extent through their highlights, comments, and responses. In online settings, these tools allow learners to annotate, comment, and respond without the need for frequent file exchanges. In addition, learners can easily identify the specific segments referred to in their peers' remarks.

Our DSR pedagogy underpins these eight tasks by illustrating how to effectively enhance digital social reading tasks for the purpose of facilitating source-based writing. This includes the components of NICER (Noticing grammatical structures, Instigating conversations on reading content, Crafting source-based writing, Engaging critical analysis of arguments, and Reconstructing ideas). Furthermore, we stress the importance of implementing VIM (Vocabulary glossing, making Inferences, and dissecting Model texts) with diligence when analyzing and interpreting model texts to reinforce the core principles of our DSR pedagogy. Importantly, our pedagogy promotes the utilization of collaborative reading strategies to improve comprehension, bolster writing skills, and equip teachers with procedures and prompts that guide learners in assisting each other.

In no way do we wish to suggest that these eight DSR tasks encompass all potential ways DSR can support the achievement of learning objectives or the various strategies teachers can employ to scaffold source-based writing instruction and enhance learners' socio-pragmatic interactions and engagement. However, the list of DSR tasks provides examples of pedagogical activities to initiate discussions on how to effectively promote the ways in which learners interact with digital texts, utilize linguistic and semiotic resources for meaning construction, and, importantly, engage in multimodal communication within these dynamic contexts.

We organized the DSR tasks into three phases of escalating complexity so that teachers who aim to implement learner-centered activities in online collaborative learning settings could have multiple valuable assessment points to verify that their learners are making progress toward the learning objectives outlined in the curriculum or course syllabus. While the tasks are introduced sequentially, it is important to highlight that each task stands alone and is independent of the next one. Even so, many a task can complement each other and be carried out concurrently. Second language learners may start to recognize the advantages of participating in one or more DSR tasks during online learning. The tasks are categorized based on their function in either processing or transforming knowledge (refer to Table 1). Nonetheless, teachers have the freedom to select from among them, taking into account the unique requirements of their particular context. This flexibility has the potential to enhance source-based writing by aligning it with students' actual task performance and social annotation behaviors. Following a brief rationale, argument, or example, each of the eight DSR tasks to be discussed next is summarized in a tabular format for easy presentation and subsequent analysis.

Noticing grammatical structures

Schmidt (1990) suggested that learners need to consciously notice the input before they can be expected to improve their linguistic abilities. Accordingly, when learners begin to read L2 texts without explicit emphasis, the noticing of specific grammatical structures is not always guaranteed. This is especially crucial for learners with low proficiency levels since it may be their first time encountering a particular grammar point. In some cases, especially when working with texts specifically written to introduce a grammatical structure, DSR tools can be an excellent vehicle towards guiding learners in noticing said grammatical structure on a conscious level. A DSR task so conceived exemplifies the productive use of the highlighting feature, which, in turn, prompts learners to attend to the form: highlighting increases the likelihood of noticing it. Jourdenais and colleagues (1995) examined college students' experience in a Spanish course where the experimental group received reading texts that included highlighted preterit and imperfect verbs as opposed to the control group who did not receive any textual enhancement. Following the reading activity, the groups were asked to write a piece similar to what they had read. The participants in the experimental group were able to produce target forms more than the group who did not receive textual enhancement. All participants participated in a think-aloud protocol during the writing stage where they talked about how they were making choices as they formed their sentences. The analysis of this think-aloud data showed that textual enhancement can indeed promote noticing as experimental group talked more about the use of preterit and imperfect forms (Jourdenais et al., 1995). With teacher's guidance, learners' annotations in DSR environments could be used as the textual enhancement that could assist learners with noticing target forms.

Helping learners to consciously notice the target input is thus a necessary first step towards raising their awareness of a specific grammatical structure. Thereafter, learners should be asked to construct hypotheses on its usage. Once learners are familiar with how a structure is used in natural contexts, they could then be asked to notice any violations needing correction. Their attempts at using the target form independently completes the cycle of noticing and awareness-raising. Important to note here is the observation that by gradually increasing the level of task difficulty, learners are afforded distinct occasions to first become familiar with the structure targeted before being asked to form their own utterances. The assistance of MKOs in their respective online collaboration groups both strengthens and enhances the development and acquisition of the form/structure(s) under discussion. Learners' confidence may improve as well.

Table 2. Noticing grammatical structures

Rationale and Purpose: Awareness of grammatical structures is best noticed in the input learners receive. This task recognizes the importance of authentic input, brings conscious understanding to observed structures, and fosters the development and acquisition of the form/structure(s) under discussion.
Phase 1: Learners demonstrate noticing of grammatical structure(s).   – Highlight all gerunds and verbs preceding them.   – Highlight passive voice structures in paragraph. Who is carrying out the action? Highlight information where available and as needed.   – Highlight plural marker at end of plural nouns without including letters from singular noun. How many versions do you see? Do you notice a spelling pattern?   – Highlight relative pronouns in paragraph. What are they referring to?
Phase 2: Learners receive new reading input that includes errors regarding the target form. They correct the mistakes that they could see. This phase could be recycled at the end of Phase 3 as a peer-feedback exercise for learner-created output.   – Pay attention to plural nouns. Some of them contain errors. Use comment feature to suggest corrected versions.   – Confirm whether the subjects carry out the action in the following sentences. Do you need to change the sentences from active voice to passive voice?

Table 2. *(continued)*

– Paragraph contains mistakes in terms of subject-verb agreement. Find and correct the mistakes therein.
– Some sentences have incorrect relative pronouns. Find and write the correct pronouns in your comments.

– Phase 3: Learners construct new sentences by employing grammatical structure(s) targeted. Choose two sentences in passive voice. In your comments, write the negative versions of them.
– Choose another sentence and pose a question in passive voice using a question word (e.g., where, how, why, when, what, how often).
– Respond to your group members' questions in full sentences by referring to the information present in the paragraph.
– These statements contradict the information in a passage. In your comments, negate statements and write another full sentence containing the correct information.

Applying vocabulary glossing

In our second language classes, we invariably encourage our students not to get stuck on words they do not know, but instead carry out lexical inferencing (Haustrup, 1991, as cited in Prior et al., 2014) by referring to the available linguistic cues surrounding the word. Cultivating this skill is a profitable investment for future reading practices since using contextual clues for lexical inferencing makes texts more comprehensible (Ilahude et al., 2021; Oclarit & Casinillo, 2021; Stevani et al., 2022; Tuyen & Huyen, 2019) and thus possibly less intimidating. In fact, involving learners in the steps required to identify the words that appear to play a key role in understanding the message the author is trying to convey is an intervention that requires serious consideration. Couched in the pedagogical principles of a learner-centered approach, such meaningful interventions/scaffolds allow teachers to address specific vocabulary items and, importantly, show the contribution these words make to text coherence and text cohesion, respectively. Prompts in the first stage direct learners' attention to words with particular functions. Attending to transitional words or phrases (also called linking words or connecting words) is particularly helpful in critical thinking exercises since such words help carry thoughts forward from one sentence to another and one paragraph to another. They are the 'cues' that help the reader interpret the author's ideas, that is, how authors piece together their ideas into a logically coherent argument. Studying them closely helps learners see how transitional words link sentences and paragraphs together smoothly so that there are no abrupt jumps or breaks between ideas. In the next stage, we recommend that teachers model how to select unknown words that are likely to impede text understanding. The final stage invites learners to look at the contextual clues surrounding unknown words to guess their meanings, a much helpful strategy when reading texts containing unknown lexemes or other linguistic/semiotic structures.

Table 3. Applying vocabulary glossing

Rationale and Purpose: Inferring meaning from context makes deconstructing author meaning possible. This task helps learners explore and discover text cohesion and text coherence as exemplified in the logical flow of ideas and selected words/phrases.

Phase 1: Learners identify words or phrases used for specific functions. They also search for keywords based on teacher's brief descriptions or clues.
– Highlight and label...
  – words or phrases indicating sequence.
  – transitional words or phrases used for connecting contrasting ideas.
  – transitional words or phrases used for adding more items or ideas.
  – transitional words or phrases used for connecting cause-and-effect.
  – words or phrases implying generalization.
  – words or phrases expressing frequency.
  – words or phrases introducing examples.
– Highlight two words or phrases describing quality of food.
– Highlight words or phrases suggesting uncertainty.

Phase 2: Learners highlight unknown words or phrases impeding understanding.
– Highlight unknown words or phrases making understanding of text difficult.

Phase 3: Learners use contextual clues to guess the meaning of highlighted words or phrases.
– Look at the words/phrases your group members and I [the teacher] highlighted. Refer to the rest of the sentence, the previous sentence, and the following sentence. Are there any transition words/phrases between those sentences that give you some idea about the logical flow of ideas here?
– Add a comment and guess the meaning of the highlighted words/phrases. Tell your group members what aided your guess(es).
– Consult an online dictionary. Were your group's guesses correct? If not, clarify why not.
– Do you know any synonyms for the words/phrases highlighted? If yes, write them in your comments.

Instigating reading content conversations

For collaboration to be both effective and efficient, peer interactions need to lead to reciprocal dialogues that enrich learners' thinking on an issue under discussion. Peer interaction among learners can promote a learner-centered environment because it allows learners to negotiate meaning and think critically, the combination of which invites knowledge building and deeper understanding of the material (Scardamalia & Bereiter, 2006). Following a social constructivism perspective, learners often offer different viewpoints and frames of reference shaped by their cultural and historical backgrounds. Consequently, uncovering alternative perspectives to grasp the complexities of an author's argument is key to engaging learners in socially anchored interactions. Learners could be asked to disclose surface-level knowledge present in the text by generating a list of items, pointing at key ideas, and defending textual evidence. In particular, the highlighting and underlining features of the DSR tools are most helpful at this stage because learners can employ them as they see fit when they are responding to a prompt encouraging them to highlight/underline the textual chunk in question. The next stage involves use of the commenting feature as learners present their opinions and stances. Finally, learners engage in a discussion of their positionality by responding to each other's comments. They are thus encouraged to make connections to prior knowledge and take advantage of any other multimodal resource available to them other than the reading text. We note here that these interactions not only help guide learners in forming their understanding of the text, but, even more importantly, perhaps, also refine insights gained whilst applying the new lexical items in the text.

Table 4. Instigating reading content conversations

Rationale and Purpose: Understanding learner meaning-making processes both enhances and undergirds knowledge building and critical thinking. This task focuses cognitive energy on the options to be considered and their evaluations during socially anchored learner interactions.
Phase 1: Learners identify opinions and/or issues present in the reading passage. – According to the author, what are the advantages and disadvantages of decreasing the sales tax? Indicate them in the text. – What does the author think about the cultural impact of partaking in the European Union? Support your answer by referring to the relevant parts of the text. – How does the author feel about implementing a carbon tax to fight climate change? What benefits and/or downsides does the text address? – Does the author acknowledge or refute counterarguments? – According to the author, what problems do online multiplayer games present? – What solutions does the author offer to ease the unemployment problem caused by artificial intelligence which is already replacing certain jobs humans perform?
Phase 2: Learners share opinions regarding the issue(s) discussed. – Do you agree with the author's stance against carbon tax as a viable measure to slow down global warming? – In your opinion, does playing video games influence teenagers? Is there any research to back up your rationale?

Table 4. *(continued)*

- What do you think about the author's predictions concerning the changes in our future lives as a result of improved robots and artificial intelligence? Are they realistic? Do you have any other predictions of your own? What would you tell the author about these concerns?
- Do you think the author's suggestions are effective? What are some of the shortcomings in addressing this problem?

Phase 3: Learners respond to their group members' opinions and provide supporting evidence for their own stance.
- Explain your agreement or disagreement with your group members' perspectives.
- Engage in internet research and present the evidence you find to support your opinion.
- If the evidence you gathered contradicts your group members' arguments, see if your group members would consider it.
- Respond to your group members' comments. Do you think the evidence they shared with you refutes the integrity of your position? Why or why not? Explain your rationale.

Engaging critical thinking on arguments

Kuhn (1991) offers some key skills of argument including differentiating between opinions and evidence, supporting a perspective with evidence, acknowledging other perspectives and possible evidence, evaluating the credibility of evidence, and forming relations between counterarguments and rebuttals. Engaging learners in critical thinking exercises where they implement these skills is crucial for their reading comprehension and ability to form sound arguments. Accordingly, the prompts in this task help guide learners how to think about data objectivity in texts they are asked to read. By asking learners to deconstruct the components of an argument, their ability to judge the linguistic/semiotic functions present in an argument is maximized. Additionally, learners refine their perception of how best to evaluate argument credibility. In so doing, learners also learn how to justify their own positions with details supporting dialogic exchanges the DSR tool facilitates ever so readily. The quality of their writing output, too, is likely to be influenced by such tactful engagement as they will transform knowledge from reliable sources and incorporate them to support their points.

Table 5. Engaging critical thinking on arguments

Rationale and Purpose: Critical thinking is a fundamental by-product of refined understanding and deep reflection. This task forges linkages between the deconstruction of multimodal texts and the reconstruction of evidence-based arguments and axiological stances learners are able to negotiate and defend during dialogic exchanges.

Phase 1: Learners identify argument components.
- Are there analogies present in the text? If yes, clearly indicate what is being compared here.

Table 5. *(continued)*

- Locate cause-and-effect relationships suggested in the text. Label the cause and the effect accordingly.
- Label facts.
- Label subjective statements (e.g., beliefs, opinions, feelings).
- Label generalizations. What is the sample in those generalizations? What is the population?
- What are the underlying assumptions in the [highlighted] statement?
- What seems to be the primary cause of the stated problem?

Phase 2: Learners examine text tone.
- What is the author's purpose in writing this essay?
- What is the author's stance against the problem presented?
- Does the author address counter perspectives to the issue? If yes, locate and label rebuttal accordingly.
- How does the author support the argument(s) presented? What kind of supports are used herein? Label them accordingly.
- What is the author's conclusion?

Phase 3: Learners critique argument strength by examining line of logic.
- Add comments on the supports: Are they relevant or valid to the argument made? Think here about the context, sources of authority, objectivity, and truth.
- Are the situations in this [highlighted] analogy really similar?
- Does this [highlighted] premise lead to the author's conclusion? Are there any logical fallacies?
- How would you strengthen this argument? Would you omit or modify any of the supports present? What would you add as new support? How would you change the conclusion?

Making inferences

As expected, in a DSR setting, learners are afforded ample opportunities to demonstrate their abstract thinking moves in a transparent manner: highlighting, underlining, responding. Learner interactions with texts and each other thus provide teachers with valuable data concerning performance and learning progress. At the same time, annotations produced can serve both as snapshots and as formative assessments of overall learner performance and progress. In order to determine whether learners comprehend the text or not, teachers are advised to structure discussions in ways that encourage astute reasoning with evidence and build-in explanations. Learners who are unable to summarize the text they just read are learners who failed to understand the text (Hedgecock & Ferris, 2009). It stands to reason then that guiding learners on the why's and how's of creating summaries may well be a productive and meaningful way for them to check and confirm anew their comprehension of the text(s) read. Furthermore, learners need to make text connections beyond mere surface features in order to reach viable conclusions and interpretations befitting the meaning the author had in mind when writing the text. For best results, we advise teachers provide learners with the support structures they are likely to need to attain deep understanding. When looking "below the surface of things," it is advisable that learners generate their own set of questions to answer. Specifically, interpreting metaphors (or any other type of figurative or idiomatic language) or making inferences based on the clues present in the text pushes learners to become more deeply immersed in the text — a reading behavior that should be replicated again and again when reading culturally authentic texts rich in idiomatic knowledge (see, for example, Liontas, 2018, 2019, 2021a, 2021b, 2021c). Concurrently, teachers are advised to closely monitor learners' in-group interactions and support individual learners or groups as needed should difficulties with summarizing or interpreting ideas arise.

Table 6. Making inferences

Rationale and Purpose: This task encapsulates learner behavior during reading comprehension and the ways learners can profitably apply their thinking skills to generate nuanced enquiries, information processing and reasoning constructs, and, finally, evaluative and creative stances befitting reading comprehension and writing growth.

Phase 1: Learners show evidence of reading comprehension as they answer teacher's questions and respond to prompts. Should confusion arise, they can pose their own questions.
- What factors increase the risk of wildfires? Locate these factors in the text.
- What accelerates the spread of wildfires? How could wildfires be prevented? Find strategies named in the text.
- Why did the author include this [highlighted] section? Does it help readers understand the passage better?
- What are the pros and cons of _____? Mark them in the text.
- Show the sentence supporting the idea that global warming increased the frequency of wildfires.
- Write a title for each section.
- Why does the author compare forests to lungs?

Phase 2: Learners summarize text.
- What is the text's main idea? Rewrite main idea in your own words.
- Which parts of this article do you consider the most important ones? Why? Explain.
- What are the three stages of _____? / What are the three reasons behind _____?
- Write a brief summary of this article by referring to your group's annotations. Include the author's motivation, the main idea, the causes of ___, and the author's final suggestion.

Phase 3: Learners make inferences from text.
- In your opinion, why did the author include this [highlighted] graph? What role does the information included play here?
- Do you think the author would agree with the following statement? _____ Provide evidence from the text.

Table 6. *(continued)*

– What do you think motivated the author to write this essay? What does the author want to accomplish with this essay?
– Based on the statistics given by the author, can you reasonably predict the future of _____?

Dissecting model texts

Genre-based writing pedagogy suggests that organizational and linguistic elements in written work need to be explicitly shown to learners through deconstruction (Martin, 1999; Rothery, 1996) so that learners can effectively engage in joint and independent writing in the target genre. Dissecting model texts could be a useful exercise that enables learners to see stylistic patterns in the format and enhance their vocabulary choices (Andrade et al., 2010; Kang, 2020; Tieu & Baker, 2023). To go from conceptual knowledge to procedural knowledge in source-based writing tasks, learners would need to read model texts and even become familiar with the organizational patterns therein. Exemplary texts in the target genre could thus provide the necessary insights they would need to construct their own essays. Even so, without proper scaffolding or teacher guidance, some learners may fail to recognize patterns of usage or outlines of convention within the text. In this task, therefore, DSR tools are employed as the vehicle for 'collective scaffolding.' Learners identify the location of the main idea and the evidence supporting it, highlight the marked use of transition words, and make comments as needed regarding the outline of the sample text. In case they fail to notice certain textual features on their own, an MKO in their groups could reveal those elements that would otherwise be missed. In keeping with a proactive DSR pedagogy where learners are empowered to develop their own agency, they should feel free to ask each other questions sans preconceived judgments to affirm their understanding of any technical concepts regarding writing. It stands to reason that encouraging learners to apply analytical thinking on the model texts selected for training may better prepare them to become autonomous writers, indeed skillful writers, who could actually produce texts in the target genre following preestablished cultural norms and practices.

Table 7. Dissecting model texts

Rationale and Purpose: Learner familiarity with text structure and writing conventions is intended to contribute to their autonomy in writing. This task encourages several annotation moves learners could make when asked to produce their own texts featuring target genre norms and practices. The sample prompts in this task are geared towards argumentative essays but they could be adapted to requirements of other genres.

Table 7. *(continued)*

Phase 1: The instructor forms small groups of three or four, uploads a model text for each group, and provides a preliminary list of items learners need to locate in the text.
- Highlight the main idea in each paragraph.
- Identify the thesis statement.
- Find representative sentences and determine, based on the supporting evidence presented, if these sentences can be regarded as statistical data, examples, anecdotes, research studies, expert opinions, or historical facts.

Phase 2: Learners work in groups to highlight transition words and comment on the strength of the supporting evidence the author provided.
- Highlight the verbs the author uses when introducing support structures.
- Is there a direct connection between supporting evidence and main idea?
- Are the sources of support credible?
- Do you think you need to know more details about the supporting evidence?
- Find the transitional words and determine if they signal similarities, contrasts, cause-and-effect relationships, sequences, examples, or additional support.

Phase 3: Learners discuss connections between ideas and the rhetorical style of model text(s).
- What does the author wish to achieve in writing this essay? How would you characterize the overall tone?
- In what specific ways does the author apply in the essay his/her logos, pathos, and ethos?
- Is the author's reasoning in the essay inductive or deductive in nature?
- Does the author elaborate on the supports provided in a coherent manner?
- Referring to your annotations, create an outline of this essay in a shared document.

Note: Following completion of model text analysis via the DSR tool, encourage learners to brainstorm their own text and create an outline for it.

Reconstructing ideas

The ability to reconstruct an idea has long been a fundamental skill in L2 writing. A textual borrowing technique could equip learners with lexical and syntactical resources that they could transfer into their written pieces (Allen & Goodspeed, 2018; Maxim, 2009). Learners with diverse academic and cultural backgrounds in online learning settings may need explicit instruction and deliberate practice in paraphrasing/reconstructing techniques, especially if they are to write well-supported essays without committing acts of plagiarism in the process since they may not know how to identify important elements to borrow and how to use them in their writing (Maxim, 2009). Currie (1998) suggests teachers look at plagiarism critically from the perspective of a language learner and offers helpful advice on how best to support students who struggle to cope with the demands of a new academic community. She argues that second language learners may be committing plagiarism not necessarily to copy certain ideas, but instead to implement the linguistic properties their fields require. At the same time, teachers may be reinforcing plagiarism unintentionally when they fail to provide adequate guidance in the construction of an assignment, thereby leaving learners with nothing else but their textbook(s) serving as models. A process-based approach to writing assignments with a purpose and for a purpose can aid students' confidence and skills in the tasks they are expected to complete. According to Hirvela and Du (2013), engaging learners in paraphrasing exercises requires close reading of the very texts students are likely to use as prime sources to enhance their reading and writing skills. Through paraphrasing, students prepare for even more comprehensive and efficient writing assignments. Indeed, by prompting learners to change sentence speech, voice, and lexical elements, learners are afforded ample opportunities to creatively construct and reconstruct multiple versions of the same idea while also participating in constructive peer feedback which could increase their awareness of the qualities of a good paraphrase.

Table 8. Reconstructing ideas

Rationale and Purpose: Plagiarism, as unintentional as it may often be, is the result of learners trying to rewrite in their own words a particular source statement. This task encourages the use of specific reading-writing strategies learners can employ when composing novel paraphrases befitting their collective interpretations of source texts such as research articles and public reports.
Phase 1: Learners identify parts of speech in a given sentence that describe research findings. Thereafter, they suggest synonyms, antonyms, or both, for each chunk identified.   – Divide information into smaller units by highlighting responses to these questions: Who did the research? Where did the research take place? When was this research conducted? Who were the participants? What did they find?   – Highlight the subject, verb, object, and adverb in the sentences.   – Provide a synonym or antonym for each chunk you and your group members highlighted.
Phase 2: Learners change the structure of the original sentence and rewrite the chunks.   – Convert the verb of the sentence into a noun.   – Change passive voice into active voice.   – Change sentence tense to past from present.   – Use a relative clause to describe the study's participants.   – Write a sentence that begins with "According to Dr. Bright, ...".   – Write another sentence that begins with "Dr. Bright concluded/claimed/argued that..."
Phase 3: Learners select the most crucial information to (re)construct their paraphrases. Responding to the paraphrases/reconstructions of their peers, they make modifications and offer alternatives using different structures and vocabulary.   – You will use this information to support the following main idea: "...."

Table 8. *(continued)*

– Choose the most relevant pieces of information in this sentence and eliminate the rest.
– Tell your group members why you think you should exclude any chunks.
– Write a new sentence using the chunks you just wrote.
– Respond to your group members' sentences. Are they elaborate enough to support the main idea? Do you need to add or remove anything here?
– Modify as needed your group members' versions by using different vocabulary and/or grammatical structures.

Crafting source-based writing

The ability to use source texts for textual borrowing establishes the basis for academic writing and reading, so Hirvela and Du (2013) advise us. Indeed, learners are expected to distinguish relevant and important ideas within the source texts as they begin to plan their writing. To this end, Bai and Wang (2020) proposed a framework for self-regulated reading-to-write in ESL/EFL. Said framework involved the strategies of "mining reading, writerly reading, cognitive strategies, purposive reading, recalling while writing, and peer revision reading" (p.1). The authors posited that when learners were self-regulated during source-based writing task, they would be motivated to search for reading materials, evaluate the reading source and its components, and select information pertinent to their written product. So contextualized, this DSR task aims to promote the use of the aforementioned self-regulation strategies along distinct pathways of learning involving pre-writing, during-writing, and post-writing. The annotation functions of DSR tools constitute a feasible environment for making the use of such strategies both visible and accessible. Learners can easily search for sources, evaluate their relevance and credibility, and pay close attention to important writing conventions as discussed earlier in the 'dissecting model texts' task. Further, learners can employ cognitive strategies while also extracting lists of information from the source texts. Information collected can then be used to create summaries and synthesize information and interpretation of ideas into plausible explanations befitting a logical line of argumentation and justification. Lastly, learners can evaluate their own writing as well as that of their peers, thereby improve their output in significant ways.

Table 9. Crafting source-based writing

Rationale and Purpose: Source-based writing requires learners engage in purposive reading, critical thinking, and paraphrasing. This task supports these behaviors and provides learners with repeated opportunities to self-regulate their learning progress as they reflect on learning, engage in shared negotiations, and analyze, reason, and evaluate each other's communicative intents.

Table 9. *(continued)*

Phase 1: Learners read source texts and determine which information they wish to integrate into their arguments by highlighting phrases as needed. Following that, they evaluate the credibility of the source content in their comments.

– Consider your argument and essay topic. As you read this passage, highlight and label the information that supports your point of view.
– Is there any information contradicting your stance? If yes, label it accordingly.
– In your comments, discuss if these sources are objective. Address any potential biases therein.
– Find another source about this issue. Provide the link here. [Phase 1 will be initiated for these additional resources.]

Phase 2: Learners paraphrase chunks they decide to integrate into their group essay. They highlight vocabulary they can use in their writing. They then compose their first draft using an online word processor.

– Which key terms do you plan to include in your essay? Highlight them.
– Use your own words and rewrite the information you plan to transfer to your essay.
– Read your peers' paraphrases. Do they cover all the essential information in the original text? Revise as necessary.
– Use this Google Docs link to create an outline of your essay.
– Consider your thesis statement and write a main idea for each paragraph. Are the main ideas directly related to your thesis?
– Discuss with your group members and decide where in the plan you intend to place your paraphrases.

Phase 3: Groups exchange essays. Learners give and receive peer feedback on first drafts. At the end, they revise their essays and reflect on progress.

– What is the tone of the essay?
– Highlight the supporting evidence. Is the evidence clearly linked to the main ideas?
– Highlight the rebuttals the authors addressed. Did they respond to the rebuttal effectively? (If there is none, think about how you would oppose such theses statements. Thereafter, leave a comment asking group members to respond to your point.)
– Leave a comment pointing out sections needing further elaboration.
– Leave a comment pointing out confusing segments needing further clarification.
– Read your classmates' feedback. Discus how you would improve this essay and revise it accordingly.

Challenges and pedagogical implications

Even though annotation tasks through DSR tools constitute a viable platform where learners can display their thinking on the text in a social constructivist paradigm, researchers and language practitioners alike intending to incorporate them into their teaching need to first consider plausible challenges impacting peer interaction processes and then develop the strategies needed to mitigate such difficulties. To be more precise, unfamiliarity with the tool, location-based restrictions, and lack of mutuality of contributions in the group may well interrupt the expected collaboration among learners heretofore explicated. In anticipation of such shortcomings, we offer next a few suggestions researchers and language practitioners may want to consider prior to forging ahead with plans intended to exploit the benefits of applying DSR in online collaborative contexts.

First, scaffolding needs to be initiated by familiarizing learners with using the DSR tool, particularly when learners have no prior experience with DSR. In order for online collaboration to proceed smoothly, learners need to be equipped with digital literacy skills necessary to download and/or sign-up to the DSR environments. Teachers are advised to organize an informational session to familiarize learners with the DSR tool of choice and prepare guiding documents as needed in case tutorial or troubleshooting solutions are called for. Screen recorded tutorials may be helpful resources as well. The initial stages of annotation should include simple prompts that only practice the functions of the tool with everyone in class. Learners should be grouped only after making sure they are able to highlight and add comments independently. Otherwise, the instructor may experience difficulty in guiding the struggling learners in multiple small groups at the same time. Consequently, some learners may be unfairly deprived of the opportunity to demonstrate their thinking and share their perspectives in groups, which could impede their collaboration due to reduced mutuality in their interactions. By ensuring everyone's mastery at various interaction types, lack of command of a newly introduced tool does not act as a hindrance on learning.

Second, in online collaborative contexts requiring dialogic interactions, location-based restrictions may unnecessarily challenge learners' access to the DSR tools. In our experience, some countries have been known to ban access to certain foreign applications and platforms. DSR tools may well be among those banned or restricted. Learners may need to circumvent these bans or restrictions by resorting to VPNs that are notoriously complicated or expensive to use. Teachers interested in applying DSR in distance learning contexts should first confirm everyone's access before deciding which DSR tool to use. Time-zone differences between learners' locations may yet be another location-based restriction that needs to be considered here as some learners may end up with less time to respond to their peers. However, grouping learners according to analogous time zones may well remedy such a challenge.

Third, peer interaction, when executed with care and forethought, is expected to contribute to language learning (Erdemir & Brutt-Griffler, 2020; Jacob et al., 1996; Pinter, 2007; Zeng & Takatsuka, 2009). Even so, teachers are asked to bear in mind that despite evidence to the contrary, some learners' need for assistance may not be fully met if they fail to ask the right questions, or if their peers do not respond to their calls for help in a way that benefits knowledge building in general and second language acquisition in particular, irrespective of the context or the opportunities strategically created for them. It thus behooves teachers to monitor the progress of collaboration and, furthermore, structure — to the extent possible — all cooperative learning tasks in a dynamic way that epitomizes socially anchored discussions promoting learner agency and development of research-rich reading practices. For that purpose, teachers can guide learners with prompts that first demand noticing ideas, concepts, or components, then ask for elaboration, interpretation, or revision, and finally synthesize information and exchange opinions. While doing so, reading across various research articles, books, and websites may allow students to explore various perspectives, develop a deeper understanding of the subject matter and develop a more nuanced viewpoint. In turn, students may transfer the knowledge they acquired from reading into their writing and employ stylistic patterns relevant to the genre of their writing. To promote everyone's engagement in knowledge formation and transfer, it may be necessary to give learners specific instructions and create assessment criteria requiring individuals to contribute in distinct forms (e.g., responding to peers, interpreting statements, asking for clarification, etc.) could easily prevent the domination of annotations by only a few learners.

Finally, as learners work in groups to annotate the text, they may experience difficulty in finding new ideas to share (Thoms & Poole, 2018). Providing a variety of prompts and encouraging opinion-sharing may well expand the scope of things learners are asked to address in their respective annotations. Moreover, some learners may not even revisit the text after posting their comments, as laconic as they may well be, thus interrupting the dialogic space envisaged herein. Assigning multiple deadlines within a single task stage may curtail such learner disposition while also increasing the likelihood that everyone's contribution to shared learning is valued and acknowledged. Limiting group membership to either three or four students may yet be another feasible strategy to employ here to avoid the replication of similar contributions resulting from groups larger than five members.

Conclusion

The employment of DSR tools has a lot of potential for online collaborative learning as it makes learners' thinking visible on the texts. Source-based writing requires learners to engage in many reading and writing moves. Although we have structured the eight DSR tasks in isolation, it is equally possible to follow an eclectic approach permitting the cultivation of procedures and prompts addressing two or more tasks in parallel in classroom practice. Choice selection aside, it is important to reiterate that language learners will continue to face comprehension difficulties for as long as the learning gaps resulting from lexical, linguistic, or semiotic choices made are allowed to exist. Therefore, it is crucial for educators to guide learners to address these gaps and help learners employ moves to overcome comprehension difficulties. By implementing a diverse range of DSR prompts, teachers can equip learners with the necessary tools to achieve comprehension and critique of given ideas.

For students to become efficient readers in the target language, explicit instruction in (meta)cognitive and social/affective strategies is therefore paramount. Reading strategies often include previewing, skimming and scanning, identifying textual components, guessing from the context, and paraphrasing. Asking learners to interact with reading texts is not enough. All interactions, from the simplest to the most complex, must have purpose and be defined by purpose. For optimal results, teachers should carefully pick among proposed tasks whose prompt complexity align with the learners' proficiency levels, their needs, and the learning objectives. Each task learners are asked to perform must be preceded by a purpose learners can name, explain, and evaluate at a moment's notice. To appreciate the functions performed, learners must know the purpose(s) these tasks fulfill either individually or in combination. To establish a solid foundation for dynamic online collaborative contexts in the future, it is essential to comprehend the task, approach, purpose, and expected dialogue interactions. This understanding offers a clear sense of direction and meaning.

In sum, the socially anchored interactions discussed heretofore function as a collective scaffold that helps learners of varying abilities and dispositions advance in their ZPD with the assistance of MKOs. Integrating structured prompts with gradually increasing complexity in DSR tasks, despite noted challenges in facilitating meaningful collaboration, can promote learner autonomy within the affordances and constraints the efficient use of DSR tools presents in dynamic online settings.

References

Allen, H., & Goodspeed, L. (2018). Textual borrowing and perspective-taking: A genre-based approach to L2 writing. *L2 Journal*, 10(2), 87–110.

Andrade, H., Du, Y., & Mycek, K. (2010). Rubric-referenced self-assessment and middle school students' writing. *Assessment in Education: Principles, Policy & Practice*, 17, 199–214.

Chapter 7. Developing digital social reading in source-based writing

Bai, B., & Wang, J. (2020). Conceptualizing self-regulated reading-to-write in ESL/EFL writing and investigating its relationships to motivation and writing competence. *Language Teaching Research*, 27(5).

Beauvois, M. (1995). E-talk: Attitudes and motivation in computer-assisted classroom discussion. *Computers and the Humanities*, 28(2), 177–190.

Chun, D. (2011). Computer assisted language learning. In E. Hinkel (Ed.), *Handbook of research in second language teaching and learning* (Vol. II, pp. 663–680). Routledge.

Currie, P. (1998). Staying out of trouble: Apparent plagiarism and academic survival. *Journal of Second Language Writing*, 7(1), 1–18.

Donato, R. (1994). Collective scaffolding in second language learning. In J. Lantolf & G. Appel (Eds.), *Vygotskian approaches to second language research* (pp. 33–56). Ablex.

Dooly, M. (2017). Telecollaboration. In C.A. Chapelle & S. Sauro (Eds.), *The handbook of technology and second language teaching and learning* (pp. 169–183). Wiley-Blackwell.

Erdemir, E., & Brutt-Griffler, J. (2020). Vocabulary development through peer interactions in early childhood: A case study of an emergent bilingual child in preschool. *International Journal of Bilingual Education and Bilingualism*, 25, 834–865.

Gay, G. (2018). *Culturally responsive teaching: Theory, research, and practice* (3rd ed.). Teachers College Press.

Haastrup, K. (1991). *Lexical inferencing procedures or talking about words: Receptive procedures inforeign language learning with special reference to English*. Gunter Narr.

Hedgcock, J., & Ferris, D. (2009). *Teaching readers of English: Students, texts, and contexts*. Routledge.

Hill, J., & Hannafin, M. (2001). Teaching and learning in digital environments: The resurgence of resource-based learning. *Educational Technology Research and Development*, 49(3), 37–52.

Hirvela, A. (2016). *Connecting reading and writing in second language writing instruction* (2nd ed.). University of Michigan Press.

Hirvela, A., & Du, Q. (2013). "Why am I paraphrasing?": Undergraduate ESL writers' engagement with source-based academic writing and reading. *Journal of English for Academic Purposes*, 12(2), 87–98.

Ilahude, F., Fatsah, H., Luwiti, S., & Otoluwa, M. (2021). The influence of the use of context clues strategy on reading comprehension. *International Journal of Education and Social Science Research*, 4(6), 166–180.

Jacob, E., Rottenberg, L., Patrick, S., & Wheeler, E. (1996). Cooperative learning: Context and opportunities for acquiring academic English. *TESOL Quarterly*, 30, 253–280.

Jourdenais, R., Ota, M., Stauffer, S., Boyson, B., & Doughty, C. (1995). Does textual enhancement promote noticing? A think-aloud protocol analysis. In R. Schmidt (Ed.), *Attention and awareness in foreign language learning* (pp. 183–216). University of Hawai'i, Second Language Teaching & Curriculum Center.

Kang, E. (2020). Using model texts as a form of feedback in L2 writing. *System*, 89, 102196.

Kelm, O. (1998). The use of electronic mail in foreign language classes. In J. Swaffar, S. Romano, P. Markley, & K. Arens (Eds.), *Language learning online: Theory and practice in the ESL and L2 computer classroom* (pp. 1–15). Daedalus.

Kern, R. (1995). Restructuring classroom interaction with networked computers: Effects on quantity and characteristics of language production. *Modern Language Journal*, 79, 457–476.

Kiili, C., Laurinen, L., Marttunen, M., & Leu, D. J. (2012). Working on understanding during collaborative online reading. *Journal of Literacy Research*, 44(4), 448-483.

Klingner, J., Vaughn, S., & Schumm, J. (1998). Collaborative strategic reading during social studies in heterogeneous fourth-grade classrooms. *The Elementary School Journal*, 99(1), 3–22.

Klingner, J., & Vaughn, S. (2000). The helping behaviors of fifth graders while using collaborative strategic reading during ESL content classes. *TESOL Quarterly*, 34(1), 69–98.

Kroonenberg, N. (1994). Developing communicative and thinking skills via electronic mail. *TESOL Journal*, 4(2), 24–27.

Kuhn, D. (1991). *The skills of argument*. Cambridge University Press.

Lee, L. (2010). Fostering reflective writing and interactive Exchange through blogging in an advanced language course. *ReCALL*, 22(2), 212–227.

Liontas, J. (2018). Refocusing the digital lens of idiomaticity: A second look at understanding idiomaticity in CALL. *Iranian Journal of Language Teaching Research*, 6(2), 1–21.

Liontas, J. (2019). Teaching idioms and idiomatic expressions across the second language curriculum. In E. Hinkel (Ed.), *Teaching essential units of language: Beyond single-word vocabulary* (pp. 55–105). Routledge.

Liontas, J. (2021a). Figures of speech? Go figure! A baker's dozen should do it: Imagining figurative language. In I. Galantomos (Ed.), *L2 figurative language teaching: Theory and Practice* (pp. 28–64). Cambridge Scholars.

Liontas, J. (2021b). A baker's dozen plus one for the road: Reimagining figurative language. In I. Galantomos (Ed.), *L2 figurative language teaching: Theory and Practice* (pp. 65–84). Cambridge Scholars.

Liontas, J. (2021c). Attaining knowledge of idiomatics in the age of Corona and beyond. In K. Kelch, P. Byun, S. Safavi, & S. Cervantes (Eds.), *CALL theory applications for online TESOL education* (pp. 1–34). IGI Global Publishing.

Lo, J., Yeh, S., & Sung, C. (2013). Learning paragraph structure with online annotations: An interactive approach to enhancing EFL reading comprehension. *System*, 41(2), 413–427.

Lotman, Y. (1988). Text within a text. *Soviet Psychology*, 26(3), 32–51.

Martin, J. (1999). Mentoring semogenesis: 'genre-based' literacy pedagogy. In F. Christie (Ed.), *Pedagogy and the shaping of consciousness: Linguistic and social processes* (pp. 123–155). Continuum.

Maxim, H. (2009). "It's made to match": Linking L2 reading and writing through textual borrowing. In C. Brantmeier (Ed.), *Crossing languages and research methods: Analyses of adult foreign language reading* (pp. 97–122). Information Age Publishing.

Meunier, L. (1998). Personality and motivational factors in computer-mediated foreign language communication. In J.A. Muyskens (Ed.), *New ways of learning and teaching* (pp. 145–197). Heinle & Heinle.

Nor, N., Azman, H., & Hamat, A. (2013). Investigating students' use of online annotation tool in an online reading environment. *3L: Southeast Asian Journal of English Language Studies*, 19(3), 87–101.

Norris, J.M. (2009). Task-based teaching and testing. In M.H. Long & C.J. Doughty (Eds.), *The handbook of language teaching* (pp. 578–594). Wiley-Blackwell.

Oclarit, R., & Casinillo, L. (2021). Strengthening the reading comprehension of students using a context clue. *Journal of Education Research and Evaluation*, 5(3), 373–379.

Piaget, J., & Inhelder, B. (1969). *The psychology of the child* (H. Weaver, Trans.). Basic Books.

Pinter, A. (2007). Some benefits of peer — peer interaction: 10-year-old children practising with a communication task. *Language Teaching Research*, 11, 189–207.

Prior, A., Goldina, A., Shany, M., Geva, E., & Katzir, T. (2014). Lexical inference in L2: Predictive roles of vocabulary knowledge and reading skill beyond reading comprehension. *Reading and Writing*, 27, 1467–1484.

Rothery, J. (1996). Making changes: Developing an educational linguistics. In R. Hasan, & G. Williams (Eds.), *Literacy in society* (pp. 86–123). Longman.

Salaberry, R. (2000). L2 morphosyntactic development in text-based computer communication. *Computer Assisted Language Learning*, 13(1), 5–27.

Scardamalia, M., & Bereiter, C. (2006). Knowledge building: Theory, pedagogy, and technology. In R.K. Sawyer (Ed.), *The Cambridge handbook of the learning sciences* (pp. 97–119). Cambridge University Press.

Schmidt, R. (1990). The role of consciousness in second language learning. *Applied Linguistics*, 11, 17–46.

Stevani, M., Prayuda, M.S., Sari, D.W., Marianus, S.M., & Tarigan, K.E. (2022). Evaluation of contextual clues: EFL proficiency in reading comprehension. *English Review: Journal of English Education*, 10(3), 993–1002.

The New London Group. (1996). A pedagogy of multiliteracies: Designing social futures. *Harvard Educational Review*, 66(1), 60–92.

Thoms, J., & Poole, F. (2018). Exploring digital literacy practices via L2 social reading. *L2 Journal*, 10(2), 36–61.

Tieu, L., & Baker, J. (2023). Using model essays in conjunction with noticing as a feedback instrument in IELTS writing preparation. *Innovation in Language Learning and Teaching*, 17(2), 380–392.

Tseng, S., Yeh, H., & Yang, S. (2015). Promoting different reading comprehension levels through online annotations. *Computer Assisted Language Learning*, 28(1), 41–57.

Tseng, S., & Yeh, H. (2018). Integrating reciprocal teaching in an online environment with an annotation feature to enhance low-achieving students' English reading comprehension. *Interactive Learning Environments*, 26(6), 789–802.

Tuyen, L., & Huyen, V. (2019). Effects of using contextual clues on English vocabulary retention and reading comprehension. *International Journal of English Literature and Social Sciences (IJELS)*, 4(5), 1342–1347.

Vygotsky, L. (1978). *Mind in society: The development of higher psychological processes*. Harvard University Press.

Warschauer, M. (1996). Comparing face-to-face and electronic discussion in the second language classroom. *CALICO Journal*, 13(2), 7–26.

Yang, Y. (2016). Teaching Chinese college ESL writing: A genre-based approach. *English Language Teaching*, 9(9), 36–44.

Yasuda, S. (2011). Genre-based tasks in foreign language writing: Developing writers' genre awareness, linguistic knowledge, and writing competence. *Journal of Second Language Writing*, 20(2), 111–133.

Yeh, H., Hung, H., & Chiang, Y. (2017). The use of online annotations in reading instruction and its impact on students' reading progress and processes. *ReCALL*, 29(1), 22–38.

Zeng, G., & Takatsuka, S. (2009). Text-based peer-peer collaborative dialogue in a computer-mediated learning environment in the EFL context. *System*, 37, 434–446.

CHAPTER 8

Conclusion
Insights for research and praxis around DSR

Kristen Michelson
Texas Tech University

In this chapter, I present an overview of where we currently sit with respect to research in digital social reading (DSR) in L2 contexts by providing a critical synthesis of the findings and implications of the chapters in this collection and making a case for future research areas around DSR. Next, I offer an overview of technical and pedagogical considerations practitioners might wish to make when selecting a DAT for integrating DSR activities into L2 teaching and learning. Technical issues such as cost and accessibility, privacy and visibility, text types supported, and user experience are discussed, followed by pedagogical considerations for optimally matching texts, tools, and techniques. Finally, I showcase several methods and techniques from multiliteracies pedagogies, demonstrating their compatibility with DSR.

Introduction

This book emerged out of a desire to bring together research around digital social reading (DSR) in second language (L2) contexts into one collection, with the broad intentions of documenting the empirical work around DSR and providing models for practitioners who might wish to implement DSR in L2 educational settings. Although DSR is by no means a novel pedagogical activity, and research around DSR in L2 contexts has been ongoing for at least a decade, much of this work has been descriptive in nature, and scattered across isolated journal articles or book chapters.

The collected chapters in this book present empirical studies and pedagogical guides from a range of educational contexts, learner levels, L2s, pedagogical purposes, and research paradigms. In this concluding chapter, I begin with a synthesis of the collected chapters and their major contributions to the field and discuss the current state of research around DSR. Next, I synthesize the different digital annotation tools (DATs), text types, and pedagogies employed in the projects

https://doi.org/10.1075/aals.21.08mic
© 2024 John Benjamins Publishing Company

presented in this book. Finally, I discuss technical and pedagogical considerations for practitioners who might wish to implement DSR in L2 teaching and learning, including demonstrating how multiliteracies-based methods and techniques can be combined with DSR.

The affordances of DSR: Amplifier of social relations and learner behaviors

Several themes emerge from the findings across the chapters and converge around three broad areas. First, DSR can be an important site for the construction of identity and establishment of community norms of interaction. Chapters 2 and 3 each explore how learners position themselves vis à vis each other and in relation to the ideas and knowledge they are encountering in texts and demonstrate how learners enact various identities and stances through their comments and dialogues. Burhan-Horasanlı's chapter (2) demonstrates through a fine-grained discourse analysis of learners' comments in a DSR activity how these learners construct and enact positioning identities through their comments. At the same time, the DSR activity implemented in the course set up a context where learners were not only reading in community but were now engaging in a more social form of note-taking in community, as one participant noted. The contribution by Lynn and Sayılı-Hurley (Chapter 3) demonstrates, through a linguistic analysis of learners' dialogues around key texts, how DSR can mediate the development of community norms of interaction, where learners build on collective knowledge, rather than individual knowledge, demonstrating alignment with one another.

Second, learner behaviors in DSR-mediated reading are highly sensitive to the entire classroom ecology including the complex relationships that emerge in the learning setting, and the pedagogical designs around DSR. Blyth (Chapter 4) noted that his "students did not seem to pay much attention to each other's annotations while using a DAT when I first taught the course in 2021. In retrospect, this does not seem to be the fault of the DAT, but rather how I had asked my students to use the tool." Similarly, in Lynn and Sayılı-Hurleys' study (Chapter 3), even with key questions from the course professor, students did not demonstrate consistent or persistent ways of historical thinking. Although they showed movement toward the kind of thinking that is desirable in foreign language (FL) classes for developing transcultural knowledge, the tool alone cannot do the work of fostering different ways of thinking. Law, Barny, and Dorsey's study (Chapter 5) demonstrated that very few literary affordances emerged in students' annotations for texts with more metaphorical complexity, and they concluded that, "even when learners are given support in this area via glosses, they still require overt instruction and critical framing in order to take full advantage of the literary affordances that some texts offer" (Chapter 5).

Third, DSR can serve as an important site for research around text difficulty, learner characteristics, and assessment of language development. While DSR is ostensibly a tool for fostering collaborative reading, studies in this volume nevertheless demonstrate its utility as a tool for research and assessment. In Chapter 5, Law, Barny, and Dorsey demonstrate the importance of looking at text difficulty not only as a function of text-based factors — as has been traditionally done — but as a function of how learners engage with texts, thus expanding theoretical notions of text difficulty into a realm of a dynamic rather than static construct. The authors' use of the construct of affordances allows the key finding that text difficulty ultimately is not an essential property of a text but rather one that is relative to the learners engaged in the task, and the way in which the task is constructed (e.g., with the addition of glosses in this case). Chapters 2 and 3 demonstrate DSR's optimal pairing with discursive approaches to analyzing identity construction and intersubjectivity. In Chapter 2, we saw how a DAT can become a productive site of research to better understand the socially situated identity positions that learners take up in the course of their learning activities; in this case, reading scholarly articles in applied linguistics. Chapter 4 shows how DSR can foster mindful reflection on both the self and on collective learning goals. Chapter 6 demonstrates the usefulness of DSR in assessing language learners' performances over time through analysis of written comments.

In terms of pedagogical practice, Fred Poole and Joshua Thoms (Chapter 7) and Inanç Karagöz and John Liontas (Chapter 8) have provided sample activities and actionable guides through clearly articulated sets of tasks at different levels. While Karagöz and Liontas present tasks in terms of degrees or levels of cognitive complexity, Poole and Thoms present tasks in terms of ACTFL performance indicators. In both cases, the authors provide concrete ideas for instructors wishing to implement DSR with their students or use DSR tasks as a formative assessment lens.

Within the chapters in this book, innovative — and in some cases, counterintuitive — approaches to implementing DSR demonstrate its potential for driving learning and development, particularly around fostering critical thinking, and slowed down thinking and reading. The collection of chapters illuminate how DSR can serve as a companion — not replacement — for in-class work, emphasizing the continued importance of human interactions in learning. Overall, the chapters in this book collectively demonstrate that reading — as learning activity and as social activity — is more than an exercise in merely understanding words or exchanging facts, but rather it is highly sensitive to relationships between learners and the community that emerges in online and offline settings, to the semiotic affordances of texts, and to the ways that reading is scaffolded within the learning setting.

Future research directions

Despite advances in research around DSR, several questions remain in terms of the contributions of DSR to student learning processes and outcomes, students' L2 development, and to teacher effectiveness. In terms of learner processes, future research might examine the technical affordances used by L2 readers in a DSR activity. For example, in addition to glosses that are determined and provided by teachers, what additional supports do learners seek out to enhance their textual understanding? Such supports might include looking up lexical items or involve translation assistance of syntactically complex sentences, thus unblocking potential processing obstacles. Online supports might also involve looking up cultural references that would help scaffold background knowledge needed for interpretation of a text. Processes research around DSR might also investigate readers' use of peer or instructor annotations in their reading. Eye tracking methods could potentially provide rich insights into the usefulness of peer and/or instructor annotations for students' textual understanding.

Beyond solely focusing on how cognitive processes manifest themselves in DSR contexts, it would also be instructive to learn how these processes are tied to learning outcomes, whether language development, reading comprehension, or general knowledge acquisition. Relatedly, while DSR is primarily a learning tool that fosters collaborative activities (in this case, reading), DSR might also serve as a valuable research methodology in exposing and capturing cognitive processes while reading, by operating, in a way, as a think-aloud activity, however with more slowed down reflection that emerges through written instead of oral comments.

In terms of implications for teachers and learners, the field would benefit from empirical research on the effectiveness of various techniques and tools for assessing students' DSR activity. What forms of assessment capture the comprehensive ecology of learning that is taking place? What kinds of assessments drive students' actions and interactions in DSR, and how do these actions and interactions contribute, in turn, to learning? Finally, what kinds of in-the-moment teacher interaction and scaffolding are helpful for learners, and how might we train teachers in effectively interacting in DSR discussions, in terms of the frequency, length, and focus of comments? How might we train students to use DSR in different stages of their reading, such that they make the leap from close reading of isolated passages to global synthesis of an entire text?

Finally, in terms of research settings, there remains a dearth of research on DSR in L2 contexts other than English. Additionally, more research could be carried out in different L2 learning settings, such as hybrid and fully online contexts, via a wider age range of research participants, for example, understanding younger learners in immersion programs who are simultaneously developing their L1 and L2 literacies via DSR activities. These are just a few of the areas that remain elusive within the field of research around DSR in L2 contexts. I now turn to a synthesis of the texts, formats, and tools employed by the studies in this volume.

Overview of texts, tasks, and tools

The chapters in this volume represent DSR projects across a range of learning contexts, learner levels, and languages. Table 1 presents an overview of the levels, languages, tools, and configurations used in Chapters 2 through 6. Chapter 7 is omitted from this table, as it presents a more general set of pedagogical sequences for fostering literacy development that can be applied to a range of DATs and educational settings.

Table 1. Overview of learning contexts and DSR configurations

Chapter number	Course level	L2	Text types	DAT	Configurations
2	Graduate; PhD in Applied Linguistics	English	Articles from scholarly journals in Applied Linguistics	Live Margin (aka Social Book)	Three learners to a group; asynchronous, out of class; regular FTF course
3	Undergraduate; advanced collegiate German Studies course	German	Scholarly texts related to culture, identity, and history in Germany	Perusall	Three learners to a group; asynchronous, out of class; regular FTF course
4	Undergraduate; advanced collegiate French course	French	Multilingual narratives of multilingual authors writing in French; course syllabus	Google Docs	Synchronous, in class; whole class and small groups

Table 1. *(continued)*

Chapter number	Course level	L2	Text types	DAT	Configurations
5	Undergraduate; beginning collegiate French course	French	Song lyrics in French	eComma	Asynchronous; out of class; small groups
6	Undergraduate; beginning and advanced collegiate Chinese courses in language and literature/film	Chinese	Newspaper article; poems, song lyrics, and excerpts from a novel	eComma; Classroom Salon	Asynchronous; out of class; small groups

In terms of course levels, one study involved graduate students, while four studies involved undergraduate students. Of the projects involving undergraduate students, one project involved beginning language students; while two projects involved advanced L2 students, and one incorporated learners at both beginning and advanced levels. The L2s represented across the studies were Chinese, English, French (2x), and German. Configurations of reading groups were small groups, where asynchronous reading took place primarily outside of class. In one case, DSR was conducted as a synchronous activity within the space of the classroom. In all cases, DSR was a companion activity to a traditional FTF course, rather than an online course. DATs used in these studies include: Live Margin (aka, Social Book), Perusall, Google Docs, eComma (2x), and Classroom Salon. Text types involved: articles from scholarly journals in Applied Linguistics; scholarly texts related to culture, identity, and history in the context of Germany; multilingual narratives of multilingual authors writing in French; the course syllabus; song lyrics (2x); newspaper articles; poems; and excerpts from a novel.

While technology affords possibilities for expanding enrollments or co-convening learners across disparate geographical spaces, ironically, the chapters in this collection do not aim to promote DSR for these ends. In all cases, DSR was used in classroom contexts where learning took place primarily in a face-to-face environment, and the DSR activity was one of many learning activities. DSR platforms were not used to co-convene learners, but rather to create different opportunities for engagement among learners, between learners and teachers, and between learners and texts. Forms of engagement for students included co-constructing meanings around texts (Chapters 2 and 3); understanding the course syllabus and generating collective course goals (Chapter 4); slowing down reading such that it could become a mindful practice (Chapter 4); and reading with glosses (Chapter 5). For teachers, we saw how DSR can create opportunities for formative assessment (Chapter 6) and how textual awareness can be raised through guiding questions (Chapter 7). Together these studies represent specific combinations of pedagogical purposes, L2s, text types, and DATs, however, insights from these studies can be applied across a range of L2 educational settings.

Designs and considerations for implementing DSR

I turn now to an overview and discussion of technical and pedagogical considerations for implementing DSR with the intention of paving the way for other researchers and practitioners who wish to take up this topic. Several considerations come into play when selecting a DAT, including cost and accessibility, privacy and visibility, text types supported, and user experience — both in terms of the interface used by student readers, and the ease of reviewing or downloading students' comments by instructors or researchers. While some DATs have been designed specifically to support DSR (e.g., Hypothes.is and Perusall), other familiar digital tools can also be leveraged for annotation (e.g., Google Docs). The Center for Open Educational Resources and Language Learning at the University of Texas at Austin (COERLL, n.d.) maintains a wealth of resources related to digital social reading, including a list of social annotation tools, use cases from scholars and practitioners who have employed DSR in L2 educational settings, and a pedagogical guide for instructors implementing DSR.

Technical considerations: Important questions to ask when selecting a DAT

Cost and accessibility

Many DATs are free to use, while some operate on a freemium basis, and others may be available via licensing agreements. For example, Hypothes.is is a free tool that operates via a Google Chrome extension, however licensing agreements for LMS integration are available and provide additional features. Those wanting to implement DATs might consider the following questions when deciding which tool to use: Does the tool afford LMS integration or is a separate login necessary? Is a subscription necessary or can the tool be used for one-off activities? Is there a limit to the number of DSRs in which one user can participate?

Privacy and visibility

In terms of privacy, it is important to consider whether interactions take place in a closed or open network or both. Are learners reading within a private community or with anyone and everyone on the open web? If a closed network configuration is possible, is this feature included in a free version of the DAT? How easy is it to set up groups? Within a closed network setting where groupings consist of learners familiar with one another within the same class, can learners in one group see the comments of learners in another group? When the instructor responds to comments, can learners in one group see the instructors' comments made for a different group?

Supported text types

Another important technical consideration of a DAT is what text types are supported. For example, does the tool support written language? Multimodal texts? Videos? Is there an optimal text length? Additionally, what is the preferred medium of the text for a particular DAT? For example, Hypothes.is affords annotation of websites, but can also support annotation of PDFs if they are stored on a web-based platform such as Google Drive. Perusall affords annotations of PDFs. What modes are supported in the commenting features of the DAT? Can users post multimodal annotations?

User experience

One of the most important considerations contributing to student perceptions of DSR is ease of access to source texts, and ease of annotating, commenting, and reading others' comments. Users might ask: are notifications internal to the tool, requiring a user to log back into the platform to read comments, or can notifications be channeled to a users' email or phone? For instructors, what is the process for uploading texts to the DAT? Can PDFs be uploaded to the DAT or must they be converted to another format such as ePub? What is the process for creating groups? Can groups be kept intact for subsequent DSR activities throughout the term? Can changes be made easily? Finally, what affordances are there for reading or aggregating students' comments for the purposes of grading? Can transcripts be downloaded? When downloading comments is possible, does the transcript retain the originally highlighted passage, such that an instructor or researcher can evaluate or analyze a comment in light of the passage which prompted it? Figures 1 through 3 illustrate three different DATs and some of their affordances: Hypothes.is, Perusall, and Live Margin (aka Social Book).

Chapter 8. Conclusion 187

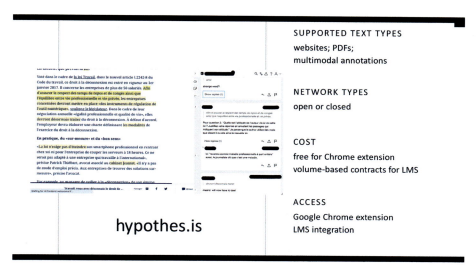

Figure 1. Hypothes.is affordances and interface

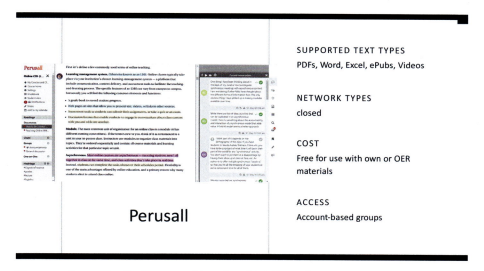

Figure 2. Perusall's affordances and interface (Bruff, 2020)

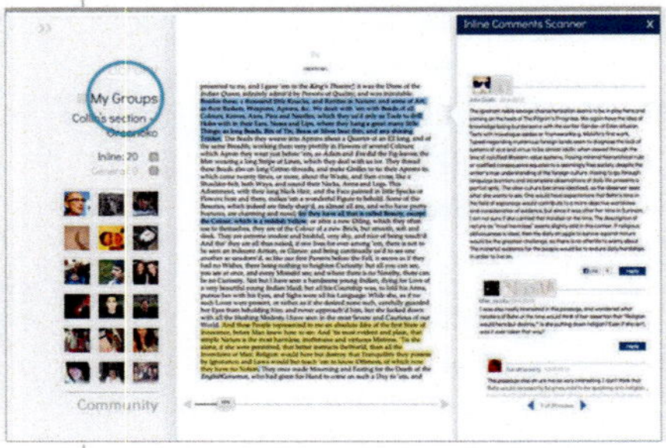

Figure 3. Social Book's affordances and interface (Social Book, 2024)

Pedagogical considerations

Beyond technical considerations, it is arguably more important to consider how the tools will be integrated with sound pedagogical design. As the chapters in this volume corroborate, the tool alone cannot do the work of scaffolding reading. Theoretically, one can combine any pedagogical techniques and methods with digital annotation tools. However, as scholarship from educational contexts beyond L2 learning has demonstrated, different tools and technologies will be more or less well-suited to particular pedagogical and/or literacy purposes. For example, Gao, Zhang, and Franklin (2012) demonstrated that anchored discussion (e.g., digital social reading) seems to be well-suited for close reading of texts and for comments on specific passages, but less effective for synthesizing across texts. Inanç Karagöz' and John Liontas' chapter offers a wide range of literacy tasks that can be flexibly applied to different educational settings and language levels, and productively combined with DSR. In addition to these pedagogical considerations and suggestions, COERLL maintains a variety of pedagogical accompaniments for DSR, including a guide for instructors addressing choosing a text, preparing a text for teaching, deciding on lesson objectives, and structuring a social reading lesson (COERLL, n.d.).

Multiliteracies as method

Overall, many of the chapters in this volume draw on multiliteracies (ML) pedagogies in the design of classroom activities with which DSR tools were integrated. Essential to ML is a grounding in textual analysis, making DSR tools especially compatible with ML pedagogies due to the affordances of DATs for close reading. The Multiliteracies Framework by Paesani, Allen, and Dupuy (2016) provides theoretically well-grounded teaching sequences based on principles of exploring textual designs and analyzing how those designs contribute to meanings. In their five-stage lesson template for reading, the interpretation of texts is scaffolded through pre-reading, initial reading, during reading, critical reading, and post-reading phases. Each phase orients readers' attention to different parts of text, focusing on learners' engagement with texts through linguistic, cognitive, socio-cultural, and affective dimensions of literacy. Drawing on the original ML proposal by the New London Group (1996), Paesani, Allen, and Dupuy (2016) explain and model ways of incorporating the four curricular components (i.e., situated practice, overt instruction, critical framing, transformed practice) across all phases of their templates for different literacies (e.g., reading, writing, oral language development, video-mediated listening).

Multiliteracies as techniques

An epistemologically related but practically different project is the Learning by Design (Cope & Kalantzis, 2015) project, which foregrounds the four curricular components, renamed as experiencing, conceptualizing, analyzing, and applying. The New Learning Online website related to Learning by Design (https:// newlearningonline.com/learning-by-design/the-knowledge-processes) offers valuable techniques for scaffolding reading, including techniques for close reading. The following techniques have been selected for their compatibility with DSR, and are re-copied here. (New Learning Online, n.d.). Curriculum designers and instructors could begin with the multiliteracies-framed template for reading by Paesani, Allen, and Dupuy (2016), slotting into this template some of the techniques from "The Knowledge Processes" of the New Learning Online website.

Connecting with text

"Connecting with text" invites learners to "record any personal connections...while reading or viewing a text. Their personal connections could be about similar experiences, people they know, similar images, links to other texts they have read/viewed or information they recall". (New Learning Online, n.d.; Experiencing the Known). This technique could be used as an initial reading technique, as it invites readers to take note of their first thoughts and feelings.

Text annotation strategy

"Text annotation strategy" offers concrete prompts that could also be integrated into an initial reading phase. These include: inviting learners to acknowledge any moments of limited understanding ("In the margins record a question mark (?) for any questions you have about what is happening or about the vocabulary."); noticing and reacting affectively to elements of style ("Underline aspects of the writing style. This could be a line or phrase that you think is beautifully worded or makes you think. It could be something about the style or tone that strikes you or that you like or dislike. Put a double line under what you think is the best written sentence in the story"); making connections with other texts and ideas or with personal experiences ("Draw a 'C' for your connections when the story reminds you of something you have read or seen or done in your own life."); reflecting on affective responses ("Write ! when something is interesting, important, unusual and it surprises or even shocks you"); and predicting content ("Share any other opinions, ideas or predictions about what will happen next.") (New Learning Online, n.d.; Experiencing the New). This heuristic for initial reading with DSR may be especially suited to novice language learners, as the suggested annotation codes might mitigate pressure to produce target language forms, keeping the task focused on reading and interpreting. This sort of initial reading and annotating activity could then be productively integrated with a later phase in which students would select the coded passages that most resonated with them and expand on their reflections and reactions.

Reciprocal teaching

The "reciprocal teaching" technique is designed — through concrete prompts — to invite students to summarize, question, clarify, and predict. Prompts might be given to readers in advance as they embark on a DSR activity, or the text could be pre-annotated by instructors with the prompts. Thinking about the social aspects of digital social reading, different roles could be assigned to readers in a group and rotated for subsequent DSR activities with different texts (New Learning Online, n.d.; Experiencing the New). In short, the techniques presented are especially well suited to close reading of a text and can be productively combined with DSR.

Regardless of the DAT used and the instructional techniques adopted, what is perhaps most important in leaning upon scholarship in this field and ultimately in one's own implementation of DSR is a critical reflection on and attention to aligning one's views of learning, teaching, and language with the pedagogical designs around the selected tool.

Conclusion

The contributions in this volume corroborate the usefulness of DSR in L2 learning contexts and expand scholarship in this field through innovative and counterintuitive uses of the tool. Together, they demonstrate that DSR does more than just expose — through margins comments and dialogues — the reactions and interpretations of students as they read. What is more, DSR sets up a social space where learners' readings are mediated by their sense of community and where learners' actions and dialogues emerge with respect to the broader classroom ecology and the relationships with the learning spaces. With rapid developments in online tools and increasing concerns about human actions being replaced by new technologies, the collection of work in this volume demonstrates just the opposite: that digital tools can be leveraged as a companion to teaching and learning — to foster identity development, interpersonal interactions, textual understanding, or teachers' reading of students' learning — but ultimately cannot replace humans in the design of instructional activities nor in creating the dialogical spaces that emerge in communities of learners.

References

Bruff, D. (2020, September 23). Teaching with Perusall and Social Annotation – Highlights from a Conversation. Vanderbilt University Center for Teaching. https://cft.vanderbilt.edu/2020/09/teaching-with-perusall-and-social-annotation-highlights-from-a-conversation/

Center for Open Educational Resources and Language Learning (COERLL). (n.d.). *Planning a social reading lesson.* eComma: Digital Social Reading.

Cope, B., & Kalantzis, M. (2015). *A Pedagogy of multiliteracies: Learning by design.* Palgrave Macmillan.

Gao, F., Zhang, T., & Franklin, T. (2012). Designing asynchronous online discussion environments: Recent progress and possible future directions. *British Journal of Educational Technology, 44*(3), 469–483.

New Learning Online. (n.d.). *The knowledge processes. Experiencing the known.* Retrieved on 6 June 2024 from https://newlearningonline.com/learning-by-design/the-knowledge-processes/activities

New Learning Online. (n.d.). *The knowledge processes. Experiencing the new.* Retrieved on 6 June 2024 from https://newlearningonline.com/learning-by-design/the-knowledge-processes/experiencing

New Learning Online. (n.d.). *The Knowledge Processes*. Retrieved on 6 June 2024 from https://newlearningonline.com/learning-by-design/the-knowledge-processes

New London Group. (1996). A pedagogy of multiliteracies: Designing social futures. *Harvard Educational Review*, 66(1), 60–92.

Paesani, K., Allen, H., & Dupuy, B. (2016). *A multiliteracies framework for collegiate foreign language teaching (theory and practice in second language classroom instruction)*. Pearson.

Social Book. (2024, July 29). Social Book. https://www.livemargin.com

Index

A

Affordances, 6, 7, 8, 11, 13–14, 27,
105–108, 111–113, 114–115
Assessment, 11–12, 14
conceptual, 145
of learning (AoL), 130–131
for learning (AfL), 131–132
Integrated Performance
Assessment (IPA), 129,
147–148
performance-based,
128–129, 133

C

Collaboration, 67, 154, 162,
172–174
Computer-mediated
communication (CMC),
154–155

D

Digital annotation tool (DAT),
2, 22, 109, 134, 136

Digital literacy, 82, 156
Digital social reading, 2, 23, 104,
134, 153

E

Ecological theory/approaches,
11, 105–106, 119
Evidence-centered design, 145

G

Genre, 90, 109
Genre-based pedagogy, 167
Gloss/glossing, 57–58, 86, 105,
110, 112–113

L

Learning by design, 75, 94, 189

M

Mediation, 9, 54, 69
Multiliteracies, 8–9, 99, 104–105,
117, 120, 156, 189

Multimodal, 22, 25–26, 54,
117–118

P

Perezhivanie, 11, 78, 80–81, 91
Positioning, 10, 24–26
Proficiency, 79, 128–129, 133–135,
139, 146–147, 157

S

Social constructivism, 155–156
Sociocultural theory, 8, 13, 80,
104, 106, 108, 155
Source-based writing, 153–154,
170–171
Standards, 132–133

T

Translanguaging, 91–92

Z

Zone of proximal development
(ZPD), 107, 155